EXCAVATIONS AT
QASRIJ CLIFF
AND
KHIRBET QASRIJ

THE STATE ORGANIZATION OF
ANTIQUITIES AND HERITAGE, BAGHDAD

SADDAM DAM
REPORT 10

MINISTRY OF CULTURE AND INFORMATION
REPUBLIC OF IRAQ

BRITISH MUSEUM
WESTERN ASIATIC EXCAVATIONS
I

EXCAVATIONS AT QASRIJ CLIFF AND KHIRBET QASRIJ

JOHN CURTIS

WITH CONTRIBUTIONS BY

DOMINIQUE COLLON

AND APPENDICES BY
R. K. UPRICHARD, M. S. TITE,
I. C. FREESTONE AND M. J. HUGHES

PUBLISHED FOR
THE TRUSTEES OF THE BRITISH MUSEUM
BY BRITISH MUSEUM PUBLICATIONS

Published by British Museum Publications Ltd
46 Bloomsbury Street, London WC1B 3QQ

British Library Cataloguing in Publication Data
Curtis, John, 1946–
    Excavations at Qasrij Cliff and Khirbet Qasrij
    1. Mesopotamia. Antiquities. Excavation of remains, history
    I. Title   II. Collon, Dominique
    935

    ISBN 0-7141-1123-6

Printed in Great Britain
by Henry Ling Ltd, The Dorset Press, Dorchester, Dorset

Contents

Foreword

As part of the archaeological rescue operations in the dam regions in Iraq, the State Organization of Antiquities and Heritage organized and launched in 1983 and the following years an Iraqi–International rescue excavation campaign in which many well-known archaeologists participated. More than fifty tells have been excavated and there are a further fifty awaiting completion.

Dr John Curtis, director of the British Museum expedition, excavated at Qasrij near Tell Mohammed 'Arab, where a stone-built building dated to the Neo-Assyrian or the beginning of the Neo-Babylonian period was discovered.

The following report is the final result of the excavations with appendices on the results of the atomic absorption analysis and thin-section analysis of the pottery. Dr Curtis has completed his archaeological work with the help of recent scientific methods which provide us with a better picture of the site and its history, especially as it relies on analysis and comparative studies.

The work at Qasrij is indicative of the spirit of cooperation between Iraq and friendly foreign expeditions, and also proof of the success of such ventures in large-scale rescue operations.

Dr Mu'ayyad Sa'id Damerji
President, State Organization of Antiquities and Heritage

المقدمة

ضمن المشاريع الانقاذية للاثار في مناطق غمر السدود في العراق ... قامت المؤسسة العامة للاثار والتراث في عام ١٩٨٣ وفي السنين التي تلتها باعداد حملة عراقية وعالمية شارك بها مجموعة ممتازة من الاثاريين المعروفين دولياً ... واستطاعت هذه المجموعة التنقيب وحتى الآن في اكثر من خمسين تلاً وموقعاً اثرياً بشكل كامل ... كما تقوم بالانتهاء في اعمالها في خمسين تلاً اثرياً اخر .

ولقد قام جون كيرتس على رأس بعثة من الاثاريين البريطانيين بالتنقيب في موقع قصريج بالقرب من تل (محمد عرب) ... وعثر على بناية مشيدة بالصخر ... من العصر الاشوري المتأخر وبداية العصر البابلي الكلدي ...

ان التقرير المعمد امامكم هو النتيجة النهائية لاعمال التنقيبات ملحق بها نتائج الابحاث المختبرية لفحص الفخار بواسطة جهاز الامتصاص الذري الطيفي ... وبذلك يكون السيد جون كيرتس قد قام بانجاز عمل من اعمال البحث الاثاري بالطرق الحديثة محاولاً تقديم صورة افضل عن الموقع وتاريخه معتمداً على دراسات علمية .

ان نجاح العمل في هذا الموقع هو ودليل على نجاح العمل المشترك بين العراق والبعثات الاجنبية الصديقة ... ودليل على نجاح تطبيق اسلوب العمل المشترك في الحملات الانقاذية للاثار على هذا النطاق الواسع .

د . مؤيد سعيد دميرجي
مدير عام
دائرة الاثار والتراث

Preface

The present volume forms the first of a new series entitled *British Museum Western Asiatic Excavations* which will publish final reports on excavations carried out on behalf of the Trustees of the British Museum by members of the staff of the Department of Western Asiatic Antiquities. At present departmental expeditions are working in Iraq, Jordan and Oman: subsequent volumes will report on these and will be numbered in sequence of publication.

This volume is the first of four in the series which will report on the work carried out by Dr J. E. Curtis, Assistant Keeper in the Department, at sites in the area of the Saddam Dam Salvage Project in Northern Iraq. In this work he was greatly helped by the State Organization of Antiquities and Heritage of Iraq under its Director–General Dr Mu'ayyad Sa'id, who contributed accommodation and valuable labour.

In this first volume Dr Curtis deals with his excavations carried out in 1983 and 1984 at the Late Assyrian site of Qasrij Cliff and at the post-Assyrian site of Khirbet Qasrij.

T. C. Mitchell
Keeper of Western Asiatic Antiquities, British Museum

Acknowledgements

In the first place, proper acknowledgement must be made of the help and assistance provided by the Iraqi State Organization for Antiquities and Heritage, without which no excavations would have been possible. At Qasrij Cliff and Khirbet Qasrij, as elsewhere in the Saddam Dam Salvage Project, the Iraqis paid the wages of the workmen and provided accommodation and some equipment. Thanks are due to many officials of the SOAH, but particular mention should be made of Dr Mu'ayyad Sa'id, the President, Dr Behham Abu al-Soof, then the Director-General of the Northern Region, and our representatives, Sd Mohammed Zekki and Sd Abd al-Salaam.

The work was done in close co-operation with the British Archaeological Expedition to Iraq, and we are grateful to them for generously providing facilities and lending some equipment, as well as many other kindnesses, both on site and in Baghdad. In various ways Dr Michael Roaf, the Director of the BAEI, Dr Jeremy Black, the Assistant Director, and Dr Robert Killick, the Secretary-Librarian, all contributed to the success of the expedition, and their help is gratefully acknowledged.

In the preparation of this report, we were greatly helped by Ann Searight of the Department of Western Asiatic Antiquities in the British Museum, who inked for publication drawings done in the field and prepared the layout of the plates. The photographs were printed by Jim Hendry of the British Museum Photographic Service from negatives taken in the field by the author. We are also grateful to have had the collaboration of the British Museum Research Laboratory, who have carried out scientific examinations of samples brought back to the British Museum. Last, but by no means least, thanks are due to Velina Taylor and Yvette Taylor, who transferred an untidy typescript onto a word processor for publication, and to Teresa Francis of British Museum Publications, who has edited the text.

Abbreviations

BM	British Museum		L.	length
b.s.	below surface		MM	Mosul Museum
diam.	diameter		veg.	vegetable (temper)
frag.	fragment		W.	width
H.	height		wt	weight
IM	Iraq Museum, Baghdad			

Part 1

EXCAVATIONS AT QASRIJ CLIFF

a. Introduction

Excavations at the Late Assyrian site of Qasrij Cliff were undertaken in the early spring of 1983 when I was staying with the British Archaeological Expedition to Iraq at Babneet. Under the direction of Dr Michael Roaf they were working at the nearby site of Tell Mohammed 'Arab. I had gone to Iraq on a reconnaissance trip to identify a site within the Saddam Dam Salvage Project for future excavation by the British Museum, and I am much indebted to Dr Roaf for the help and hospitality that he liberally extended to me. It was due to his initiative that other British expeditions were able to work in the rescue project under the umbrella of the British Archaeological Expedition; in addition to the British Museum, expeditions from the Universities of Edinburgh and Manchester took advantage of the scheme.

The Saddam Dam Salvage Project came about through the construction of a new dam on the River Tigris near the town of Eski Mosul (Fig. 1). The dam itself was previously called the Eski Mosul Dam, but is now known as the Saddam Dam. The construction of this dam caused the formation of a large lake stretching almost as far as the Turkish-Syrian frontier and up to 4.5 km wide at its maximum extent. Many archaeological sites have now been flooded, but before the waters started to back up behind the dam the Iraqi authorities drew up a detailed map of known archaeological sites in the area and took steps to ensure that as many as possible of them were excavated, or at least partially excavated, before they disappeared beneath the water. In a spirit of true international co-operation, the Iraqis invited foreign teams to participate in the project, paid the wages of the local workmen and provided accommodation for the visiting teams.

The site that we called Qasrij Cliff is located in the south-east part of the flooded area, on a low cliff that forms the east bank of the Tigris. It is about 1500 m east of the village of Babneet, and about 250 m west of the modern, but then (1983) already deserted, village of Qasrij (Fig. 2). The site is on a promontory, bounded on the east side by a branch of the Wadi Qasrij (Fig. 3). It is not marked on the SOAH map of sites in the Saddam Dam Salvage Project, but had first been noticed by Dr Geoffrey Summers, a member of Dr Roaf's team at Tell Mohammed 'Arab, while walking upstream from Babneet alongside the Tigris. At this point the cliff is very eroded, and potsherds could be seen leaching out of the eroded section. This discovery was kindly brought to my attention by Dr Roaf, and I first visited the site with him on 5 March 1983. Careful inspection on the surface seemed to indicate that the sherds were coming from what appeared to be a large pit several metres deep that had been eroded away on the north-eastern side, and it was decided that this feature should be investigated in a small excavation.

b. The excavation [1]

The work was completed in five days between 10 and 22 March 1983, with a maximum of three workmen, including one Sherqati. Sd Mohammed Zekki was the representative of the Iraqi State Organization for Antiquities and Heritage, and best thanks are due to him for his help. Initially, the ground-surface of the area to be excavated was cleared of loose and recently fallen earth (batch M = Mixed), and then we proceeded to cut back to a section (Figs 4-5) so that the nature of the feature could be better understood. Pottery from this operation was divided into three batches (batches 1-3), corresponding to stratigraphical divisions in the pit-fill. After the section had been cut and recorded, the remaining pit-fill was removed, observing the same stratigraphical divisions as before.

Total excavation showed that the feature was indeed a pit, straight-sided and approximately circular, with a maximum diameter of about 3.70 m (Pls Ia-b). The sides of the pit were best preserved in the western part, where they reached a height of 2.25 m. The bottom of the pit was flat, and into it had been dug two smaller pits, one of them (pit A) with a diameter of about 95 cm and a depth of about 20 cm and the other (pit B) about 45 cm in diameter and about 35 cm deep (Fig. 4). The bottom of the main pit (in the centre of the section-line) was found to be 7.96 m above river level (on 29 March 1983 when the River Tigris was high) and 4.50 m below the headland at the top of the cliff. However, as the pit was on a steep slope going down to the river, it was not necessarily this deep when it was dug. The process of erosion could already have started in Assyrian times, in which case the pit could have been dug down not from the top of the headland but from a surface that was even

1. Preliminary reports about the excavation at Qasrij Cliff have appeared in Roaf 1983: 78-9, fig. 7, and Killick and Black 1985: 237.

then sloping down towards the river.

The fill of the pit was mixed, but predominantly ashy. At the bottom was a thick layer of dark grey ash, and above this were levels of broken-down brick mixed with ash, separated by bands of light grey ash. Lenses of dark grey ash were a prominent feature. In a few places on the sides of the pit there was ash with flecks of charcoal, but no clear evidence was found for remains of chaff or grain, either here or on the bottom of the pit. Throughout the pit-fill, but predominantly in batches 2-3, were a large number of pot sherds, more than 1,000 in total. No pottery vessels were preserved intact, but it was possible to reconstruct a number of profiles, and a wide range of forms is represented. Bowls were particularly numerous, but jars and some comparatively fine wares, such as cups and beakers, were also present. Also in the pit-fill, but restricted entirely to batches 2-3, were a number of bones. Most of these came from sheep or goats, but pig, dog and cat bones have also been identified. The majority of these bones presumably came from animals that were butchered for food. The presence of pig bones is interesting, and in modern times wild boars are said to have lived on nearby Babneet Island. In 1983 the rumoured existence of these beasts occasioned a hunting expedition to the island, but although an intensive search was made, no trace of them was found. Other noteworthy inclusions in the pit-fill were two large fragments of unbaked brick (*libn*), about 10 cm thick but otherwise of undeterminable dimensions, and one side of a baked brick, unfortunately uninscribed, 6 cm thick and 33 cm wide. This baked brick was near the top of the dark grey ashy deposit on the floor of the pit (see section, Fig. 5). Small finds comprised a cylindrical glass bead, a section of iron rod, a core of red chert and a terracotta chariot wheel (Fig. 6a).

Clearly the pit at Qasrij Cliff was used for domestic rubbish, presumably after it had ceased to fulfil its original function. But the circumstances in which it was filled and over what period of time are obscure. In spite of the fact that no joins were observed between potsherds from different batches (i.e. batches 1-3), the pottery as a whole presents a unified appearance. This would suggest that the pit was filled up fairly quickly, during a relatively short period of time.

What was the original purpose of the pit at Qasrij Cliff? Most probably, it was a silo for storing grain. There is extensive evidence from Western Asia for the storage of grain in subterranean pits dug down from the surface, both in antiquity and in modern times. In Iraq the practice is attested as early as the Hassuna period (Lloyd and Safar 1945:268). Often, but not always, these grain silos had lined walls. Thus at Tell Hassuna the walls were lined with bitumen on the outside and sometimes white gypsum on the inside (*ibid.*); in Anatolia pits were sometimes lined with matting (Mellaart 1967: 62-3), and at Tepe Yahya in Iran a large

grain silo in Level IVA was lined with bricks (Lamberg-Karlovsky 1976:77). Close to Qasrij Cliff and also within the Saddam Dam Salvage Project, grain silos of Hellenistic date were found at Tell Mohammed 'Arab (Roaf 1984: 144). These are cut down from the surface to a depth of about 3 m; they are bell-shaped, about 3 m in diameter at the bottom and 1 m or less in diameter at the top. A whitish deposit was sometimes observed on the walls of these silos, suggesting that they might have been lined with chaff. By contrast, pits probably for storing grain in the Middle Assyrian period at Tell Mohammad 'Arab were straight-sided and cylindrical (Michael Roaf, pers. comm.). Grain silos of Hellenistic date were also found in the British Museum excavations at Grai Darki, also part of the Saddam Dam Salvage Project.

Particularly good evidence for grain silos in the Iron Age comes from Tell es Sa'idiyeh in Jordan, where nearly a hundred were found in Stratum IV (Pritchard 1985: 39-42, fig. 180). Like the pit at Qasrij Cliff, most of them were circular with vertical walls, and none had plastered walls. None was quite so large as the pit at Qasrij, however, the largest having a diameter of 2.7 m and the deepest a depth of 1.77 m. In several of the pits at Sa'idiyeh there were samples of grain, confirming their identification as grain silos.

Interesting evidence for the use of grain storage pits in modern times was noted by Patty Jo Watson at Hasanabad in Western Iran (Watson 1979: 125-6). There, the pits are usually bell-shaped and about 1 m in diameter at the mouth and 1 m deep. The sides of the pits are lined with plaster, and the bottom covered with straw or chaff before the grain is put in. Surplus unmilled grain is stored in these pits from harvest time until it is needed. Lamberg-Karlovsky remarks that the villagers near Tepe Yahya store grain for up to a year in underground silos. [2]

If the pit at Qasrij Cliff was indeed a silo for storing grain, how was it roofed? For this, of course, we have no evidence, and are obliged to turn to modern ethnographic parallels. At Hasanabad, for example, the grain in the silo was covered over with straw or chaff; this was held down with a layer of dung cakes, and finally the pit was sealed with a mud capping.

Assuming that our pit is indeed a grain silo, it must have belonged to a nearby settlement. It could be argued that a silo need not necessarily have been located in or close to a village but might instead have been situated in open country near the supply of grain. This seems unlikely, however, for reasons of security. There should, then, have been some habitation close to the silo but I was unable to find any evidence for this. In an attempt to find occupation levels associated with the silo, a 2 m

2. He also provides some statistics about the amount of grain that could have been stored in the silo of Level IVA at Tepe Yahya and how many people it might have provided rations for.

x 2 m sondage was dug on top of the cliff as near to the pit as possible (Fig. 3). This proved to be quite sterile, and no evidence was found for any ancient (or modern) occupation. A second 2 m x 2 m sondage was dug on the cliff-top 86 m to the west, but this again was sterile. These sondages were dug on 13 and 14 March 1983.

The conclusion seems inescapable that any ancient occupation originally associated with the pit has been completely eroded away. It could have been removed by the river, for the cliff does not in fact face the main stream of the Tigris but a secondary channel that only contains running water when the river is high. This channel has the appearance of being a comparatively recent phenomenon caused by the meandering of the river, and is already silting up. A second possibility is that the site has been swept away by the wadi immediately to the east of the pit, and a third, less likely, explanation may be that vestiges of ancient occupation have been removed from the top of the cliff through erosion. Any of these factors, or indeed a combination of all three, could account for the lack of associated material in the vicinity of the pit.

c. Catalogue of small finds from Qasrij Cliff

QC1   Fig. 6a; Sulaimaniya Museum. Registered in SOAH files as KQ26. Cylindrical glass bead, L. 2.5 cm, diam. 1.05 cm. Now yellowish-white in colour with two yellow bands running around it. QCM.

QC2   Fig. 6a; Sulaimaniya Museum. Registered in SOAH files as KQ28. Red chert bladelet core, L. 4.0 cm, max. diam. 1.4 cm. Probably prehistoric, perhaps dating between the 7th and 3rd millennium BC; see comments below in section d. QC2.

QC3   Fig. 6a; MM for study no. 279. Registered in SOAH files as KQ27. Terracotta chariot-wheel with pronounced hub, presumably from a child's toy. Parts chipped away, max. diam. 7.05 cm, max. thickness 4.3 cm. QC2.

QC4   Fig. 6a. A section of iron rod, fractured at both ends, L. 2.5 cm, diam. 1.0-1.3 cm. QC2.

d. Flints from the vicinity of Qasrij Cliff

1   Fig. 6b. Single-platform bladelet core, flint, L. 4.6 cm, diam. 1.8 cm. Found on surface by St. John Simpson on 27 February 1985, *c*.40 m to the south-east of Sondage QC2.

2   Fig. 6b. Opposed-platform blade core, flint, L. 8.1 cm, max. thickness 6.8 cm. Found on surface in vicinity of Qasrij Cliff.

These flint cores were drawn by Dr Marie-Louise Inizan of the Centre National de la Recherche Scientifique, and I am most grateful to her for permission to reproduce the drawings in this report. I have shown the drawings to Jill Cook of the Quaternary Section in the British Museum, and received valuable advice from her about how to describe them. Both of these flint cores are likely to be prehistoric, and could date from any time between the seventh and the third millennium BC. Although they have no association whatsoever with the Late Assyrian deposit at Qasrij Cliff, they are included here because they were found in the vicinity of that site and demonstrate that there was earlier occupation in the area. Also, they provide interesting comparative material for the red chert core actually found in the pit at Qasrij Cliff (see above, QC2).

e. Qasrij Cliff bones

The bones from Qasrij Cliff have been identified by Miss Marie-Odile Saacké (now Mrs Alastair Killick). Mr Keith Dobney, of the Institute of Archaeology, London, kindly gave advice as to the best way to present the evidence.

The bones were found only in batches 2 and 3 and seem to have been thrown into the pit as rubbish, probably, in some cases, after eating. There are no traces of burning on the bones, so those which were cooked were probably stewed rather than roasted.

		Cattle	Sheep/Goat	Pig	Dog	Cat	Unidentifiable
Horn			XX				
Skull frags							XXXX
Jaw frags			XXXXX	XXXXX	X		
Humerus			XXX				
Scapula			XX			X	
Calcaneus			X				X
Astragalus			X	X			
Phalanx			X				
	M		XXXXXXXX				
Loose Teeth	P		XXX				
	I		XX	X			
Rib			XXXXXX				

X = single example
M = molars
P = premolars
I = incisors

f. Catalogue of pottery from Qasrij Cliff

In the catalogue, frequent reference is made to what appeared to be a slip or wash. It has been pointed out in Appendix III (section on surface coats) that these surfaces were almost certainly not deliberately added. It has been decided to retain the descriptions, however, as they convey an impression of what the sherds actually looked like. Descriptions of fabric colours are according to *Munsell Soil Colour Charts*.

Bowls

1   Fig. 7. Rim frag., L. 3.5 cm. Fabric 5YR 6/4 light reddish brown, surface 2.5Y 6/6 light red. Grit temper. QC3.

2   Fig. 7. Rim frag., L. 4.2 cm, diam. 22.0 cm. 10YR 8/2 white. Veg. and grit temper. QCM.

3   Fig. 7. Half of rim preserved, diam. 22.0 cm. 2.5YR 6/6 light red. Veg. temper. QC2. Sample BM 1984-5-12, 2; see Appendix III.
Two similar rim frags:
a. L. 3.1 cm, diam. 23.0 cm. 5YR 7/4 pink. QCM.
b. (thinner than example illustrated) L. 3.9 cm, diam. 18.0 cm. 7.5YR 8/4 pink. Veg. temper. QCM.

4   Fig. 7. Rim frag., L. 6.5 cm, diam. 22.0 cm. 10YR 7/3 very pale brown. Veg. temper. QCM.

5   Fig. 7. Rim frag., L. 11.0 cm, diam. 23.8 cm. 5YR 7/4 pink. Veg. temper. QCM.

6   Fig. 7. 3.5 cm of rim and one-sixth of base preserved, H. 8.2 cm, diam. 24.4 cm. 7.5YR 7/4 pink. Veg. temper. QCM.

7   Fig. 7. Rim frag., L. 10.0 cm, diam. 24.0 cm. 5YR 7/4 pink firing in middle of core to 7.5YR 7/ light grey. Veg. temper. QCM. Sample BM 1984-5-12, 1; see Appendix III.
A similar rim frag.:
a. L. 5.8 cm, diam. *c.*28.0 cm. 5YR 7/3 pink. Veg. temper. QCM.

8   Fig. 7. Rim frag., L. 8.0 cm, diam. 24.0 cm. 10YR 7/3 very pale brown. Veg. temper. QC3

9   Fig. 7. Rim frag., L. 2.4 cm, diam. 20.0 cm. 10YR 8/2 white. Veg. temper. QCM.

10   Fig. 7. Rim frag., L. 3.6 cm, diam 25.0 cm. 10YR 8/2 white. Veg. temper. QC2.

11   Fig. 8. One-third of rim preserved in three frags, diam. 26.0 cm. 10YR 7/3 very pale yellow. Veg. temper. QC2.
A similar rim frag.:
a. L. 6.4 cm, diam. *c.*20.0 cm. 10YR 7/2 light grey. Veg. temper. QCM.

12   Fig. 8. Rim frag., L. 15.0 cm, diam. 26.0 cm. 7.5YR 7/4 pink. Veg. temper. QCM.
A similar rim frag.:
a. L. 8.2 cm, diam. *c.*30.0 cm. 2.5YR 6/6 light red. Veg. and slight grit temper. QCM.

13   Fig. 8. Rim frag., L. 16.0 cm, diam. 26.0 cm. 7.5YR 7/4 pink. Veg. temper. QC3.

14   Fig. 8. Rim frag., L. 18.0 cm, diam. 26.0 cm. 10YR 7/4 very pale brown. Veg. and white grit temper. QCM.
A similar rim frag.:
a. L. 11.5 cm, diam. 27.0 cm. 10YR 8/3 very pale brown. Veg. and white grit temper. QC2.

15   Fig. 8. Rim frag., L. 7.0 cm, diam. 26.6 cm. 5YR 7/6 reddish yellow. Veg. temper. QCM. Sample BM 1984-5-12, 17; see Appendix III.

16   Fig. 8. Rim frag., L. 9.0 cm, diam. 26.0 cm. 5YR 7/4 pink. Veg. temper. QCM.

17   Fig. 8. Bowl, three-quarters preserved, H. 11.5 cm, diam. 26.4 cm. 2.5YR 6/6 light red. Veg. and fine grit temper. QC2. Sample BM 1984-5-12, 3; see Appendix III.
Three similar rim frags:
a. (thicker than example illustrated) L. 10.6 cm, diam. *c.*39.0 cm. 5YR 7/4 pink. Veg. temper. QC2.
b. L. 5.8 cm, diam. *c.* 30.0 cm. 10YR 8/3 very pale brown. Veg. temper. QCM.
c. L. 3.9 cm, diam. *c.* 26.0 cm. 10YR 7/3 very pale brown. QCM.
A similar base frag.:
d. W. 7.3 cm, diam. 9.0 cm. 10YR 7/4 very pale brown. Veg. temper. QCM.

18   Fig. 9. Bowl with 17.0 cm of rim and half of base preserved, H. 9.1 cm, diam. 29.0 cm. Fabric 2.5YR 5/8 red, surface wash/slip 10YR 7/3 very pale brown. Veg. and fine grit temper. QC2.

19   Fig. 9. Bowl, three-quarters preserved with most of base missing, H. 12.0 cm, diam. 29.0 cm. Fabric 10YR 6/4 light yellowish brown, surface 10YR 7/3 very pale brown. Veg. temper. QC3.
A similar rim frag.:
a. (thicker than example illustrated) L. 3.7 cm. 7.5YR 7/4 pink. Veg. temper. QC3.
A similar base:
b. Diam. 6.5 cm. 10YR 8/3 very pale brown. Veg. temper. QCM.

20   Fig. 9. Rim frag., L. 8.0 cm, diam. 30.0 cm. Fabric 5YR 7/4 pink, slip 2.5Y 8/2 white on inside and outside. Veg temper. QC3. Sample BM 1984-5-12, 19; see Appendix III.
A similar rim frag.:

a. (smaller than example illustrated) L. 2.6 cm. 7.5YR 7/2 pinkish grey. Veg. temper. QC3.

21   Fig. 9. Rim frag., L. 5.7 cm, diam. 32.8 cm. 10YR 7/3 very pale brown. Veg. temper. QC3.

22   Fig. 9. Rim frag., L. 7.0 cm, diam. 27.0 cm. 5YR 7/4 pink. Veg. temper. QCM.

23   Fig. 9. Rim frag., L. 11.0 cm, diam. 34.0 cm. Fabric 5YR 7/4 pink, surface 10YR 7/3 very pale brown. Veg. temper. QC3.

24   Fig. 9. Rim frag., L. 23.0 cm, diam. 38.0 cm. 10YR 7/3 very pale brown. Veg. and grit temper. QCM. Sample BM 1984-5-12, 9; see Appendix III.

25   Fig. 9. Rim frag., L. 12.5 cm, diam. 38.0 cm. 7.5YR 8/4 pink. Veg. temper with conspicuous white grits. QCM.

Fine wares

26   Fig. 10. Rim frag. of bowl, L. 2.5 cm. 7.5YR N8/ white, light burnish on outside. Veg. temper. QCM.

27   Fig. 10. Rim frag. of bowl, L. 7.5 cm, diam. 12.0 cm. 2.5Y 8/2 white. Veg. temper. QC2. Sample BM 1984-5-12, 24; see Appendix III.
   A similar rim frag.:
   a. L. 4.2 cm, diam. 18.0 cm. 10 YR 8/2 white. Veg. temper. QCM.

28   Fig. 10. Rim frag. of bowl, L. 2.6 cm, diam. 15.0 cm. 2.5Y 8/2 white. Veg. temper. QC3.

29   Fig. 10. Bowl with parts of rim missing, H. 6.0 cm, diam. 13.0 cm. 2.5Y 8/2 white. Veg. temper. QC3. Sample BM 1984-5-12, 14; see Appendix III.
   Five similar rim frags:
   a. L. 3.1 cm, diam. *c*.13.0 cm. 10YR 6/3 pale red. Small white grit temper. QC2.
   b-c. L. 0.7 cm and 1.9 cm. 10YR 7/4 very pale brown. Veg. temper. QCM.
   d. (thicker than example illustrated) L. 3.0 cm, diam. 22.0 cm. Fabric 2.5YR 6/6 light red, surface slip inside and outside 10YR 8/3 very pale brown. Veg. temper. QC2.
   e. (larger than example illustrated) L. 3.4 cm, diam. *c*.17.0 cm. 10YR 7/4 very pale brown. Veg. and sparse grit temper. QC3.
   A similar base:
   f. Diam. 4.3 cm. 2.5YR 6/6 light red. Veg. and sparse grit temper. QC3.

30   Fig. 10. Bowl with parts of rim and wall missing, H. 6.2 cm, diam. 14.1 cm. Fabric 2.5YR 6/6 light red, surface 10YR 7/3 very pale brown. Veg. temper with sparse white calcareous grits. QC3. Sample BM 1984-5-12, 4; see Appendix III.

Three similar rim frags:
   a. L. 3.0 cm, diam. *c*.14.0 cm. 5YR 6/4 light reddish brown. Veg. temper. QC2.
   b. L. 3.8 cm, diam. 12.0 cm. 10YR 8/2 white. Veg. temper. QC2.
   c. L. 4.1 cm, diam. *c*. 15.0 cm. 5YR 8/3 pink. Veg. and some grit temper. QCM.
   A similar base frag.:
   d. W. 5.0 cm, diam. 7.0 cm. 10YR 8/3 very pale brown. Veg. temper. QC1. Sample BM 1984-5-12, 16; see Appendix III.

31   Fig. 10. Rim frag. of bowl, L. 5.0 cm, diam. 16.0 cm. 10YR 7/4 very pale brown. Veg. temper. QC3.

Four similar rim frags:
   a. L. 5.8 cm, diam. 16.0 cm. 2.5YR 8/2 white. Veg. temper. QCM.
   b. (thicker than example illustrated) L. 2.0 cm. 10YR 8/3 very pale brown. Veg. temper. QCM.
   c-d. (thicker than example illustrated) L. 3.7 cm and 4.5 cm, diam. *c*.19.0 cm. 10YR 7/3 very pale brown. Veg. temper. QCM.

32   Fig. 10. Rim frag. of cup (?), L. 4.0 cm, diam. 7.0 cm. 5YR 7/6 reddish yellow. Veg. and fine white grit temper. QC3.

33   Fig. 10. Rim frags of cup (?), L. 2.4 cm and 1.8 cm, and part of wall, diam. 8.6 cm. Fabric 7.5YR 8/4 pink, surface 7.5YR 8/2 pinkish white. Fine veg. temper. QC3.

34   Fig. 10. Base of cup, diam. 6.1 cm. Fabric 5YR 7/4 pink, surface 7.5YR 7/4 pink. Veg. and fine white grit temper. QC3.

35   Fig. 10. Base of cup, diam. 8.0 cm. 2.5Y 7/2 light grey. Veg. temper. QCM.
   A similar base frag.:
   a. W. 3.6 cm, diam. *c*.6.0 cm. 10YR 7/3 very pale brown. White grit temper. QCM. Sample BM 1984-5-12, 18; see Appendix III.

36   Fig. 10. Base of cup, diam. 8.0 cm. 2.5Y 8/2 white. Veg. temper. QC3. Sample BM 1984-5-12, 13; see Appendix III.

37   Fig. 10. Base of cup, part missing, diam. 7.6 cm. 7.5YR 8/2 pinkish white. Veg. temper. QC2.

38   Fig. 10. Rim frag. of jar, L. 5.2 cm, diam. 6.5 cm. 2.5Y 7/4 pale yellow. Fine grit temper. QC2.

39   Fig. 10. Rim frag. of jar, L. 2.5 cm, diam. 8.0 cm. Fabric 5YR 7/3 pink, surface 2.5Y 8/2 white. Fine grit temper. QCM.

40   Fig. 10. One-third of rim of jar preserved, diam. 7.9 cm. 10YR 8/2 white. Fine grit temper. QCM. Sample BM 1984-5-12, 6; see Appendix III.

41 Fig. 10. Rim frag. of beaker (?), L. 3.0 cm, diam. 8.0 cm. 5Y 7/3 pale yellow. Fine grit temper. QC3.

42 Fig. 10. Rim frag., L. 4.3 cm, diam. 9.1 cm, and sections of wall and base of a beaker. 2.5Y 8/2 white. Very fine, mainly veg. temper. QC3. Sample BM 1984-5-12, 8; see Appendix III.
Two similar rim frags:
a. L. 4.3 cm, diam. 11.0 cm. 5Y 7/4 pale yellow. Veg. temper. QC3.
b. L. 2.9 cm, diam. *c*.5.5 cm. 5Y 8/1 white. Sparse veg. and grit temper. QCM.
Two similar base frags:
c. Fabric 5YR 6/4 light reddish brown, surface 10YR 7/3 very pale brown. Veg. temper. QC2.
d. Fabric 5YR 8/4 pink in centre, surface 7.5YR 8/2 pinkish white. White grit temper. QC2.

43 Fig. 10. Rim frag. of jar, L. 1.0 cm, diam. 3.6 cm. 5YR 7/4 pink. Veg. temper. QCM.

44 Fig. 10. Rim frag. of bowl, L. 5.4 cm, diam. 7.4 cm. Fabric 7.5YR 7/4 pink, surface 10YR 6/2 brownish-grey. Veg. and fine white grit temper. QC3.

45 Fig. 10. Lower part of jar, rim missing. 2.5Y 8/2 white. Veg. temper. QCM.

46 Fig. 10. Parts of body of jar only. 10YR 7/3 very pale brown. Veg. temper. QCM.

47 Fig. 10. Frags of beaker (?), only two short sections of rim preserved, L. 1.6 cm and 1.0 cm, diam. 8.5 cm. 2.5Y 8/2 white. Very fine, mainly veg. temper. QC3.
A similar rim frag.:
a. L. 4.6 cm, diam. 33.0 cm. 10YR 7/4 very pale brown. White grit temper. QC2.

48 Fig. 10. Rim frag. of jar (?), L. 5.0 cm, diam. 9.6 cm. Fabric 7.5YR 6/ grey, surface 7.5YR 4/ dark grey. Fine white grit temper. QC3.

Jars

49 Fig. 11. Rim frag., L. 4.5 cm, diam. 14.0 cm, and part of wall. 5YR 7/3 pink. Veg. temper. QCM.
A similar rim frag.:
a. L. 4.2 cm, diam. *c*.12.0 cm. 5YR 7/2 pinkish grey. Veg. and white grit temper. QCM.

50 Fig. 11. Rim frag., L. 7.0 cm, diam. 14.0 cm, and parts of wall. 10YR 7/3 very pale brown. Veg. temper. QC3.

51 Fig. 11. Three-quarters of rim preserved, diam. 14.0 cm. 7.5YR 7/4 pink. Veg. temper. QC3. Sample BM 1984-5-12, 12; see Appendix III.

52 Fig. 11. Half of rim preserved, diam. 15.3 cm. 2.5Y 8/2 white. Veg. temper. QCM. Sample BM 1984-5-12, 5; see Appendix III.
A similar rim frag.:
a. L. 4.8 cm, diam. *c*.29.0 cm. 2.5Y 8/2 white. Veg. temper. QC2.

53 Fig. 11. Top part of jar only, diam. 15.9 cm. 7.5YR 6/4 light brown. Veg. temper. QC3. Sample BM 1984-5-12, 21; see Appendix III.
A similar rim frag.:
a. L. 3.5 cm, diam. 16.0 cm. 7.5YR 8/2 pinkish white. Veg. temper. QC3.

54 Fig. 11. Rim frag., L. 5.5 cm, diam. 13.2 cm. 2.5YR 6/6 light red. Veg. temper. QCM.
A similar rim frag.:
a. L. 5.7 cm, diam. 15.0 cm. 5YR 6/4 light reddish brown. Veg. temper. QC1.

55 Fig. 11. Rim frag., L. 7.0 cm, diam. 12.8 cm. 10YR 8/3 very pale brown. Veg. and grit temper. QC2.
A similar rim frag.:
a. L. 3.8 cm, diam. *c*.13.0 cm. Fabric 10YR 7/4 very pale brown, surface slip 10YR 8/2 white. Veg. temper. QC2.

56 Fig. 11. Whole rim preserved, diam. 12.1 cm. Fabric 5YR 7/4 pink, surface 2.5Y 7/2 light grey. Veg. temper. QCM.

57 Fig. 11. Whole rim preserved, diam. 10.3 cm. 2.5Y 7/4 pale yellow. Veg. temper. QC3.
Three similar rim frags.:
a. L. 3.2 cm, diam. *c*.10.0 cm. 10YR 8/4 very pale brown. Veg. temper. QC2.
b. L. 2.3 cm. 2.5Y 8/2 white. Veg temper. QC2.
c. L. 5.2 cm, diam. *c*. 32.0 cm. 5YR 6/4 light reddish brown. Sparse veg. temper. QCM.

58 Fig. 11. One-third of rim preserved, diam. 11.0 cm, and part of wall. 2.5Y 8/2 white. Veg. temper. QC3.
A similar rim frag.:
a. L. 4.6 cm, diam. *c*.12.0 cm. 2.5Y 7/4 pale yellow. Veg. temper. QCM.

59 Fig. 11. Most of rim preserved, diam. 12.0 cm, and part of wall. 7.5YR 7/4 pink. Veg. temper. QC2.

60 Fig. 11. Rim frag., L. 5.5 cm, diam. 16.2 cm. Fabric 10YR 7/4 very pale brown, surface wash 10YR 8/3 very pale brown. Veg. temper. QC3.

61 Fig. 12. Rim frag., L. 5.0 cm, diam. 8.0 cm. 2.5Y 7/4 pale yellow. Fine grit temper. QC3.

62 Fig. 12. One-third of rim preserved, diam. 9.2 cm. 10YR 7/4 very pale brown. Veg. temper. QCM.
A similar rim frag.:

a. (thicker than example illustrated) L. 4.8 cm, diam. 21.0 cm. 7.5YR 7/4 pink. No temper (?). QCM.

63 Fig. 12. One-third of rim preserved, diam. 10.5 cm. 5YR 6/4 light reddish brown. Veg. and sparse white grit temper. QC3. Sample BM 1984-5-12, 7; see Appendix III.

64 Fig. 12. Rim frag., L. 8.0 cm, diam. 12.8 cm. 10YR 7/3 very pale brown. Veg. and grit temper. QCM. Sample BM 1984-5-12, 22; see Appendix III.

A similar rim frag.:
a. (thicker than example illustrated) L. 4.1 cm, diam. *c*.24.0 cm. 7.5YR 8/4 pink. Veg. and grit temper. QC3.

65 Fig. 12. Rim frag., L. 2.6 cm, diam. 14.0 cm. 7.5YR 8/2 pinkish white. Veg. temper. QCM.

66 Fig. 12. Rim frag., L. 4.6 cm, diam. 15.0 cm. 2.5YR 6/8 light red. White grit temper. QC3.

67 Fig. 12. Rim frag., L. 8.0 cm, diam. 17.0 cm. 2.5Y 7/4 pale yellow. Veg. temper. QC2. Sample BM 1984-5-12,15; see Appendix III.

68 Fig. 12. Rim frag., L. 1.7 cm, diam. 18.0 cm. 2.5YR 6/8 light red. Sparse grit temper. QCM.

69 Fig. 12. Rim frag., L. 4.8 cm, diam. 20.0 cm. 10YR 7/3 very pale brown. Veg. temper. QCM.

70 Fig. 12. Rim frag., L. 4.8 cm. Fabric 5Y 6/3 pale olive, surface 5Y 7/3 pale yellow. Veg. temper. QC2.

71 Fig. 12. Rim frag., L. 6.8 cm, diam. *c*.45-50 cm. Fabric 5Y 8/4 pink firing at surface to 10YR 8/2 white. Veg. temper. QCM.

72 Fig. 12. One-third of rim preserved, diam. 14.0 cm. 5Y 8/2 white. Veg. and grit temper. QC3. Sample BM 1984-5-12,10; see Appendex III.

73 Fig. 12. Rim frag., L. 8.0 cm, diam. 22.0 cm. 10YR 7/4 very pale brown. Veg. temper. QCM.

74 Fig. 12. Rim frag., L. 13.0 cm, diam 25.8 cm. 10YR 7/3 very pale brown. Veg. and grit temper. QCM.

Six similar rim frags:
a. L. 4.4 cm, diam. *c*.25.0 cm. 7.5YR 7/4 pink. Veg. and white grit temper. QCM.
b. L. 5.5 cm, diam. *c*. 37.0 cm. 10YR 8/3 very pale brown. Veg. temper. QCM.
c. (thicker than example illustrated) L. 3.7 cm. 10YR 8/3 very pale brown. Veg. temper. QCM.
d. L. 2.4 cm. 5YR 7/3 pink. Veg. temper. QCM.
e. L. 4.5 cm, diam. *c*.23.0 cm. 5YR 7/4 pink. Veg. temper. QC1.
f. L. 4.3 cm, diam. *c*.27.0 cm. 7.5YR 7/4 pink. Veg. temper. QC3.

75 Fig. 12. Rim. frag., L. 5.6 cm, diam. 28.0 cm. 7.5YR 7/4 pink. Veg. temper. QC2.

76 Fig. 12. Rim frag., L. 8.3 cm, diam. 31.4 cm. 10YR 7/4 very pale brown. Veg. and grit temper. QCM.

77 Fig. 13. One-third of rim, diam. 27.0 cm, and parts of wall preserved. 5YR 7/4 pink. Veg. temper. QCM.

78 Fig. 13. Rim frag., L. 18.0 cm, diam. 52.2 cm. 10YR 8/2 white. Veg. temper. QC2.

Cooking-pot wares

79 Fig. 13. Rim frag., L. 5.6 cm, diam. *c*.26.0 cm. Fabric 10YR 4/1 dark grey, surface 2.5Y N2/ black. Exterior, light horizontal burnishing. Numerous large white grit inclusions. QC2.

80 Fig. 13. Rim frag., L. 7.2 cm, diam. 25.2 cm, and large part of wall. 7.5YR N3/ very dark grey. Numerous large white grit inclusions. QC2.

81 Fig. 13. Half of jar preserved, diam. 24.0 cm. Fabric 10YR 6/4 light yellowish brown, surface 10YR 4/2 greyish brown. Large white grit inclusions. QC3. Sample BM 1984-5-12, 20; see Appendix III.

Bases

82 Fig. 14. Small part of base, diam. 8.0 cm, and section of wall. 10YR 6/4 light yellowish brown. Exterior, very lightly vertically burnished. Groups of scored lines inside. White grit temper. QC3.
Two similar base frags:
a. Half preserved, diam. 8.6 cm. Fabric 10YR 6/1 grey in centre, 5YR 7/4 pink at edges, 5YR 7/1 light grey on surface. Groups of scored lines on outside. Veg. and grit temper. QCM.
b. W. 5.5 cm, diam. 8.0 cm. 7.5YR 8/4 pink. Sparse white grit temper. QC3.

83 Fig. 14. Base, diam. 5.6-6.0 cm. Fabric 10YR 7/4 very pale brown, surface burnt. Veg. temper. QC2.
A similar base frag.:
a. W. 5.1 cm, diam. 12.0 cm. 5YR 7/1 light grey. Veg. temper. QC2.

84 Fig. 14. Base frag., W. 5.6 cm, diam. 10.0 cm. Fabric and exterior surface 2.5Y 8/2 white, interior surface 5YR 8/2 pinkish white. Veg. temper. QC3.

85 Fig. 14. Base, diam. 7.9 cm. QCM.

86 Fig. 14. Base, diam. 9.0 cm. 10YR 6/4 light yellowish brown. Veg. temper. QC3.
Three similar base frags:
a. Half, diam. *c*.5.5 cm. Fabric 7.5YR 7/6 reddish yellow, surface slip 10YR 8/4 very pale brown. Veg. and white grit temper. QC2.

b. W. 5.6 cm, diam. 6.0 cm. 7.5YR 7/4 pink. Veg. temper. QCM.

c. W. 4.0 cm, diam. *c*.10.0 cm. 7.5YR 7/2 pinkish grey. Veg. and grit temper. QC3.

87   Fig. 14. Base, diam. 5.0 cm. 5YR 7/6 reddish yellow. Veg. temper. QC1. Sample BM 1984-5-12, 23; see Appendix III.

88   Fig. 14. Half of base, diam. 6.2 cm. Fabric 5YR 7/4 pink, surface 5YR 7/6 reddish yellow. Veg. temper. QCM.

89   Fig. 14. Base, diam. 5.9 cm. Fabric 10YR 7/3 very pale brown, surface 10YR 8/3 very pale brown. Veg. temper. QC2.

Three similar base frags:
a. Base, diam. 5.5 cm. Fabric 5YR 7/3 pink, surface slip 10YR 8/2 white. Veg. temper. QCM.
b. Frag., W. 3.7 cm., diam. *c*.8.0 cm. 10YR 7/2 light grey. Veg. temper. QCM.
c. Base (in poor condition), diam. 5.1 cm. 10YR 8/3 very pale brown. Veg. temper. QC2.

90   Fig. 14. Base, diam. 9.6 cm. Fabric 5YR 7/6 reddish yellow, surface slip 10YR 8/3 very pale brown. Veg. temper. QC2.

Two similar base frags:
a. W. 7.4 cm, diam. 9.0 cm. Fabric 5YR 6/6 reddish yellow, surface slip 10YR 6/4 light yellowish brown. Veg. temper. QCM.
b. W. 4.6 cm, diam. *c*.8.0 cm. 10YR 7/2 light grey. Veg. temper. QCM.

91   Fig. 14. Half of base, diam. 9.6 cm. 10YR 7/3 very pale brown. Veg. and fine grit temper. QC2.

92   Fig. 14. Half of base, diam. 10.0 cm. Fabric 5YR 7/4 pink, surface 7.5YR 8/2 pinkish white. Veg. temper. QC2.

93   Fig. 14. Half of base, diam. 8.4 cm. 2.5Y 8/2 white. Veg. temper. QC2.

94   Fig. 14. Most of base, diam. 9.1 cm. Fabric 2.5YR 6/6 light red, slip on exterior 10YR 8/2 white, slip/wash on interior 7.5YR 8/4 pink. Veg. temper. QC1.

95   Fig. 14. Half of base, diam. 7.8 cm. Fabric 10YR 7/3 very pale brown, surface 5YR 7/4 pink. Veg. temper. QC3.

Three similar base frags:
a. W. 4.3 cm, diam. 8.0 cm. Fabric 10YR 7/4 very pale brown, surface 10YR 4/1 dark grey. Veg. temper. QC3.
b. W. 4.1 cm, diam. *c*.6.0cm. 5YR 7/3 pink. Veg. temper. QCM.
c. W. 4.1 cm, diam. *c*.10.0 cm. 7.5YR 7/4 pink. Veg. and white grit temper. QCM.

96   Fig. 14. Most of base preserved, diam. 2.8 cm. 2.5YR 6/6 light red. Veg. temper. QCM.

Three similar base frags:
a. W. 4.8 cm, diam. 11.0 cm. 5YR 6/4 light reddish brown. Veg. temper. QCM.
b. W. 4.7 cm, diam. 8.0 cm. 10YR 6/4 light yellowish brown. Veg. temper. QCM.
c. (thinner than example illustrated) L. 2.3 cm, diam. *c*.20.0 cm. 10YR 7/4 very pale brown. Veg. temper. QCM.

97   Fig. 14. Half of base, diam. 3.4 cm. 7.5YR 7/4 pink. Veg. temper. QCM.

98   Fig. 14. Base, diam. 4.4 cm. Fabric 10YR 7/4 very pale brown, surface 10YR 8/3 very pale brown, light wash on exterior. Veg. temper. QC3. Sample BM 1984-5-12, 11; see Appendix III.

A similar base frag:
a. W. 2.7 cm, diam. *c*.7.0 cm. 10YR 7/4 very pale brown. Veg. temper. QC3.

99   Fig. 14. Quarter of base, diam. 14.0 cm. Fabric 5YR 7/4 pink, surface 10YR 7/3 very pale brown. Veg. temper. QC3.

Two similar base frags:
a. W. 5.3 cm, diam. 8.0 cm. 10YR 6/4 light yellowish brown. Veg. temper. QC3.
b. W. 5.8 cm, diam. 6.0 cm. 7.5YR 6/4 light brown. Veg. temper. QCM.

Qasrij Cliff sherd-count

	Mainly vegetable temper	Mixed vegetable and grit temper	Mainly grit temper	Temper unobservable/ undetermined	Totals
QC1	18	-	1	-	19
QC2	171	19	16	-	206
QC3	265	36	19	-	320
QCM	218	49	19	4	290
Totals	672	104	55	4	835

N.B.   These totals represent a combination of *unjoined* body sherds and diagnostic pieces, listed in the catalogue, that are counted as single items even when they are made up of a number of sherds.

g. Discussion of pottery from Qasrij Cliff

Bowls (1-25)

Apart from nos 1-2 which are apparently plain types with simple, curving walls, nos 3-25 are all carinated bowls of standard Late Assyrian type. There is some variation in the rim shape, but most commonly it is thickened and slightly everted. Of the four complete profiles, one (no. 6) has a flat bottom and three (nos 17-19) have a ring-base. These bowls are predominantly vegetable-tempered, and have a fabric colour generally varying between very pale brown, pink and light red. Normally, there is no observable surface treatment. Carinated bowls of this type are well attested at Nimrud, where they were found in large quantities (Joan Oates 1954: pl. XXXVII, 4-5, 10; 1959:132, pls XXXV-XXXVI) and at Ashur (Haller 1954: pl. 6, *passim*).

Fine wares (26-48)

Gathered in this section are vessels of various types that are either small or thin-walled and so qualify for the description of 'fine wares'; the term is not used here as a description of the fabric. The bowls nos 29-30 are smaller versions of the carinated bowls with ring-base discussed above. The cups nos 34-7, of which unfortunately only bases survive, may be compared with the 'istikans' from Nimrud published by Joan Oates (1959: pl. XXXVI, 37-49), but ours appear to be larger and rather more coarse than the Nimrud examples. The beaker no. 42, plus pieces from four related beakers, belongs to a type well represented at Nimrud both in 'palace ware', generally with dimpled bodies (Joan Oates 1959: pl. XXXVII, 60-67), and in more common fabric such as ours (Joan Oates 1959: pl. XXXVII, 79). The rim fragments no. 47 may also be from a beaker.

Jars (49-78)

There is an interesting range of jar forms from Qasrij Cliff, but unfortunately no complete profiles. The best-preserved example (no. 53), with bevelled rim, neck thickening towards the top and a slight collar, belongs to a type 'occurring frequently in both Late Assyrian and squatter occupation debris' at Nimrud (Joan Oates 1959: 145, no. 93, pl. XXXVII, 93). The Nimrud examples have a ring-base. Other related forms from Qasrij Cliff include nos 51-2 and 60. The forms nos 49-50, with collar and flaring mouth, the rims slightly thickened and rounded, belong to large storage jars of a type that also seems to occur at Nimrud (Joan Oates 1954: pl. XXXIX, 1-3). Generally, however, few of the Nimrud jars have been published, and so it is not possible to find precise parallels for all the Qasrij Cliff types. However, there is no reason to suppose that any of them are not Assyrian in date or manufacture. As with the bowls, the vast majority of the jar fabrics are vegetable-tempered. The commonest colour-range is from light brown to pink.

Cooking-pot wares (79-81)

These are characterised by their coarse fabrics with large white grit inclusions; the colour of the fabric varies from black to brown. Amongst the forms there is a hole-mouth jar (no. 80) and a jar with one or two small handles at the rim (no. 81).

Bases (82-99)

Flat bases, ring-bases and round bases are all attested, belonging variously to bowls and jars. Nos 96-7 and related examples may belong to beakers.

h. Conclusions

The large circular pit at Qasrij Cliff was almost certainly a grain silo that, after it had fallen into disuse, was filled with rubbish, principally pottery and bones. This process seems to have been completed in a fairly short period of time, as there was no great distinction between the various strata in the pit and nothing to show that it had been open to the elements for a long period, such as would be demonstrated by layers of mud or silt. No occupation levels were found associated with this pit, and it is presumed they had been eroded away, either by the River Tigris itself or by the wadi immediately to the east of the site.

A large quantity of pottery was recovered from the pit - well over 1,000 sherds - and it was possible to reconstruct a number of complete profiles and some nearly complete. Consistent with having been thrown into a pit, the pottery was all fragmentary when found. Without exception all this pottery seems to be Late Assyrian in date, and there are close connections with material from sites such as Nimrud. A notable feature was the remarkable extent to which vegetable temper (chaff etc.) had been included in the fabric; grit-tempered wares were far less common, and relatively unusual (see Qasrij Cliff sherd-count). This was so much the case that when the pottery from Qasrij Cliff and from the later site of Khirbet Qasrij was being processed at the same time in Babneet it was usually possible to tell at a glance from which site a particular potsherd came. The pottery from Qasrij Cliff could in theory date from anywhere between the ninth and seventh centuries BC. However, because of its dissimilarity to the pottery from Khirbet Qasrij, and because a number of the forms apparently from the destruction levels at Nimrud (and therefore dating from 614-612 BC or later) are not present at Qasrij Cliff, I would incline towards a relatively early date, probably in the eighth century BC. A date in the ninth century BC is less likely, particularly as a small iron rod was found in the pit, and it is generally assumed that iron was not common in the ninth century.

Apart from the pottery, the few small finds from Qasrij Cliff are all consistent with a date in the Late Assyrian period. An exception here is the red chert bladelet core (QC2; Fig. 6a) that is almost certainly earlier. The presence of prehistoric occupation in the area is also suggested by the discovery, in the vicinity of the pit but on the surface of the ground, of two more flint cores (Fig. 6b).

What is the significance of Qasrij Cliff? In the first place, no corpus of Late Assyrian pottery from this area has yet been published, although there are other sites with Late Assyrian levels in the vicinity. Within the Saddam Dam Salvage Project, and on the east bank of the Tigris, these include Tell Baqaq 2 and Tell Ronak (Killick and Black 1985: 228, 238; Yusif 1987) and Khirbet Khatuniyeh (Curtis and Green 1987), but the pottery from these sites has not yet been fully published and in any case they are not necessarily of precisely the same date as Qasrij Cliff. Secondly, in spite of the large amount of excavation undertaken on Assyrian sites, Late Assyrian pottery as a whole is poorly dated. It still remains difficult to distinguish between ninth-century and seventh-century types. This is partly because at sites such as Nimrud, where Late Assyrian pottery occurs in greatest abundance, the majority of material has been found in late seventh-century contexts, although some of it may be substantially earlier. At Ashur the problem is rather different, in that most of the published pottery comes from graves and tombs. It is evident, then, that a homogeneous collection of pottery, spanning a relatively short period of time and coming from an undisturbed context, even though it is only a small group, will in due course be useful for a better understanding of the typology of Late Assyrian pottery. When more work is undertaken on Late Assyrian pottery, as it inevitably will be, it is to be hoped that the pottery from Qasrij Cliff will find its proper niche in the sequence and thereby justify the excavation of this small site.

1. It used to be thought that there was late Assyrian occupation at the large site of Tell Jikan, but this seems to be due to a misunderstanding arising from the publication of a photograph showing objects from Jikan in association with a Late Assyrian brick (Pillet 1962: fig. 28). The brick, however, is almost certainly from Khorsabad.

Part 2

EXCAVATIONS AT KHIRBET QASRIJ

a. Introduction

The site of Khirbet Qasrij ('ruins of Qasrij') is a little inland from Qasrij Cliff, and is bounded on the east side by the Wadi Qasrij (see Fig. 3). The size of the site is substantial, and it may extend to the west as far as Wadi Kharabeh. To the north it does not seem to go as far as the bank of the Tigris, as two sondages dug on the cliff-top in association with the work at Qasrij Cliff (QC1 and QC2) were found to be quite sterile. To the south, the site appears to be delimited by the track crossing over Wadi Kharabeh and going round Wadi Qasrij. The main part of the site is situated just above the 270 m contour. It is presumably the site marked no. 12 on the map of 'Archaeological sites at the Mosul Dam reservoir' produced by the State Organization of Antiquities and Heritage. Periods represented there are described as XVI-XVIII (Parthian-Islamic), and the site is named as 'Kharab Shatani'. This should not be confused with the site that was excavated by the University of Edinburgh, known as 'Kh. Kharab Shatani', which is no. 10 on the map.[1] On the east side of Wadi Qasrij, and therefore opposite the site, is the village of Qasrij. It appears to be comparatively modern, and according to local tradition it was founded in 1945 by people from the nearby village of Babneet. It was abandoned in 1982, and by 1984 the only building left standing was a mosque.

The origin of the name Qasrij is obscure, and it is not known whether the village gave its name to the wadi or vice versa. The local villagers, usually a good source of speculation, have no suggestions to offer about the etymology of the name. It may perhaps be derived from the word *qasr*, but it would then be difficult to account for the final consonant in the name. Michael Roaf suggests it may be a contracted form of 'Qasr Serij' (castle of [St] Sergius). At first I thought this a little unlikely, as the well-known Qasr Serij, the Church of St Sergius (David Oates 1968 : 106-17), is not only on the other side of the Tigris but is some 25 km from Qasrij as the crow flies. I have since discovered, however, that the monastery on Jebel Butmah is also sometimes known as Qasr Serij (Fiey 1958 : 126),[2] but is in fact dedicated to a different Sergius. This was an anchorite known as

'St Sergius of the Arid Mountain', as opposed to the Roman officer who was martyred in about AD 303 and to whom a number of eastern churches are dedicated. Jebel Butmah is also on the other side of the Tigris, but it is relatively close to Qasrij and is clearly visible from the site. Given this, Dr Roaf's suggestion is far from implausible.

I first visited the site of Khirbet Qasrij on 10 March 1983 in the company of Dr Geofffrey Summers and his wife Françoise, while I was staying at Babneet with the British Archaeological Expedition to Iraq. We walked along the west bank of Wadi Qasrij, inland from Qasrij Cliff, and about 285 m to the south-east of the cliff site we noted that there was a cluster of sherds on the high ground about 10 m from the edge of the wadi. Most of these sherds were undistinctive, but a few looked as if they could belong to the post-Assyrian period. This was significant, as I was looking for a site that might cast light on this rather obscure period. Writing in 1957, David Oates had remarked that the dating of post-Assyrian pottery constituted 'one of the most serious gaps in our knowledge of the history of Northern Iraq' (David Oates 1957 : 38). Subsequent work has done a little to improve the situation, but the statement is still valid. I therefore determined to dig a sondage on the site, and between 14 and 20 March 1983 a 2 m x 4 m trench was dug, comprising the northern half of what was later to be termed trench A1 (Fig. 14). Evidence was found for a single period of occupation only, represented by the stone footings of a wall running diagonally across the trench, that is to say in a NE-SW orientation. The associated pottery was indeed post-Assyrian, and as the wall-footings were not far below the surface it was felt that a larger area of the settlement could be cleared relatively quickly and cheaply.

Consequently, full-scale excavations were carried out in the early spring of 1984 by a British Museum team consisting of myself and Dr D. Collon (archaeologists) and R.K. Uprichard (conservator). Sd Abd al-Salaam was the representative of the State Organization of Antiquities and Heritage, and best thanks are due to him for his constant help and encouragement. During the 1984 season we stayed at Babneet with the British Archaeological Expedition who were working at Tell Mohammed 'Arab. We are grateful to them for their hospitality and co-operation, particularly to their then Director, Dr Michael Roaf.

1. For a report on the Halaf levels at this site, see Watkins and Campbell 1986.

2. It is more commonly known as 'Deir al mu'allaq' or 'the hanging monastery'.

b. The excavation [1]

As stated above, an initial sondage at Khirbet Qasrij was dug in March 1983; this operation was effected with a workforce of three men, including one Sherqati. The main excavation took place between 13 February and 27 March 1984, and the workforce consisted of one Sherqati and up to nine local workmen drawn from the nearby villages of Babira and Kharabeh Shattani. On one exceptional day the number of workmen was boosted to twenty-one, when operations were temporarily suspended at Tell Mohammed 'Arab. During this season efforts were concentrated on the area adjacent to the sondage dug in 1983, and an area with maximum dimensions of 26 m x 14 m was completely cleared. In addition, two 2 m x 1 m sondages were dug at intervals of 30 m and 50 m respectively from the north-west corner of the main excavated area, and two outlying trenches were dug in an effort to determine the size of the settlement (Fig. 3). Each of these measured 4 m x 2 m, and they were named PF (ploughed field) and WR (wadi road) respectively.

Main area The 4 m x 2 m sondage dug in 1983 was enlarged into a 4 m x 4 m trench (A1) and a further ten 4 m x 4 m trenches were opened (A2-5, B1-5, C1) (Pl. IIa). After the sections had been drawn, all the baulks between these trenches were removed, and trench B1 was extended 2 m to the east in order to complete a section of the plan. In this way, an area measuring up to 26 m x 14 m was completely cleared (Pls IIb, IIIa-b). Over the whole area the topsoil was soft and medium brown in colour. It varied in depth between 6 cm and 48 cm, but both these extremes were exceptional. Generally, it was about 16 cm deep. The area had recently been ploughed, and 16 cm or a little less probably represents the average depth of ploughing. In a few places where the soft brown topsoil appeared to go much deeper there could have been animal disturbance or levelling action by the plough. Where the topsoil was very shallow and the underlying deposit undisturbed, the plough had apparently jumped, probably because of the presence of stones close to the surface.

Beneath the layer of topsoil was a hard-packed light brown deposit that extended down to the pavements which covered much of the area. These stone pavements were very shallow at the east end of the excavation, in the east end of B1 being just 8 cm below the surface in places, and becoming deeper at the west of the excavation, reaching a depth of 59 cm below surface in trench A5. This discrepancy is explained by the fact that the modern contours were rising slowly towards the west. The hard-packed light brown deposit presumably represents broken-down mud-brick, although no forms were discernible and the deposit generally had a fine, even consistency. No evidence was actually found for mud-bricks above the wall foundations, but they must once have existed. There were no floor deposits as such, in the form of decayed organic matter or ash above the pavements, probably for two reasons. First, much of the area was probably open in antiquity and never roofed over; secondly, the pavements are so close to the surface that the survival of such deposits is hardly to be expected. Occasionally stones were found above the level of the pavements, but none of them appeared to be *in situ*, and some had clearly been pulled out of position by the plough. Over the whole of the main area no evidence was found for more than one level of occupation with the exception of a few stray Islamic sherds, notably the 'turban handle' (pottery catalogue no. 361) and possibly a couple of glazed sherds. Also, apart from ploughing, there were no indications of any other sort of disturbance, such as man-made pits or graves. There was, however, occasional evidence of animal activity, such as in trench A1.

Therefore, in most trenches the pottery, bones and small finds were removed in two batches, batch 1 representing the topsoil and batch 2 the hard-packed light brown deposit beneath. There were a few exceptions to this, mainly in the areas around the kiln and in the trenches at the east end of the excavation. The latter were dug at an early stage in the excavation when we were still feeling our way and unsure of the stratigraphy. Thus, in trench A1, batch 2 represents material from above the pavement in the south-east corner of the trench, batch 3 material from the south-west part of the trench and around the oven, batches 3a-d pottery in close association with the oven, and batch 4 material from the central part of the trench beneath some small fallen stones. In trench A2 the batch number 3 was given to material immediately above the pavement, although there was no change in the character of the deposit. In trench C1, bones from beneath a cluster of stones in the north part of the trench were given the batch number 3. In the baulk between the trenches A3 and B3, material from beneath a diagonal line of small stones towards the west end of the baulk (see Figs 15-16) was assigned to batch 3. Elsewhere, material was divided into more than two batches in the vicinity of the kiln. Accordingly, in trench B4, batch 3 represents material from the top part of the kiln, that is after the kiln had been identified and we were clearing out the uppermost deposits inside the outline. The same applies to batch 3 from the baulk between trenches B3 and B4. The deposit from inside the kiln - collapsed debris and ash that was undoubtedly associated with this feature - was given the batch description 'kiln'. Lastly, batch 4 from trench B4 applies to a scatter of stones, burnt brick and pottery found in the south of the kiln area and pottery lying on the large

1. Preliminary reports about the excavation at Khirbet Qasrij have appeared in Curtis 1985 and Killick and Black 1985:236-7.

block of sandstone to the south of the kiln.

As stated above, much of the excavated area was covered by stone pavements; there were in addition stone wall-footings and a raised stone platform. Most of the stones used were of the local limestone which is plentiful in the area, but in addition there was quite extensive use of smoothed 'river pebbles', sometimes to fill the spaces between larger stones but also to make small areas of pavement on their own. Stones of basalt and conglomerate were also observed, but these were far less common. In drawing the plan (Figs 15-16), every effort was made to distinguish between the different types of stone. Levels were taken from a limestone outcrop to the east of the main excavated area, and figures on the plan denote levels above or below a prominent stone in this outcrop. The stone in question was 7.13 m above the bed of Wadi Qasrij. In addition to drawing a complete plan of the remains that were uncovered, some aerial photographs were taken of the area (Pl. IV). This was made possible through the good offices of Dr Roaf, who not only lent us the equipment but also provided the necessary technical expertise. The photographs were taken with a 35mm camera suspended from a large box-kite. The kite was secured to a heavy wooden winch, and the camera shutter was activated by a remote-control gadget.

The most remarkable feature in the main excavated area was a small complex centred on a kiln for firing pottery (Pl. Va). The kiln itself is mostly in square B4, and it is approximately oval in shape. Little of the superstructure was preserved, and what we actually found was the fire-pit and the collapsed floor of the kiln-chamber. This kiln will be described in more detail below.

To the north of the kiln and to the south-west of it were well-preserved stone pavements; to the north-west the pavement was poorly preserved, but originally it had probably been continuous. Beyond the pavement on the north-east side was a carefully constructed stone platform, rectangular in shape and about 15 cm higher than the pavement level. It measured approximately 3 m x 2 m. The purpose of this platform is not really clear, but one possibility is that it may have been for drying the pots prior to firing. After being fashioned by the potter, they could have been stacked here until 'green-hard' and ready to be fired in the kiln. In front of this platform, that is to the south-west of it, three of the paving-stones had regular holes in them (Pl. VIb). From west to east, the first had a hole 9 cm in diameter going right through the stone, which was 16 cm thick; the second had a shallow hole 3 cm in depth and 8 cm in diameter; and the third had a large hole - 14 cm in diameter - that again went right through the stone, but here the stone was comparatively thin. The purpose of the holes in these stones is obscure. Only one of them - that in the middle - looks like a pivot-stone of the type usually found in association with doors, but there could hardly have been a door in this position. The holes to either side of it look as if they might have accommodated poles, perhaps for an awning or some kind of structure, but again their position rather rules this out. One possibility, suggested by their presence in a complex apparently devoted to the production of pottery, is that these stones were used for supporting potters' wheels or turn-tables. There are two ways in which this might have been done. First, a pivot on the bottom of the turn-table or a pivot at the base of a shaft supporting a fly-wheel and wheel-head could have rotated in the hole, or second, the holes might have supported a stationary post on which the turn-table revolved (for illustrations of the latter technique, see Childe 1955: figs 120, 123). If our interpretation of these holes is correct, the second method is more likely in view of the depth of the holes. On the platform itself, which we have suggested might have been used for drying pots preparatory to firing, none of the stones had holes in them.

To the west of the platform, the pavements and the kiln, and running in a NE-SW direction for a distance of about 11 m, was a wall represented by stone foundations and preserved to a maximum height of about 25 cm above the level of the pavement. On average it was more than 80 cm wide. At its south-west end the wall turned a 90° angle and after a distance of approximately 2.30 m turned back again and ran towards the kiln, thus forming three sides of a rectangle. It stopped short of the kiln, however, leaving a gap of approximately 1.15 m between the end of the wall and the kiln. In the long part of the wall there are two gaps, or doorways, one 1.30 m wide, opposite the pavement in front of the platform, and the other, of approximately the same width, about 3 m to the south. In the northern doorway was found a cluster of bones at a comparatively high level (about 37 cm below surface), but no evidence of a pit. This wall has some puzzling features. Of course, we do not know how high it stood in antiquity: it could have been a low boundary-wall, much as it was when discovered, or there might have been mud-bricks on top of the stone foundations. But in either case one might have expected the wall to have enclosed the compound containing the kiln, that is to have returned to the east of the kiln rather than stopping short on a direct line with the front of it. However, it is possible that because of the heat and smoke generated and the need for a good draught it was desirable to have an open space on one side of the kiln. In any case, even today industrial areas in towns or villages in the Middle East are difficult to interpret exactly; the plan is seldom tidy, and there are frequently stumps of walls and other features whose purpose is unclear, at least to an uninformed outsider.

Immediately to the south of the kiln there was no pavement as such, but we found here, at a distance of 65 cm from the kiln, an extensive mass of sandstone, light red in colour and up to 10 cm thick (Pl. VIa). It was irregular in shape, and measured about 1.85 m by 90 cm. When found, it had a fairly homogeneous appearance, suggesting it was a single slab, but the stone was actually very weathered and broken down and it could originally have been a number of different slabs that in the process of time had merged together. Initially I was inclined to associate the presence of this sandstone with the production of pottery that we know to have taken place in the vicinity, and assumed that it might have been for the use of the potters, possibly as a temper for the clay. However, I am informed by my colleague Ian Freestone in the British Museum Research Laboratory that there was no evidence of sandstone having been used to temper the pottery in the samples examined in the British Museum. He thinks it more likely that this large, flat stone was the surface on which the potters would have wedged and kneaded their clay to get the air out and make it workable. This essential process needs a firm, clean, flat surface. Another possibility is that the sandstone was simply used as paving. In the vicinity of Qasrij there are a number of outcrops of sandstone, so it was presumably of local origin. Apart from this sandstone, in the southern part of trench B4 various pieces of slag and fragments of burnt brick were found, all of which presumably originated from the kiln. The greatest number of wasters, though, was found in square A3 and in the kiln itself. A glass bead (KQ14; Fig. 21) was found in the space between the kiln and the wall to the south-west at a depth of 34 cm below surface.

Another interesting object found in the vicinity of the kiln was the base of a large pottery container. This was to the east of the kiln, at a distance of 2.25 m. This container, or jar, was circular, and had a flat bottom, diameter 75 cm, and straight sides preserved to a maximum height of 39 cm. It is tempting to suppose that it was for the use of the potters, perhaps as a water container. A stone duck-weight (KQ1; Pl. XII) was found 16 cm to the west of the jar; it was lying on its side, at the same level as the base of the large jar and the nearby paving-stones, at 50 cm below the surface. It was overlaid and surrounded by the same hard-packed brown deposit that was observed elsewhere in this area.

To the west of the enclosure-wall partially screening the kiln was another stone pavement, on the same level as that to the east of the wall. It was particularly well preserved in the south-western part of the main excavated area. Here, at a high level, on top of the hard-packed deposit and 24 cm below surface, was found a dentalium shell bead (KQ13; Fig. 21). In the extreme west of the excavated area, centred on the baulk between trenches A5 and B5 but extending into these two trenches, was a further pavement, or work-surface, separated from that just described and at a slightly higher level (Pl. Vb). It was approximately square in outline,

and measured about 2.50 m x 2.30 m. On the south-east side of this pavement one of the stones had a deep, regular hole in it similar to those observed in the stones in front of the platform in trench A3 and the baulk A3-A4. Here the hole was 9 cm in diameter and was at least 10 cm deep, going right through the stone. We suggested above that such stones might have been used for supporting potters' wheels. Another stone in this pavement, to the north of the other, had an irregular depression in it, measuring 10 cm x 7 cm and 5 cm deep. It did not appear to have served any particular function.

To the north-east of this pavement, in the south-east corner of trench A5, were a number of stones, some of them quite large, roughly arranged in a circle about 2.30 m in diameter. Within this circle there were practically no stones, and the deposit, although of the same nature as elsewhere, was comparatively soft. This, combined with the fact that the surface dipped down towards the centre of the circle, suggests that the feature may have been a sump or soakaway. Near the centre of the feature, at a depth of 50 cm below surface, was found an iron pin (KQ5; Fig. 21).

To the north of this feature, that is in the north part of trench A5, was a cluster of stones, some of them extremely large, with the biggest measuring 119 cm x 108 cm. These stones were not all lying flat and were at different levels. A small iron peg (KQ4; Fig. 21) was found in the vicinity of the stones in the north-east corner of the trench at a depth of 55 cm below surface. More large stones were found in the northern part of trench A4, and those in the north-eastern section of the trench in particular were at a high level. Other stones were clearly running underneath them, and the upper stones were separated in places by 40 cm of hard brown deposit from the floor or surface beneath. None of these stones was lying flat, and they are presumably in a secondary context, but how or why they came to be in this position is unclear. Beneath these stones was found the top part of a terracotta wall-nail (KQ9; Fig. 22), and the fragment of another (KQ8; Fig. 22) was also found in trench A4. Another extremely large stone was found in the south-west corner of trench A4, this time separated from the pavement beneath by up to 10 cm of hard brown deposit. This stone was 67 cm long and was almost triangular in section, measuring 40 cm in width and 30 cm in height. Immediately next to the large stone, on the west side of it, a small fragment of glass was found in the topsoil, about 14 cm below the surface. It measured 1.65 cm x 1.7 cm, was convex in shape and was probably a neck fragment from a bottle or jar.

Turning now to the area to the east of the kiln complex, in the north part, mainly in trench A2, was another stone pavement, or work-surface. It now has a rather irregular appearance, but it may originally have been rectangular, measuring about 4.90 m x 2.70 m. On the south-west side of the platform is a rectangular projection that may have been the stump of a wall, but the stones here were not significantly higher than those belonging to the pavement. This feature extends for about 1.70 m and is up to 1 m wide. In the area of the pavement, in the eastern part of trench A2, there was a fairly dense scatter of potsherds, pithos fragments and a few small finds (Fig. 19a). These were generally slightly above the level of the paving-stones, but some of the pithos fragments at least, which fitted together with others at a higher level, were on or only slightly above the pavement and show that all this material should be regarded as contemporary with the pavement. The pithos fragments could be joined together to form a small coffin (pottery catalogue no. 290). Two complete pottery vessels were recovered from this area: a footed goblet (pottery catalogue no. 270) and a bottle with bands of dark brown paint (pottery catalogue no. 276; Pls VIIb, XIa). The small finds comprised a fashioned lump of iron that may have been a weight (KQ2; Fig. 21), a fragment of what may have been a terracotta wall-nail (KQ32; Fig. 22), and a curious, oval-shaped pottery container (KQ36; Fig. 22). To the south-west of this pavement, in the eastern part of trench B3, in the western part of B2 and in the baulk between them, was an irregular scatter of stones that constituted the remains of another pavement, but its original outline or extent could not be well established. Pottery recovered from this area included parts of a bowl with inturned rim (pottery catalogue no. 81) that was found about 65 cm to the south-east of the large jar described above and at about 40 cm below surface, definitely associated with the paving-stones and on a floor level corresponding to that on which the duck-weight was found. In the A2-A3-B2-B3 baulk, two small jars were found (pottery catalogue nos 264, 271), both upside-down with their mouths on the pavement level (Pl. VIIa). Nearby, at the north end of the B2-B3 baulk, parts of a pottery pipe lamp (KQ7; pottery catalogue no. 360) and the bottom part of a polychrome glazed jar (pottery catalogue no. 351; Pl. XIb) were at a slightly higher level but still well below the topsoil layer. Other finds from this area comprise an iron knife blade (KQ3; Fig. 21) from the southern part of B2 at 30 cm below surface, the leg from a stone tripod (KQ11; Fig. 22) from the eastern part of B3 at a depth of 36 cm, and two circular stones with holes in the centre (KQ30, 34; Fig. 22). Both of these are from the B2-B3 baulk, and while various uses may be postulated for such stones, their presence not far from the kiln suggests that they may have had something to do with pottery production, perhaps acting as bearings or miniature fly-wheels for potters' turn-tables or wheels.

In the extreme eastern part of the main excavation, chiefly in the trenches A1 and B1, part at least of the area seems to have been roofed over and to have had perhaps a domestic function. Two parallel walls running in a NW-SE direction - and thereby on the same alignment as all the other architectural features in the main excavated area - describe the two sides of what may be a room. On the north, except for a stump of wall in the NW corner, no evidence was found for a continuous wall, but to the south the wall continues on the south-east side, and in the south-west corner there is what seems to be a doorway. The stone in the extreme south-east corner of B1 is probably a pivot-stone: the hole in this stone is 7 cm in diameter and 4 cm deep. The internal measurements of this room are about 2.70 m by 3.80 m; the doorway is about 90 cm wide, and the walls are about 40-50 cm thick. These walls are not preserved to a height much greater than that of the nearby pavements, but their outline is clear enough. Inside the room there is no continuous pavement but a cluster of small stones at one end, much as one would expect to find in a room that was roofed over and not exposed to the elements. To the east of this building there is a continuous pavement, extending to the east (in the eastern extension of B1) to a point where the ground level starts to dip down towards the wadi and the ancient remains are eroded away. To the north, this pavement is delimited by a return of the wall that forms the east side of the building. To the north of this wall is a line of stones excavated in 1983 which probably constituted another wall, but its relationship to the nearby architecture is not clear. In the south-western quarter of trench A1 was an oven, 48-71 cm in diameter, apparently made up of miscellaneous sherds with a lining of burnt clay. Large body sherds from at least five separate pots were used for lining this oven.

In trench C1, where the ancient remains would have been very close to the surface, they had largely been removed by ploughing. Thus all that was found in this trench were two scatters of small stones in the western part, although the whole area was excavated to a depth of about 35 cm below surface. Below the northernmost cluster of stones a small group of bones was found, identified by Marie-Odile Saacké as part of a goat's skeleton. In this area a small lump of 'Egyptian blue' was found in the B1-C1 baulk at a depth of about 44 cm below surface (see Appendix II). A fragment of basalt saddle-quern was also recovered from this baulk. Similar fragments of quern were found in the A3-A4 baulk (two examples) and in trench B1/2.

The kiln (Figs 19b, 20a-d)   Most of the kiln was in the north-east corner of trench B4, but parts of it extended into the surrounding baulks. The existence of a kiln first became evident through the discovery of a band of highly vitrified clay, which proved on further examination to be the lining of the kiln fire-pit or combustion-chamber (Pl. IXa). This was roughly oval in shape, measuring 2.50 m x 1.38 m, and was preserved above the surrounding pavement level to a maximum height of 19 cm (35 cm below surface). The paving-stones in the centre of

B4 went right up to the vitrified lining, with no evidence of disturbance, showing that the kiln and surrounding pavements and other features are all contemporary. Also, the kiln is orientated in the same way - NE-SW - as these other features and, as we have seen, appears to be an integral part of the plan in this area. The kiln was emptied out in two halves so that a section could be drawn across it (Fig. 20c). It transpired that the fire-pit was largely subterranean, and the superstructure of this kiln, that is the oven proper, or the kiln-chamber, was scarcely preserved (Pl. IXb). Nevertheless, enough was extant to show that this kiln was a fairly simple sort of construction and belonged to the type known as 'double-chamber updraught kilns'.

The bottom of the fire-pit was roughly oval in shape, but very rounded at the south-west end and almost squared-off at the other end. The bottom was flat, measured 1.93 m x 1.12 m, and was 1.20 m below pavement level in the centre. The pit was dug out of the bedrock clay, and the bottom left untreated. The sides of the pit, however, had been smeared with mud, generally to a thickness of 5-7 cm, and in a few places finger impressions could be observed. The bottom of the pit was burnt bright orange in colour, and the sides were heavily vitrified, showing that the temperature in the fire-pit had reached a high level.

The sides of the fire-pit were approximately vertical everywhere except at the south-west end, which was slightly sloping. At 80-90 cm above the floor, however, the sides started to converge slightly: this was particularly noticeable on the south-east side, where there was quite an overhang in the middle. Clearly, this was to support the floor of the oven proper. At the south-west end of the fire-pit, there was a gap in the vitrified pit lining that was preserved above pavement level. Instead the plastered side of the pit rose smoothly and without interruption to ground level. Here, then, was the stoke-hole for the kiln, the aperture through which the fuel was thrown in and the ashes raked out. Behind the plaster at the stoke-hole end, at the top of the wall, three courses of baked brick were noted, each measuring approximately 25 cm x 10 cm. Their purpose is not clear, as no bricks were observed elsewhere behind the plaster, and they only extended to a depth of 36 cm below pavement level. Possibly the stoke-hole was at one time a sloping chute into the kiln that was subsequently blocked, but no other evidence was found for this and there are paving-stones quite close to the edge of the fire-pit at this point. Alternatively, it may be that a 'step' was left at one end when the kiln was being dug out, and that this was subsequently bricked up.

At the bottom of the fire-pit was a layer about 35 cm deep of fine, light grey ash mixed with flecks of charcoal and a few potsherds. A sample of this deposit was taken for Carbon 14 analysis, but unfortunately there was not enough carbon present in the sample for the test to be done in the British Museum Research Laboratory. Above this layer, the fire-pit was filled with a soft reddish brown deposit, with extensive patches of burnt reddish clay and some pockets of ash. Mixed in with this deposit were pieces of burnt brick, mostly irregular in shape, and fragments of burnt yellow clay. These had apparently fallen into the fire-pit at random. At the top of the fire-pit, in addition to the pieces of burnt brick there were a few irregularly shaped stones. Most interestingly, at this level some six of the burnt bricks were found lying on their sides in a horseshoe shape (Fig. 20b). This seems to be clear evidence that the roof of the fire-pit, or the floor of the oven itself, was barrel-vaulted, using pieces of mud-brick and stones, held together by mud plaster. There would have been a number of holes in this floor to allow the heat to rise up from the fire-pit. Scattered throughout the deposit in the fire-pit were potsherds, pottery wasters and some collapsed jars (Pls VIIIa-b). These were mostly above the layer of fine ash at the bottom of the fire-pit. What we found at Khirbet Qasrij, then, was the fire-pit of a kiln, into which had collapsed the floor of the oven, some pottery that had probably been in the oven, and perhaps some parts of the kiln superstructure.

In the fire-pit, and mixed with the debris representing the collapsed floor of the oven, was a good deal of pottery. That from the top of the fire-pit, to a depth of about 35-40 cm below the top of the lining, belongs with the batches B4/3 and B3-4/3. The remainder is labelled 'kiln'. All should be from a good, well-sealed context, but that belonging with the 'kiln' batch particularly so. Most of the pottery was mixed with the debris above the fine ash layer at the bottom of the fire-pit, and included more than thirty pottery wasters, some of them pieces of different pots fused together (Pl. Xa), and three collapsed jars (Pl.Xb), two of which could be reconstructed in drawings (pottery catalogue nos 183-4). In addition, a wide range of pottery types were recorded from the kiln, and so can be regarded as securely stratified. These include pottery catalogue nos 23, 30, 88, 107-11 and 232.

As stated above, the kiln at Khirbet Qasrij is a double-chamber updraught type. This is a comparatively simple design and there are a number of examples in the ancient Near East.[2] It is interesting, though, that here there were no pilasters or columns in the fire-pit to support the floor of the oven; instead, the fire-pit was roofed over by a barrel-vault. The absence of flues to bring oxygen into the fire-pit is surprising, but in spite of a careful search none was found. That is not to say they never existed, though, because such flues might easily have become blocked up by slag or vitrified clay. We do not know exactly what sort of fuel was used here,

2. For surveys of pottery kilns in ancient Western Asia, see Salonen 1964, Delcroix and Huot 1972, Majidzadeh 1977 and Alizadeh 1985.

but to judge from the fine ash at the bottom of the fire-chamber it was probably brushwood. As we have said, vent-holes in the floor of the oven would have allowed heat to rise from the fire-pit. It is unfortunate that practically nothing of the superstructure of the Khirbet Qasrij kiln was preserved, but it is generally supposed that the top parts of these kilns were dome-shaped (Hodges 1970:57). At the top of the dome there would have been a small opening to allow the escape of the hot gases. Very often the top parts of these kilns may have been temporary structures, made of clay, as after each firing the wall or a section of it would have had to be broken to remove the pots from inside (Hodges 1964:36).

Sondage KQ1   This 2 m x 1 m sondage was 30 m to the west of the main excavation; the north side of the sondage was aligned with the north baulk of trenches A1-A5 (Fig. 3). At a depth of about 50 cm below surface an irregular cluster of stones was found, probably part of a pavement but possibly the footings for a wall (Fig. 18a). Amongst the pottery from this sondage, types 18, 122, 188 and 325 were recorded, indicating that the occupation here was contemporary with that in the main excavated area.

Sondage KQ2   Another 2 m x 1 m sondage was laid out 50 m to the west of the main excavation (Fig. 3), again with the north side of the sondage aligned with the north baulk of trenches A1-A5. A scattering of potsherds was found in the upper levels of this sondage, but no evidence was found for permanent structures in this area. Virgin soil was found at a depth of about 50-60 cm, and digging continued to a depth of 70 cm to confirm this.

Trench PF   This 4 m x 2 m trench was laid out just over 230 m to the west of the main excavation, and about 125 m inland from the river (Fig. 3), in the middle of an area that at the time was under plough. Parts of two stone pavements were found close to the surface, the tops of the stones being between 5 cm and 20 cm deep (Fig. 18b). The pavement on the west side, measuring 1.95 m x 1.20 m, was made of large flat stones with just a few smaller stones or pebbles in the gaps between them. Three stones of basalt, found in a cluster, were probably originally quern-stones that had been re-used in the pavement. By contrast the second pavement, with a width of 80 cm and jutting into the trench to a distance of 60 cm, was made up largely of small pebbles. Both these clusters of stones were carefully laid and reasonably flat, suggesting they were pavements rather than foundations for walls. But the relationship between them was not clear, probably because, being so close to the surface, other associated stones had been ploughed up. The pottery found in this trench was similar to that recovered in the main excavation (types 57, 73, 78, 239, 315 were recorded here), and the occupation would seem to have been contemporary. No evidence was found to suggest any level of occupation earlier than the stone pavements. An interesting find in Trench PF was a large terracotta peg, broken at the top, presumably the shank from a terracotta wall-nail (KQ6; Fig. 22).

Trench WR   This was situated about 340 m to the south-west of the main excavation and 300 m inland from the Tigris (Fig. 3), just to the north of a minor east-west track that crossed over the Wadi Kharabeh and was only passable in dry weather; this was not the main track that linked Babneet and Qasrij, which went further to the south. The trench measured 4 m x 2 m. At a depth of 15-20 cm below surface stones were encountered over most of the trench, with the exception of the north-west corner. They were laid flat, obviously with the intention of forming a pavement (Fig. 18c). The stones were generally large, with just a few small stones and pebbles in the gaps between them. In two of the large stones were circular holes about 8 cm in diameter, one a deep hole and the other a shallow depression. These were reminiscent of the holes noted in a number of stones in the main excavation; they may be pivot-stones for doors (particularly the stone with the shallow hole), either *in situ* or re-used, or perhaps some other explanation is needed. As in the case of Trench PF, there were a number of parallels between the pottery recovered here and that from the main excavation (types 52, 54, 63, 73, 228, 308 were attested) and the occupation was apparently contemporary. Again, no evidence was found for earlier levels.

c. Catalogue of small finds from Khirbet Qasrij

KQ1   Pl. XII, Fig. 21; IM. Duck-weight in grey-black stone, L. 8.25 cm, H. 5.28 cm, W. 4.88 cm, Wt (after cleaning) 268.9 g. Head turned back over body, wings boldly depicted on both sides and feathers on breast indicated by two and a half registers of vertically incised lines. 'Stitching' around the edge and across the top of the beak carefully shown. Nostrils in middle of beak shown by two wedge-shaped incisions. Lightly incised lines on top of head accentuate eyes. Base flat except for four small depressions (apparently gouged out rather than chipped, perhaps to bring weight to required level). B3/2, 106 cm → N. baulk, 183 cm → W. baulk, 50 cm b.s.

Stone duck-weights were used in Mesopotamia from at least the Ur III period onwards, when there are examples inscribed with the name of Shulgi (Weissbach 1907: 394). In the Late Assyrian period they were comparatively common. Thus, from Khorsabad there are duck-weights both in bronze and stone (Loud and Altman 1938: pl. 61, 175-6, 178-87), and Layard found several stone specimens at Nimrud (Layard 1849a: I,

115-6, II, 316; 1849b: pl. 95a, 11, 17; 1853: 600-601). From Mallowan's excavations at Nimrud there are at least thirteen examples, only one of which has been published (Mallowan 1966: I, 170, 269, 337-8, n. 8; II, 420-21).[1] This duck-weight, plus the others from Nimrud that I have been able to examine and, the Khorsabad examples, are all markedly different from the Qasrij duck-weight in that they are cut off square at the end and are generally highly stylised, with few or no details added. The only possible exception is ND 2507, which looks as if it may have had elaborate decoration like the Qasrij piece, but it has been badly damaged, probably by fire, and the original appearance of the surface is now obscured. Again, however, like the other Nimrud pieces it is cut off square at the end and has a more or less rectangular profile not unlike a loaf of bread. Also cut off square at the end and comparatively plain are two seventh-century BC duck-weights from Babylon (Koldewey 1914: 190, fig. 120; Pritchard 1954: no. 120). More like the Qasrij duck-weight is a specimen from Sippar with a Neo-Babylonian inscription (De Meyer 1980: pl. 28, 70); the duck's head and neck are naturalistically modelled, and the back slopes down towards the tail-feathers although not actually coming to a point. Duck-weights are also attested in the Achaemenid period, with one stone and one bronze example from Persepolis (Schmidt 1957: pl. 82, 3-4). It is significant here that the stone duck-weight from Persepolis is much closer to the Qasrij piece than most of the Late Assyrian examples: it is carefully and naturalistically modelled, and the details on head and beak are carefully shown, even down to the 'stitching' around the edge of the beak. Given that the inscribed duck-weight from Sippar is also more compatible with our example than the Late Assyrian counterparts, it seems clear that the Qasrij duck-weight must in fact be post-Assyrian and not a survival from the Late Assyrian period.

The Qasrij duck-weight is in good condition, and the weight recorded after cleaning - 268.9 g - is probably quite close to its original weight. However, it is difficult to fit this weight into any known metrological system. If we accept for the Babylonian mina a weight of 505 g (Weissbach 1907: 389), and consequently for the shekel 8.4 g, then the Qasrij weight would represent 0.53 minas or, conversely, 32 shekels. Neither of these figures appears to be meaningful. In the Achaemenid period a new unit, the karsha, was introduced, corresponding to 10 shekels or one-sixth of a mina (Schmidt 1957: 106-7). In terms of karshas, then, the Qasrij weight would be 3.2 karshas. Again, this does not seem to be a significant figure. This is not altogether surprising, however, as it

1. Eight of the duck-weights are currently stored at the Institute of Archaeology in London. They are ND 2506-7, 5205, 7880, 7883-4, 7886 and 7888. I am grateful to Jenny Finkel for showing them to me.

has long been recognised that in many periods there was a considerable degree of variation from the national standard. In the Achaemenid period, for example, it is known that a number of different standards existed alongside one another, some of them of purely local relevance (Stern 1982: 106-7). Weights and standards are a subject on which much work remains to be done, and it is to be hoped that in due course the metrological significance of the Qasrij duck-weight will become clear; perhaps it will itself provide a pointer to a unit hitherto unattested or unremarked.

KQ2 Fig. 21; MM for study no. 282. Iron weight (?), H. 3.4 cm, max. diam. 4.25 cm, Wt (after cleaning) 217.5 g. Biconical lump of iron, flattened at top and bottom and roughly faceted, with six facets on each half. A2/2, 118 cm → N. baulk, 85 cm → E. baulk.

This is an unusual shape for a weight, as in the Late Assyrian period at least the most popular type at the lower end of the scale was the spherical bronze weight with flattened base (Curtis 1979: I, 296, II, pl. LXXI). Again, this object does not appear to fit into a known metrological scheme, nor does it seem to bear any obvious relationship to the weight of the duck-weight. Nevertheless, it is difficult to conceive of any use other than as a weight for an object of this shape.

KQ3 Fig. 21; Sulaimaniya Museum. Iron knife-blade in poor condition, with haft missing, L. 11.0 cm, max. W. 1.64 cm, max. thickness 0.3 cm. B2/2, 29 cm → S. baulk, 190 cm → E. baulk, 30 cm b.s.

KQ4 Fig. 21; MM for study no. 284. Iron 'peg', bent over at top. Mostly square in section, but tapering towards bottom. L. 6.1 cm, shank *c.*0.65 cm x 0.65 cm. A5/2, 60 cm → N. baulk, 45 cm → E. baulk, 55 cm b.s.

KQ5 Fig. 21; MM for study no. 286. Iron 'pin', square in section, tapering towards both ends. Poor condition and probably incomplete. Possibly a tool such as an awl. L. 7.05 cm, max. thickness 0.5 cm x 0.5 cm. A5/2, 120 cm → S. baulk, 80 cm → E. baulk, 50 cm b.s.

KQ6 Fig. 22; MM for study no. 268. Shank from a terracotta wall-nail, L. 15.3 cm, max. diam. 6.73 cm. Broken at top and roughly flattened at base. Circular in section, tapering towards base. Coarse fabric with vegetable temper, core 5YR 6/6 reddish yellow firing to 2.5Y 8/2 white (pale olive) on outer surface. Covered with thin, patchy layer of brown substance that may be paint or bitumen. Trench PF.

KQ7 See pottery catalogue no. 360.

KQ8 Fig. 22; MM for study no. 267. Fragment of a terracotta wall-nail, comprising upper part of shank, collar (partly broken away) and lower part of neck. L. 14.8 cm, max. W. as extant 8.9 cm. Fabric as KQ6 above, but in addition to the vegetable temper some grits, both white and micaceous. Also covered in part with a brown substance. A4/2.

KQ9   Fig. 22; MM for study no. 265. Head and neck of a terracotta wall-nail, circular in section throughout. Fabric as KQ6 above, but core 5YR 7/4 pink and no brown substance on outer surface. Max. L. 9.5 cm, diam. of head 9.0 cm. A4/2, NE corner of trench beneath high-level secondary stones.

KQ6 and 8-9 are all fragments of terracotta wall-nails (Akkadian *sikkatu*) with domed heads, short necks, circular flanges and tapering shanks. Such wall-nails are well known in Mesopotamia as early as the second millennium BC at sites such as Tell Rimah (Carter 1964: 40, top) and Nuzi (Starr 1937-9: II, pls 97, J-N, 98, A-D). They continued to be popular in the Late Assyrian period, notably at Ashur, where examples are sometimes inscribed or glazed (Andrae 1913: pls LXXX-LXXXI, CII-III, *passim;* 1923: 29, fig., pl. 36). The tradition of using wall-nails also survived into the Achaemenid period: for example, there are fragmentary wall-nails in blue composition from Persepolis, mostly inscribed with the names of Darius or Xerxes (Herzfeld 1938: 23-4, pl. VII; Schmidt 1957: 50, pl. 42, 27). Also supposedly of Achaemenid date are bronze wall-plaques with pegs in the centre from Tell ed-Daim in the Dokan (al-Tekriti 1960: pl. 9).

It is clear that these wall-nails had a decorative function and were usually associated with important administrative or religious buildings. Their use is particularly clear at Nuzi, where in one case they were found inserted in the wall 178 cm above the pavement and 95 cm apart (Starr 1937-9: I, 59).

KQ10   Fig. 21; MM for study no. 885. Medial fragment of flint blade, with no retouching. L. 4.25 cm, max. W. 2.68 cm. A3-A4/1.

KQ11   Fig. 22; MM for study no. 266. Leg from a basalt tripod, H. 11.0 cm, max. W. 9.2 cm. B3/2, 180 cm → N. baulk, 19 cm → E. baulk, 36 cm b.s.

KQ12   Fig. 21; MM for study no. 281. Cowrie shell bead, with large hole cut in back. L. 1.73 cm, W. 1.23 cm. A2/3, removal of floor.

The small cowrie shell (*cypraea moneta*), often known as the 'money cowrie' (Beck 1931: 431-2), had a wide distribution in antiquity.

KQ13   Fig. 21; MM for study no. 285. Dentalium shell bead, L. 0.75 cm, max. W. 0.55 cm. B5/2, 134 cm → N. baulk, 105 cm → E. baulk, 24 cm b.s.

Dentalium shell beads such as this are well known at a number of sites, including Nineveh (Thompson and Mallowan 1933: 180).

KQ14   Fig. 21; MM for study no. 284. Spherical glass bead, H. 1.05 cm, max. diam. 1.26 cm. In poor condition, and quite opaque. Present colour dull yellow, original colour unknown. A band of darker yellow around the middle of the bead probably indicates that glass of another colour was marverred into the surface. B4/2, 165 cm → S. baulk, 198 cm → W. baulk, 48 cm b.s.

KQ15   See pottery catalogue no. 276.

KQ16   See pottery catalogue no. 264.

KQ17   See pottery catalogue no. 271.

KQ18   See pottery catalogue no. 270.

KQ19   See pottery catalogue no. 268.

KQ20   See pottery catalogue no. 269.

KQ21   See pottery catalogue no. 184.

KQ22   See pottery catalogue no. 183.

KQ23   See pottery catalogue no. 112.

KQ24   See pottery catalogue no. 351.

KQ25   Fig. 21; MM for study no. 287. Fragmentary terracotta figurine of zoomorphic type. L. 4.25 cm, H. 2.5 cm. Head missing, fat tail probably indicating a sheep. A1/1983 sondage.

KQ26   See catalogue of objects from Qasrij Cliff (QC1).

KQ27   See catalogue of objects from Qasrij Cliff (QC3).

KQ28   See catalogue of objects from Qasrij Cliff (QC2).

KQ29   See pottery catalogue no. 110.

KQ30   Fig. 22; Sulaimaniya Museum. Circular stone with hole in centre, diam. 11.5 cm, max. thickness 4.9 cm. Dark grey stone, probably basalt. B2-B3.

Drilled stones such as KQ30 and the similar example KQ34 with which it was found had a variety of uses in antiquity. For example, they are attested as having been used as fishing-weights, loom-weights, and so on. In this case, however, the proximity of these two stones to the kiln, and the fact that they were found in an area apparently specialising in the production of pottery, suggest that they had something to do with the pottery industry. For example, they could have acted as fly-wheels, being mounted on the spindle that supported the potter's wheel. Alternatively, they could have been bearings to assist the rotation of the spindle.

KQ31   Fig. 22. Two rim fragments of a basalt bowl, diam. 21.0 cm. B1-B2/2.

KQ32   Fig. 22. A fragmentary terracotta object comprising a shank, fractured on the underside, on which is mounted a flange which is in turn surmounted by what appears to be the bottom part of a bowl. Fabric 10YR 7/6 yellow, with mainly grit and a little vegetable temper. Max. H. 6.75 cm, max. diam. 7.5 cm. A2/2, 100 cm → S. baulk, 15 cm → E. baulk, *c.*23 cm b.s.

This object is possibly part of a terracotta wall-nail as nos KQ6 and 8-9, but with a hollow head, or it could conceivably be from a pottery vessel such as a footed plate or goblet.

KQ33 Fig. 21. Tip of iron blade, probably part of an arrowhead, L. 3.29 cm, W. 1.65 cm. A2-A3-B2-B3/2, 45 cm b.s.

KQ34 Fig. 22. Circular stone with hole in centre, as KQ30. Dark grey stone, probably basalt. Diam. 11.1 cm, max. thickness 4.8 cm. B2-B3.

KQ35 Fig. 22. Rim fragment, L. 4.5 cm, of a basalt bowl, diam. 26.0 cm. C1/1.

KQ36 Fig. 22. Hollow oval-shaped object in un-baked clay with small hole, diam. *c.*1.2 cm, at top centre. Now in three fragments which do not quite join, but reconstruction is certain. The object has been carefully made, coil-built and smoothed on the interior. Fabric 5YR 7/4 pink. A2/2.

There is no doubt that this object was made for a specific purpose, but that purpose is now obscure. One possibility, however, is that it had something to do with beekeeping, and was perhaps a queen cage for housing a queen bee. The main purpose of such cages is to move the queen from one place to another and in so doing induce the worker bees to follow her. We have consulted Dr Eva Crane, the author of a recent history of bee-keeping (1983), on this matter, but she is reluctant to accept the Qasrij object as a queen cage. She points out that modern cages are usually made of textile, and believes that a solid queen cage with only a single hole for the entrance and exit of the bee would not allow enough ventilation. However, on an Egyptian wall-painting of the seventh century BC in the tomb of Pa-Bu-Sa at Thebes, a series of small cigar-shaped objects are shown in a beekeeping context (Neufeld 1978: fig. 9). These objects are usually identified as hives, but they seem to be very small and are very close in shape to the Qasrij object. Unfortunately no other evidence for beekeeping, such as would have supported our tentative identification, was found at Qasrij, so for the time being the purpose of this curious object must remain unresolved.

d. Khirbet Qasrij bones

The bones from Khirbet Qasrij were identified by Miss Marie-Odile Saacké (now Mrs Alastair Killick). Mr Keith Dobney, of the Institute of Archaeology, London, kindly gave advice as to the best way to present the evidence.

There were remains of at least two head of cattle. Only one bone, found near the oven in Area 1, showed traces of burning.

		Cattle	Sheep/Goat	Pig	Dog?	Horse	Unidentifiable
Horn							XXXX
Jaw		XX		X	X		XX
Humerus		X					
Radius		X					
Ulna		X	XX				
Tibia		X					
Astragalus		XX	XXX				
Metapodial		X	XX				
Phalanx			XX				
	M	XXXXX XXXXXX	XX		X	XX	
Loose Teeth	P	XXXXX	XXXX				
	I						
Vertebra			X				

X = single example
M = molars
P = premolars
I = incisors

e. Catalogue of pottery from Khirbet Qasrij

See introductory remarks to catalogue of pottery from Qasrij Cliff.

Bowls

1   Fig. 23. Rim frag., L. 3.0 cm, diam. *c*.15.5 cm. 5YR 7/4 pink. Veg. and grit temper. B5/2.

2   Fig. 23. Three rim frags, L. 6.3, 5.7 and 3.3 cm, diam. 24.0 cm. 10YR 8/4 very pale brown. Veg. and white grit temper. A3/2.

3   Fig. 23. Rim frag., diam. 20.0 cm. 5YR 8/4 pink, with 7.5YR 8/2 pinkish white slip on exterior and perhaps interior. Grit temper. A4-A5/2.
   Five similar rim frags:
   a. (thicker than example illustrated) diam. 12.0 cm. Pink ware. A4-A5/2.
   b. Diam. 13.0 cm. Light brown. A3/1.
   c-e. B1-B2 (two); B3 (inside large pot).

4   Fig. 23. Rim frag., L. 6.0 cm, diam. 18.0 cm. 5YR 7/6 reddish yellow. Veg. and grit temper. A1.

5   Fig. 23. Three rim frags of bowl representing half of rim, diam. 12.5 cm. 10YR 8/3 very pale brown. Grit temper. C1/1.
   Six similar rim frags: A1/B1.

6   Fig. 23. Rim frag., L. 3.5 cm, diam. 20.0 cm. 7.5YR 7/4 pink. Veg. and grit temper. A1.

7   Fig. 23. Rim frag., L. 2.8 cm, diam. 12.0 cm. 10YR 8/3 very pale brown. Heavy veg. temper and sparse white grits. Kiln. Sample BM 1984-5-12, 58; see Appendix III.

8   Fig. 23. Rim frag., L. 1.0 cm, diam. 16.0 cm. 10YR 8/3 very pale brown, with 2.5Y 8/2 white slip on exterior and interior. Grit temper. B5/1.

9   Fig. 23. Whole base and approx. half of rim preserved, diam. 12.8 cm, H. 3.45 cm. 10YR 8/3 very pale brown. C1/1.
   Four similar rim frags:
   a. 5YR 8/4 pink. Veg. and grit temper. A4/2.
   b. Diam. *c*.11.0 cm. 5Y 8/3 pale yellow. B4/2.
   c. Diam. *c*.21.0 cm. 10YR 8/3 very pale brown. Fine grit temper? B4/2.
   d. 5Y 8/3 pale yellow. B4/2.

10   Fig. 23. Three sherds representing part of base and approx. quarter of rim, diam. 17.0 cm, H. 4.5 cm. 5YR 7/6 reddish yellow. Grit temper. C1/1.

11   Fig. 23. Rim frag., L. 6.0 cm, diam 14.0 cm. 7.5YR 7/6 reddish yellow. Grit temper. A2/2.
   A similar rim frag.:
   a. Diam. *c*.12.0 cm. 10YR 8/4 very pale brown. White grit temper. B4/2.

12   Fig. 23. Rim frag., L. 2.0 cm, diam. 15.0 cm. 10YR 8/4 very pale brown. B4-B5.

13   Fig. 23. Rim frag., L. 3.0 cm, diam. 22.0 cm. 10YR 8/3 very pale brown. Mixed veg. and sparse white grit temper. B4/2.

14   Fig. 23. Rim frag., L. 4.3 cm, diam. 20.0 cm. 2.5YR 6/8 light red, surface 10YR 7/6 yellow. White grit temper. A5/2. Sample BM 1984-5-12, 57; see Appendix III.
   A similar rim frag.:
   a. Diam. *c*.14.0 cm. 2.5YR 6/8 light red. White grit temper. B3/2.

15   Fig. 23. Rim frag., L. 3.5 cm, diam. 11.0 cm. 10YR 8/3 very pale brown. Very fine grit temper. A1/3.

16   Fig. 23. Rim frag., L. 7.3 cm, diam. 18.8 cm. 5YR 8/4 pink. Veg. and white grit temper. B3/2.

17   Fig. 23. Rim frag., L. 3.0 cm, diam. 25.0 cm. 5YR 7/4 pink, with 7.5YR 8/2 pinkish white slip on exterior and interior. B1-B2.

18   Fig. 23. Rim frag., L. 7.0 cm, diam. 18.0 cm. 2.5YR 6/6 light red. Grit and some veg. temper. A5.
   A similar rim frag.:
   a. Greyish fabric fired to black on exterior. Sondage KQ1.

19   Fig. 23. Rim frag., L. 12.0 cm, diam. 30.0 cm. 5YR 6/2 pinkish grey core fired to 5YR 7/4 pink outer fabric and surfaces. Grit and some veg. temper. B1/2.

20   Fig. 24. Rim frag., L. 8.0 cm, diam. 21.0 cm. 5YR 6/6 reddish yellow. Grit and some veg. temper. A2/2.
   A similar rim frag.:
   a. 5Y 8/3 pale yellow. A4-A5/2.

21   Fig. 24. Quarter preserved, diam. 18.0 cm, H. 4.0 cm. 5YR 8/4 pink with light brown slip. Fine white grit temper. A2-A3.

22   Fig. 24. Rim frag., L. 7.0 cm, diam. 20.0 cm. 5YR 8/4 pink, with surface slip 5YR 8/2 pinkish white. Fine white and micaceous grit temper. A3/2.
   A similar rim frag.:
   a. 2.5Y 8/2 white. Veg. and grit temper. A1/3.

23   Fig. 24. Rim frag., diam. 19.0 cm. 5Y 8/3 pale yellow. Veg. and grit temper. Kiln.
   A similar rim frag.:
   a. Diam. 24.0 cm. 7.5YR 8/4 pink. Grit temper. B2/1.

24   Fig. 24. Rim frag., L. 8.0 cm, diam. 20.0 cm. 5Y 8/3 pale yellow. Very fine grit temper. A2/3.
   Five similar rim frags including carination. A2-A3.

25   Fig. 24. Rim frag., L. 6.9 cm, diam. 19.0 cm. 10YR 8/4 very pale brown. White grit temper. A3/2.

A similar rim frag.:
a. Diam. 18.0 cm. 5Y 8/3 pale yellow. Grit temper. A3/2.

26   Fig. 24. Rim frag., L. 5.5 cm, diam. 19.0 cm. 7.5 YR 7/4 pink. Veg. and sparse white grit temper. B4/2.

27   Fig. 24. Rim frag., L. 6.3 cm, diam. 17.0 cm. 5Y 8/3 pale yellow. Veg. and grit temper. Kiln. Sample BM 1984-5-12, 25; see Appendix III.

Three similar rim frags:
a. Possibly from the same vessel. Kiln.
b. 5Y 8/3 pale yellow. Kiln.
c. Pink. Sparse grit temper. Kiln.

28   Fig. 24. Rim frag., L. 6.5 cm, diam. 19.0 cm. 5YR 8/4 pink, with surface slip 5YR 8/2 pinkish white. Fine white and micaceous grit temper. A3/2.

29   Fig. 24. Rim frag., L. 5.3 cm, diam. 17.0 cm. 7.5YR 8/6 reddish yellow. White grit temper. A3/2.

30   Fig. 24. 11 cm of rim and small part of base preserved, diam. 24.0 cm, H. 9.8 cm. 5YR 7/6 reddish yellow, with surface wash 5YR 8/4 pink. Grit temper. B3/2.

Two similar rim frags:
a. Pink fabric with light brown slip. Kiln.
b. Brownish. A2-B2/1.

31   Fig. 24. Rim frag., L. 5.0 cm, diam. 17.0 cm. 10YR 7/4 very pale brown. Veg. and sparse white grit temper. B4/2.

32   Fig. 24. Rim frag., L. 6.0 cm, diam. 26.5 cm. 7.5YR 8/4 pink. Veg. and grit temper. A1/3.

A similar rim frag.: A4-A5/2.

33   Fig. 24. Rim frag., L. 7.0 cm, diam. 22.0 cm. 7.5YR 8/2 pinkish white. Grit temper. B1/1.

Two similar rim frags: B3-B4/1 and 2.

34   Fig. 24. Rim frag., L. 4.6 cm, diam. 26.0 cm. 5YR 7/6 reddish yellow. Veg. temper. A3/2.

35   Fig. 24. Rim frag., L. 6.0 cm, diam. 20.0 cm. 7.5YR 7/4 pink. Grit temper. A1.

Fifteen similar rim frags with varying diameters:
a. Diam. 12.0 cm. 5Y 8/3 pale yellow. A3-A4-B3-B4.
b-e. Two brown (one bigger); one red; one smaller and light brown. A3-A4-B3-B4.
f. Brownish. Grit temper. B4-B5.
g-o. A2-A3-B2-B3 (two); A2/2-3 (five); B1-B2; B2/2.

36   Fig. 24. Rim frag., L. 7.0 cm, diam. 25.0 cm. 5Y 8/3 pale yellow. A4/2.

Two similar rim frags from larger vessels:
a. Diam. 30.0 cm. 10YR 8/2 very pale brown. Veg. temper with micaceous grits. A4/2.

b. 5YR 7/6 reddish yellow. Veg. temper with micaceous grits. A4/2.

37   Fig. 24. Rim frag., L. 6.0 cm, diam. 24.0 cm. 10YR 8/3 very pale brown fabric with interior, top of rim and exterior slipped 10YR 8/2 white. B5/1.

Ten similar rim frags with varying diameters: A2-B2/2; B2-B3 (two); A3-B3/1; A3-A4/2 (six).

38   Fig. 24. Rim frag., L. 6.3 cm, diam. 22.0 cm. 10YR 8/4 very pale brown. Veg. and fine white and black grit temper. A4/2.

A similar rim frag.:
a. Diam. *c*.17.0 cm, 2.5YR 6/8 light red. Veg. and white grit temper. A4/2.

39   Fig. 24. Rim frag., L. 5.1 cm, diam. 25.0 cm. 5YR 8/4 pink, with surface slip 5YR 8/2 pinkish white. Fine white and micaceous grit temper. A3/2.

A rim frag. from smaller rim: B3-B4/2.

40   Fig. 24. Rim. frag., L. 4.0 cm, diam. 22.0 cm. 2.5YR 8/2 white with fine very smooth surface (slipped?). Sparse (white) grit temper. B4/1.

Two similar rim frags:
a. 10YR 7/4 very pale brown. White grit temper. B4/2.
b. Diam. *c*.21.0 cm. 5YR 7/6 reddish yellow. Mixed veg. and white grit temper. B4/2.

41   Fig. 24. Rim frag. L. 7.5 cm, diam. 26.0 cm. 5YR 7/6 reddish yellow. Grit temper. A2/2. Sample BM 1984-5-12, 28; see Appendix III.

42   Fig. 25. Rim frag., L. 7.5 cm, diam. 36.0 cm. 5YR 8/4 pink. Veg. temper and sparse white grits. B3/2.

43   Fig. 25. Rim frag., L. 3.0 cm, diam. 29.0 cm. 5YR 7/6 reddish yellow. Grit temper. A3-A4/1.

44.   Fig. 25. Rim frag., L. 7.15 cm, diam. 38.0 cm. 7.5YR 7/4 pink. Veg. and white grit temper. A3/2.

Three similar rim frags:
a. Diam. 23.0 cm. 7.5Y 8/4 pink. Veg. temper with white and micaceous grits. A3/2.
b. Diam. 25.0 cm. 2.5Y 8/4 pale yellow. No visible temper. A3/2.
c. Diam. 34.0 cm. 10YR 8/4 very pale brown. Fine. No visible temper. A3/2.

45   Fig. 25. Rim frag., L. 6.7 cm, diam. 32.0 cm. 5Y 8/3 pale yellow. Veg. temper. A5/2.

46   Fig. 25. Rim frag., L. 9.0 cm, diam. 28.0 cm. 5Y 8/3 pale yellow. Grit and some veg. temper. C1/2.

47   Fig. 25. Rim frag., L. 8.0 cm, diam. 30.0 cm. 5YR 7/6 reddish yellow. Veg. temper and sparse white grits. B4/2.

Four similar rim frags:
a. Diam. 10.0 cm. Grey. A3/1.

   b. Fabric 5YR 8/4 pink, surface 10YR 8/2 white. Fine white grit temper. B3/2.
   c. Diam *c*.31.0 cm. 2.5YR N4/ dark grey. White grit temper. B4/2.
   d. 2.5YR 6/8 light red. Fine white grit temper. B4/2.

48   Fig. 25. Rim frag., L. 6.0 cm, diam. 20.0 cm. 7.5YR 7/6 reddish yellow. Grit temper. B3-B4/1.

49   Fig. 25. Rim frag., L. 8.5 cm, diam. 24.0 cm. 7.5YR 8/4 pink. Grit temper. B2/1.

50   Fig. 25. One-third of rim preserved, diam. 33.0 cm. 10YR 8/3 very pale brown. Grit temper. B5/2.

51   Fig. 25. Rim frag., L. 5.0 cm, diam. 28.0 cm. 5YR 7/6 reddish yellow. Grit temper. A1.

52   Fig. 25. Rim frag., L. 4.0 cm, diam. 24.0 cm. 10YR 8/3 very pale brown. Veg. temper with sparse white grits. B4/2.
   Two similar rim frags:
   a. Light brown. Trench WR.
   b. Light red. Trench WR.

53   Fig. 25. Rim frag., L. 7.0 cm, diam. 26.0 cm. 7.5YR 7/4 pink. Grit and some veg. temper. C1.

54   Fig. 25. Rim frag., L. 4.5 cm, diam. 29.0 cm. 5YR 7/6 reddish yellow. Veg. and grit temper. C1.
   A similar rim frag.:
   a. 5Y 8/3 pale yellow. Trench WR.

55   Fig. 26. Rim frag., L. 6.0 cm, diam. 38.0 cm. 10YR 8/4 very pale brown. Veg. and white grit temper. A4/2.
   Two similar rim frags:
   a. Diam. 26.0 cm. 10YR 7/4 very pale brown. B4/2.
   b. Diam. 14.0 cm. 10YR 8/3 very pale brown. A5/2.

56   Fig. 26. Rim frag., L. 5.7 cm, diam. 26.0 cm. 2.5Y 8/4 pale yellow. Veg. and grit temper. A3/2.

57   Fig. 26. Rim frag., L. 10.7 cm, diam. 22.0 cm. 5YR 8/4 pink. Sparse white grit temper. A3/2.

58   Fig. 26. Rim frag., L. 3.6 cm, diam. 25.0 cm. 5YR 7/4 pink. A5/2.

59   Fig. 26. Rim frag., L. 3.0 cm, diam. 23.5 cm. 10YR 7/3 very pale brown. Veg. and grit temper. B5/2.
   Three similar rim frags:
   a. Diam. 22.0 cm. 5YR 7/4 pink. Veg. temper. With two grooves. A3/2.
   b. 10YR 8/3 very pale brown. Veg. temper. A3/2.
   c. 10YR 8/3 very pale brown. Veg. temper. Without incised grooves. A3/2.

60   Fig. 26. Rim frag., L. 5.5 cm, diam. 26.0 cm. 7.5YR 7/6 reddish yellow. Grit temper. A1.

61   Fig. 26. Rim frag., L. 5.9 cm, diam. 30.0 cm. 5YR 8/4 pink. Veg. and white grit temper. B3/2.

62   Fig. 26. Rim frag., L. 6.5 cm, diam. 36.0 cm. 5YR 7/4 pink, with 10YR 8/2 white slip on interior and exterior . Veg. and grit temper. C1/1.
   Three similar rim frags:
   a. 5Y 8/2 white. Veg. temper. A1/2.
   b. 7.5YR 7/4 pink. Veg. and grit temper. A1/3.
   c. B5/2.

63   Fig. 26. Rim frag., L. 15.0 cm, diam. 40.0 cm. 7.5YR 7/6 reddish yellow. Veg. and grit temper. A2/2.

64   Fig. 26. Rim frag., diam. 26.0 cm. 7.5YR 7/6 reddish yellow. Veg. and grit temper. A1.

65   F ig. 26. Rim frag., L. 6.0 cm, diam. 32.0 cm. 5YR 7/4 pink fired to 5YR 7/6 reddish yellow on interior and exterior. Veg. temper. A1/4.

66   Fig. 26. Rim frag., L. 11.0 cm, diam. 34.0 cm. 10YR 7/4 very pale brown. Grit temper. A3-B3/2.
   A similar rim frag.:
   a. Light brown. Veg. temper. Trench PF.

67   Fig. 27. Rim frag., L. 5.2 cm, diam. 18.0 cm. 10YR 8/3 very pale brown. Fine white grit temper. A5/2.
   A similar rim frag.:
   a. Diam. 19.0 cm. Light brown. A3/2.

68   Fig. 27. Rim frag., L. 3.0 cm, diam. 24.0 cm. 10YR 8/4 very pale brown. Fine white grit temper. B4/2.

69   Fig. 27. Rim frag., L. 6.5 cm, diam. 21.0 cm. 2.5YR 6/8 light red. Veg. and white grit temper. A4/1.

70   Fig. 27. Rim frag., L. 4.4 cm, diam. 28.0 cm. 7.5YR 8/4 pink. Veg. temper. A3/2.

71   Fig. 27. Rim frag., diam. 27.0 cm. 5YR 7/6 reddish yellow. Veg. and grit temper. B2/2.
   Four similar rim frags:
   a. Diam. *c*.13 cm. Red. B2/2.
   b. From much smaller vessel, 10YR 7/1 light grey. Veg. temper. A4/2.
   c. 10YR 7/6 yellow. Veg. and white grit temper. A4/4.
   d. B5/2.

72   Fig. 27. Rim frag., L. 9.2 cm, diam. 38.0 cm. 10YR 6/2 light brownish grey. Veg. and grit temper. A3/2.
   A similar rim frag.:
   a. Diam. 28.0 cm. 5YR 8/3 pink. White grit temper with some veg. A3/2.

73   Fig. 27. Rim frag., diam. 35.0 cm. 7.5YR 7/4 pink, 10YR 8/2 white slip on interior and exterior. Veg. temper. A4-A5/2.

74   Fig. 27. Rim frag., L. 7.5 cm, diam. 26.0 cm. 5YR 7/6 reddish yellow. Grit and some veg. temper. A1/4.

75   Fig. 27. Rim frag., L. 8.6 cm, diam. 26.0 cm. 5YR 7/4 pink. Veg. and sparse white grit temper. A3-A4/2.

76   Fig. 27. Rim frag., L. 6.9 cm, diam. 33.0 cm. 5YR 7/6 reddish yellow. Veg. and white grit temper. A5/2.

77   Fig. 27. Rim frag., L. 6.0 cm, diam. 31.5 cm. 5YR 7/4 pink, 7.5YR 8/2 pinkish white slip on interior and exterior. A3-A4/2.

78   Fig. 27. Rim frag., L. 8.0 cm, diam. 29.5 cm. 7.5YR 8/4 pink, 10YR 8/4 very pale brown slip on exterior and possibly on interior. Grit temper. B1/1.

79   Fig. 28. Rim frag., L. 7.5 cm, diam. 25.0 cm. 5YR 7/4 pink. Veg. temper with white grits. A5/2.

80   Fig. 28. Rim frag., L. 3.0 cm, diam. 23.0 cm. 7.5YR 7/4 pink. Veg. temper. A1/1.

Twenty-five similar rim frags:
A1/1; A1-B1 (two); B1-C1; A1-A2/2; A2-A3 (seven); B2-B3 (two); A3-B3/2 (two); A3-A4/2 (three); B3-B4/1; B3-B4/2 (three); A4-A5-B4-B5; A5-B5/2.

81   Fig. 28. Large frag., approx. a quarter of rim and whole of base, diam. 22.0 cm. 5YR 8/3 pink. Veg. temper and white grits. B3/2.

82   Fig. 28. Rim frag., L. 7.1 cm, diam. 26.0 cm. 10YR 8/4 very pale brown. Veg. and white grit temper. A3/2.

Three similar rim frags:
a. Diam. *c.*26.0 cm. 7.5YR 8/4 pink. Sparse veg. and white grit temper. A3/2.
b. 5YR 7/4 pink. Veg. and white grit temper. A3/2.
c. 5YR 8/4 pink. Veg. temper. A3/2.

83   Fig. 28. Rim frag., L. 8.5 cm, diam. 24.0 cm. 2.5Y 8/2 white. Coarse veg. temper. A3/2.

A similar rim frag.:
a. Diam. 28.0 cm. 5YR 8/4 pink. Veg. temper with sparse white grits. A3/2.

84   Fig. 28. Rim frag., L. 7.9 cm, diam. 24.0 cm. 5YR 7/4 pink. Calcareous and micaceous grit temper. Kiln. Sample BM 1984-5-12, 34; see Appendix III.

85   Fig. 28. Rim frag., L. 3.5 cm, diam. 15.0 cm. 5YR 8/4 pink, surface 7.5YR 8/2 pinkish white. A5/1.

A similar rim frag. from a larger vessel:
a. 10YR 7/2 light grey. Veg. and white grit temper. B3/2.

86   Fig. 28. Rim frag., L. 7.9 cm, diam. 18.0 cm. 7.5YR 8/4 pink, well finished. A few micaceous grits, no others observed. Possibly a waster, as bulges in parts. B3/2.

Two similar rim frags:
a. 5Y 8/3 pale yellow. Veg. and white grit temper. B3/2.

b. 5Y 8/3 pale yellow. Trench PF.

87   Fig. 28. Rim frag., L. 4.5 cm, diam. 18.0 cm. 7.5YR 7/4 pink. Fine grit temper. A4/2.

88   Fig 28. Bowl, incomplete, with all of base, most of wall and short sections of rim preserved, diam. 23.7 cm, H. 8.9 cm. Orange-brown fabric with veg. and a few large white grits, firing to dull grey-brown on inside. Outside of bowl coarse, with adhering clay, showing this bowl is clearly a waster. Kiln.

89   Fig. 28. Rim frag., L. 8.8 cm, diam. 24.0 cm. 10YR 8/3 very pale brown. Veg. temper and white grits. B3/2.

Four similar rim frags:
a. Diam. 23.0 cm. Light brown. Veg. temper. A3/2.
b. Diam. *c.* 26.0 cm. 10YR 8/3 very pale brown. Veg. temper and some white grits. B3/2.
c. 2.5YR 6/8 light red. Veg. and white grit temper. B3/2.
d. Diam. 32.0 cm. Dark grey. Kiln.

90   Fig. 28. Rim frag., L. 7.0 cm, diam. 27.0 cm. 5YR 8/4 pink. Veg. temper. B4/2.

Four similar rim frags:
a. 7.5YR 7/4 pink. Veg. temper with sparse white grits. A4/1.
b. 2.5YR 6/8 light red. Veg. temper. B4/2.
c. 5YR 7/4 pink. Veg. and fine white grit temper. B4/2.
d. 5Y 8/3 pale yellow. B4/2.

91   Fig. 28. Rim frag., L. 6.4 cm, diam. 24.0 cm. 2.5YR 6/8 light red. Veg. and white grit temper. A4/1.

92   Fig. 28. Rim frag., L. 5.8 cm, diam. 24.0 cm. 10YR 8/2 light grey. Veg. temper and sparse white grits. Kiln. Sample BM 1984-5-12, 37; see Appendix III.

A similar rim frag.:
a. Diam. 21.0 cm. Light red. A3/1.

93   Fig. 28. Rim frag., L. 7.3 cm, diam. 26.0 cm. 10YR 8/3 very pale brown. Veg. temper. B4/2.

Thirteen similar rim frags:
a-b. Probably from same vessel. Diam. 24.0 cm. 5Y 8/3 pale yellow. Veg. temper with sparse white grits. B3/2.
c. Diam. 29.0 cm. 2.5YR 6/8 light red. Veg. and white grit temper. B3/2.
d. 2.5YR 6/8 light red. Veg. temper and white grits. A4/1.
e. 10YR 8/3 very pale brown. Grit temper. B4/2.
f. Diam. 32.0 cm. Dark grey. Kiln.
g. Diam. 23.0 cm. 10YR 8/4 very pale brown. Veg. temper. A5/1.
h. Diam. 24.0 cm. 10YR 8/4 very pale brown. Veg. temper, some micaceous grits. A5/1.
i. Fabric 5YR 8/4 pink, surface 10YR 8/3 very pale

brown. Veg. temper with white grits. A5/2.
j-l. Light red. Trench PF.
m. Red. Veg. and grit temper. Trench WR.

94   Fig. 28. Quarter of rim, diam. 21.0 cm. 5YR 7/6 reddish yellow. Grit temper. B2/2.
Seven similar rim frags:
B1-C1 (two); A1-A2/1 (two); B3-B4/2; A4-B4/1; B5/2.

95   Fig. 28. Rim frag., L. 11.4 cm, diam. 31.0 cm. 10YR 8/3 very pale brown. Veg. temper. A3/2.
Eight similar rim frags:
a-g. Diams 24.0-27.0 cm. Pink or pale brown. Veg. temper, generally with white grits. A3/2.
h. Red. Veg. and grit temper. Trench WR.

96   Fig. 28. Rim frag., diam. 39.0 cm. 2.5YR 6/8 light red. Veg. and white grit temper. B4/4.
Five similar rim frags:
a. Cream. A2-A3-B2-B3.
b. B2-B3.
c. Diam. 26.0 cm. Brown. A3-A4-B3-B4.
d. Diam. *c.*30.0 cm. 5YR 8/4 pink. Veg. and fine white grit temper. B4/2.
e. 2.5YR 6/6 light red. B5/2.

97   Fig. 29. Rim frag., L. 7.0 cm, diam. 30.0 cm. 10YR 8/3 very pale brown. Veg. and grit temper. B2/2.
Seven similar rim frags:
a. Diam. 22.0 cm. Red. B2/2. Sample BM 1984-5-12, 51; see Appendix III.
b. Diam. 12.0 cm. Grey. B2/2.
c. Diam. 16.0 cm. Red. B2/2.
d-f. From one large and two smaller vessels. A3-B3/2.
g. B5/2.

98   Fig. 29. Rim frag., L. 5.5 cm, diam. 28.5 cm. 5YR 7/6 reddish yellow, fine grit temper. A1/3.
A similar rim frag.:
a. 5Y 8/2 white. Veg. and grit temper. A1/3.

99   Fig. 29. Rim frag., L. 5.0 cm, diam. 27.0 cm. 7.5YR 7/6 reddish yellow. Fine grit and veg. temper. A1/4.
Two similar rim frags in red ware: B1/2; B2/1.

100   Fig. 29. Rim frag., L. 14.0 cm, diam. 26.0 cm. 5YR 7/6 reddish yellow. Grit temper. B2/2.

101   Fig. 29. Rim frag., L. 9.0 cm, diam. 26.0 cm. 7.5YR 7/6 reddish yellow. Grit temper. A1.

102   Fig. 29. Rim frag., L. 10.0 cm, diam. 26.0 cm. 5YR 7/6 reddish yellow fabric, 7.5YR 8/6 reddish yellow slip on interior and exterior. Grit temper. A2-A3-B2-B3.
Nineteen similar rim frags of varying sizes and diameters. Mostly reddish or brownish, one grey, two pale yellow: B2-B3 (six); B3-B4/1; A5-B5/1 (ten); A5-B5/2 (two).

103   Fig. 29. Rim frag., L. 14.0 cm, diam. 33.0 cm. 7.5YR 7/4 reddish yellow. Veg. and grit temper. A1.
Six similar rim frags:
B1/2; A3-B3/2; B3 (inside large pot); A4-B4/2; A4-A5/2 (two).

104   Fig. 29. Rim frag., L. 11.0 cm, diam. 34.0 cm. 10YR 8/3 very pale brown, core 5YR 7/3 pink. Grit temper. B2/2.

105   Fig. 29. Rim frag., L. 4.5 cm, diam. 49.0 cm. 10YR 7/4 very pale brown. Large white grits. A1.
Two similar rim frags:
a. Diam. 46 cm. 10YR 8/3 very pale brown. Veg. and grit temper. C1/2.
b. 5YR 8/3 pink. Veg. temper. A3/2.

106   Fig. 30. Rim frag., L. 4.0 cm, diam. 24.0 cm. 10YR 8/4 very pale brown. Veg. and white grit temper. B4/2.

107   Fig. 30. Rim frag., L. 11.0 cm, diam. 22.0 cm. 7.5YR 8/4 pink. Grit and veg. temper. A3-A4/2.
A similar rim frag.:
a. Diam. *c.*20.0 cm. 10YR 8/4 very pale brown. Grit temper. B4/2. Sample BM 1984-5-12, 41; see Appendix III.

108   Fig. 30. Two rim frags, L. 9.4 cm and 4.1 cm, diam. 23.0 cm. Fabric 2.5YR 6/8 light red, surface 2.5YR 6/2 pale red. Veg. temper and sparse white grits. B3/2.

109   Fig. 30. Rim frag., L. 8.7 cm, diam. 25.0 cm. 10YR 8/4 very pale brown. White grit inclusions and sparse veg. temper A3/2.
A similar rim frag.:
a. Diam. 21.0 cm. Fabric 7.5YR 7/4 pink firing to 7.5YR 8/2 pinkish white on interior and exterior surfaces. Grit and veg. temper. B4/2. Sample BM 1984-5-12, 29; see Appendix III.

110   Fig. 30; KQ29; MM for study no. 278. Bowl, with base and one-third of wall and rim preserved, H. 6.9 cm, diam 25.0 cm. 5Y 8/3 pale yellow. Grit temper, well made, quite fine. B4/3.

111   Fig. 30. Rim frag., L. 5.2 cm, diam. 36.0 cm. 7.5YR 7/4 pink firing light grey in centre of core. Sparse white grits. A3/2.

Fifty rim sherds, in addition to nos 107-11, have been recorded in A1; A1-B1; A2-B2/2; A3/2 (ten); A3-B3/2 (two); B3/2; A3-A4/2 (three); A3-A4-B3-B4; B3-B4/1; A4/2; A4-B4/2 (nine); B4/2 (four); Kiln (seven plus one base frag.); A4-A5/2; A4-A5-B4-B5; B4-B5 (two); A5-B5/1 (two); A5-B5/2; B5/2.

Tripods

112   Fig. 30, Pl. Xc; KQ23; MM for study no. 274. Tripod, one-half preserved with two feet, H. 4.94 cm, diam. 15.0 cm. 2.5Y, N6/ light grey firing to 7.5YR 7/2 pinkish grey. Very fine fabric with no obvious inclusions, but feet crudely added, in veg. temper. Kiln.

Seven amorphous frags of rim and one body sherd probably from tripods of this sort. Kiln.
A fragment of base. A3/2.
A tripod foot. Pinkish. A3-B3/2.

113   Fig. 30, Pl. Xc. Tripod, one-third preserved, one foot broken off, edge of place where second attached visible. Diam. 17.0 cm. Fabric as no. 112. Kiln.

114   Fig. 30. Three rim frags from tripod (largest L. 4.8 cm), diam. 18.0 cm. Fabric as no. 112. Kiln. Sample BM 1984-5-12, 32; see Appendix III.

115   Fig. 30, Pl. Xc. Part of tripod with 4 cm of rim and one foot preserved, H. 5.0 cm, diam. 15.0 cm. At centre of core 2.5Y N7/ light grey, becoming 2.5Y N5/ grey at surface. Surface slipped 10YR 7/3 very pale brown, turning greyish on interior. Very fine grit temper except for foot, which is much coarser and veg.-tempered and applied to bowl with veg.-tempered clay. A2/2. Sample BM 1984-5-12, 26; see Appendix III.

Fine wares

116   Fig. 31. Rim frag., diam. 6.0 cm. 5Y 8/3 pale yellow. A3-A4/1.

117   Fig. 31. Rim frag., L. 2.4 cm, diam. 8.0 cm. 7.5YR 7/4 pink, surface slip(?) 7.5YR 8/2 pinkish white. Very fine. No visible temper. Kiln. Sample BM 1984-5-12, 27; see Appendix III.

Six similar rim frags:
a. A2-A3.
b. Diam. *c*.10.0 cm. 2.5Y 8/2 white. B2-B3.
c. Diam. 7.0 cm. 5Y 8/3 pale yellow. Fine ware. Kiln. Sample BM 1984-5-12,52; see Appendix III.
d. Diam. 7.0 cm. 10YR 7/1 light grey. Fine veg. and grit temper. Kiln. Sample 1984-5-12, 42; see Appendix III.
e. B4-B5.
f. A5-B5/1.

118   Fig. 31. Two rim frags, diam. 9.0 cm. 2.5YR 6/6 light red. A2-B2/2.

119   Fig. 31. Rim frag., L. 6.2 cm, diam 11.0 cm. 5YR 8/4 pink, surface slip 5YR 8/2 pinkish white. No visible temper. A3/2.

A similar rim frag.:
a. Veg. temper and sparse white grits. A3/2.

120   Fig. 31. Rim frag., L. 4.0 cm, diam. 7.0 cm. 5YR 7/4 pink. Sparse white grit temper. B4/1. Sample BM 1984-5-12, 43; see Appendix III.

Two similar rim frags:
a. Diam. 10.0 cm. White. Veg. temper. Kiln.
b. 10YR 8/2 white. Fine grit temper. B5/2.

121   Fig. 31. Rim frag., L. 2.0 cm, diam. 7.0 cm. 10YR 8/4 very pale brown. Fine grit temper. B4/2. Sample BM 1984-5-12, 50; see Appendix III.

A similar rim frag.:
a. Diam. *c*.6.0 cm. 7.5YR 7/2 pinkish grey. A3-A4/1.

122   Fig. 31. Rim frag., L. 5.0 cm, and two frags of rim and three body sherds from same vessel, diam. 8.2 cm. 2.5Y 8/2 white. No visible temper. A3/2.

Three similar rim frags:
a. 10YR 8/2 white. Veg. and white grit temper. A3/2.
b. Diam. 8.0 cm. 2.5Y 8/2 white. No visible temper. A3/2.
c. Very fine grey ware. Sondage KQ1.

123   Fig. 31. Rim frag., L. 5.0 cm, diam. 9.0 cm. 7.5YR 8/4 pink. White grit temper. A5/2.

124   Fig. 31. Rim frag., L. 4.5 cm, diam. 12.0 cm. 5YR 7/4 pink fabric with 2.5YR 8/2 white slip on interior and exterior. Grit temper. B2/2.

125   Fig. 31. Rim frag., L. 2.0 cm, diam. 6.0 cm. 5Y 5/1 grey fabric with 5Y 7/3 pale yellow slip on interior and exterior. Grit temper. B4/2.

126   Fig. 31. Rim frag., L. 4.0 cm, diam. 9.0 cm. 5Y 7/4 pale yellow fabric, with 5Y 8/3 pale yellow wash on interior and exterior. Fine grit temper. B4/2.

127   Fig. 31. Rim frag., L. 2.0 cm, diam. 10.0 cm. 7.5YR 7/4 pink. Grit temper. A5-B5/1.

A similar rim frag.: A3-B3/2.

128   Fig. 31. Rim frag., L. 3.0 cm, diam. 11.0 cm. 5YR 8/4 pink. Coarse white grit temper. A3/2.

129   Fig. 31. Rim frag., L. 2.5 cm, diam. 9.0 cm. 2.5Y 8/2 white. Veg. and white grit temper. A3/2.

130   Fig. 31. Rim frag., L. 3.0 cm, diam. 10.0 cm. 5YR 7/4 pink fabric, with 2.5YR 8/2 white slip on interior and exterior. Grit temper. B2/2.

131   Fig. 31. Rim frag., L. 5.3 cm, and two body sherds, diam. 11.0 cm. 2.5Y 8/2 white. No visible temper. A3/2.

132   Fig. 31. Shoulder frag., 4.6 cm x 3.4 cm, with dimple. 7.5YR 7/6 reddish yellow. Fine grit temper. B4/2.

Ten other dimple-ware sherds:
a. B2-B3/3. Sample BM 1984-5-12, 40; see Appendix III.
b. A3-A4/1. Sample BM 1984-5-12, 31; see Appendix III.

c-j. A2/2; A3-A4/1 (three); A4/2; A5/1; B3/2 (two).

133   Fig. 31. Shoulder frag., max. diam. 7.0 cm. 5YR 8/4 pink. A3-A4/1.

134   Fig. 31. Shoulder frag., max. diam. 7.0 cm. 7.5YR 7/6 reddish yellow. Fine grit temper. B4/2.

Sherds from similar straight-sided pot: A2/2 and 3.

135   Fig. 31. Shoulder frag., max. diam. 9.0 cm. 7.5YR 7/4 pink fabric, 10YR 8/4 very pale brown slip on exterior and interior. Fine ware. A3-A4/1.

A small frag. from a small globular pot with two grooves on the shoulder: B2-B3.

136   Fig. 31. Shoulder frag., max. diam. 10.0 cm. 7.5YR 7/4 pink. Grit temper. B2-B3.

137   Fig. 31. Shoulder frag., max. diam. 11.8 cm. 5YR 7/6 reddish yellow, possibly slightly darker wash on exterior. Fine grit temper. B4/2.

138   Fig. 31. Rim frag., diam. 10.0 cm. 5Y 8/2 white. A2-A3.

A similar rim frag., without grooves. 5Y 8/2 white. B4/2.

Sherds with fine grooving in A1-A2/1 (two with nine or ten grooves); B1-B2; A3-A4/1.

139   Fig. 31. Shoulder frag., max. diam. 12.0 cm. 2.5Y 8/2 white. A3-A4/1.

140   Fig. 31. Section of rim and shoulder, diam. 12.7 cm. A5/1.

141   Fig. 31. Base. 5Y 7/3 pale yellow. No visible temper. A3/2.

142   Fig. 31. Base. 5YR 7/6 reddish yellow, interior coated with black (bitumen). Fine grit temper. B4/2. Sample BM 1984-5-12, 38; see Appendix III.

143   Fig. 31. Base, most preserved. 5YR 8/4 pink fabric, 2.5Y 8/2 white slip on exterior. Grit temper. B5/2. Sample BM 1984-5-12, 49; see Appendix III.

144   Fig. 31. Base, quarter preserved. 5YR 7/6 reddish yellow fabric, 2.5Y 8/4 pale yellow slip on exterior. Grit temper. B5/2.

145   Fig. 31. Base. 7.5YR 8/4 pink. A3-A4/1.

146   Fig. 31. Frag. of base. 5Y 8/1 white. Very fine ware. No visible temper. A1/3.

A similar rim frag.:
a. 5Y 8/3 pale yellow. A1-B1.

Jars

147   Fig. 32. Part of jar, 4 cm of rim and large part of base preserved, H. 10.2 cm, diam. 12.3 cm. 7.5YR 7/4 pink. Veg. and grit temper. C1/1.

148   Fig. 32. Rim frag., L. 2.2 cm, diam. 8.0 cm. 10YR 6/4 light yellowish brown. Fine white and micaceous grits. A4/2.

149   Fig. 32. Rim frag., diam. 12.0 cm. 7.5YR 8/4 pink. Grit temper. A3-B3/3.

150   Fig. 32. Rim frag., diam. 11.5 cm. 5Y 6/3 pale olive, grit and veg. temper. A3-B3/2.

Two similar rim frags:
a-b. Diam. 13.0 cm. 5Y 8/3 pale yellow. Grit temper. A3-B3/2.

151   Fig. 32. Rim frag., L. 3.8 cm, diam. 9.0 cm. 5Y 8/3 pale yellow. Fine veg. and white grit temper. Kiln. Sample BM 1984-5-12, 56; see Appendix III.

152   Fig. 32. Rim frag., L. 4.9 cm, diam. 9.0 cm. 5Y 8/3 pale yellow. Veg. temper. A3/2.

Two similar rim frags:
a. Diam. *c*.10.0 cm. 10YR 7/3 very pale brown. Grit temper. A1.
b. A5-B5/1.

153   Fig. 32. One half of rim surviving, diam. 11.0 cm. 7.5YR 8/4 pink. Grit temper. A2/2.

A similar rim frag.: A3-B3/3.

154   Fig. 32. Rim frag., L. 3.5 cm, diam. 12.1 cm. 5Y 8/3 pale yellow. B4/2. Sample BM 1984-5-12, 54; see Appendix III.

Two similar rim frags:
a. From smaller vessel. Diam. *c*.10.0 cm. 5YR 8/4 pink, slip 10YR 8/4 very pale brown. Fine micaceous grit temper. A4/2.
b. 10YR 7/4 very pale brown. Grit temper. B4/2.

155   Fig. 32. Rim frag., L. 4.2 cm, diam. 10.0 cm. 5Y 8/3 pale yellow. Veg. temper. A4/2.

156   Fig. 32. Rim frag., diam. 12.0 cm. 5Y 8/3 pale yellow. Grit temper. B5/1.

A similar rim frag.: A3-B3/1.

157   Fig. 32. Rim frag. L. 6.5 cm, diam. 11.0 cm. 2.5Y 7/4 pale yellow. Grit temper. C1/2.

158   Fig. 32. One half of rim preserved, diam. 7.0 cm. 5YR 7/6 reddish yellow. Grit temper. A3-B3/2.

159   Fig. 32. Rim frag., L. 3.8 cm, diam. 12.0 cm. 5Y 8/3 pale yellow. B4/1.

160   Fig. 32. Rim frag., L. 2.5 cm, diam. 18.0 cm. 5YR 7/6 reddish yellow. Grit temper. B4-B5.

161   Fig. 32. Rim frag., L. 4.0 cm, diam. 18.0 cm. 2.5Y 8/2 white. Grit temper. C1/1.

162   Fig. 32. Rim frag., L. 8.0 cm., diam. 24.0 cm. 5YR 8/4 pink. Grit temper. A3/2.

163   Fig. 32. Rim frag., L. 5.7 cm, diam. 11.0 cm.

7.5YR 7/4 pink, surface 2.5Y 8/2 white. Veg. and fine white grit temper. A5/1.

164   Fig. 32. Rim frag., L. 3.2 cm, diam. 17.0 cm. 10R 6/6 light red. Veg. and fine white grit temper. B4/2.
  Two similar rim frags:
  a. 10YR 7/4 very pale brown. Grit temper. B4/2.
  b. Diam. *c.*18.0 cm. 7.5YR 7/6 reddish yellow. Fine grit temper. B4/2.

165   Fig. 32. Rim frag., L. 4.8 cm, diam. 14.0 cm. 10YR 8/3 very pale brown. Veg. and white grit temper. A5/2.

166   Fig. 33. Rim frag., L. 10.0 cm, diam. 9.0 cm. 5Y 8/2 white. Grit and some veg. temper. C1/2.

167   Fig. 33. One-third of rim preserved, diam. 11.8 cm. 10YR 6/6 brownish yellow. Coarse white and micaceous grit temper. B3/2.
  Five similar rim frags:
  a. Diam. 14.0 cm. 10YR 8/3 very pale brown. White grit temper. B3/2.
  b. Diam. 12.0 cm. 10YR 7/4 very pale brown. White grit temper. B3/2.
  c. Diam. 12.0cm. 10YR 7/6 yellow. White grit temper. B3/2.
  d. 10YR 5/1 grey. White grit temper. B3/2.
  e. 5YR 7/6 reddish yellow. Veg. and white grit temper. B3/2.

168   Fig. 33. Rim frag., L. 5.5 cm, diam. 12.0 cm. 2.5Y 7/2 light grey fabric. 2.5Y 8/2 white slip on interior and exterior. Veg. and grit temper. A1.
  A similar rim frag.: A4-A5/2.

169   Fig. 33. Rim frag., L. 3.8 cm, diam. 12.0 cm. 10YR 8/6 yellow. Veg. and white grit temper. B3/2.
  A similar rim frag.:
  a. More angular. 10YR 6/4 light yellowish brown. White grit temper. B3/2.

170   Fig. 33. Rim frag., L. 7.0 cm, diam. 9.4 cm. 5YR 7/6 reddish yellow. Grit temper. B2/1.

171   Fig. 33. Rim frag., L. 5.0 cm, diam. 9.0 cm. Fabric and interior 10YR 8/3 very pale brown, slip 5Y 8/2 white on exterior. White grits (largish) and small black grits. A1/3.

172   Fig. 33. Rim frag., L. 4.0 cm, diam. 10.0 cm. 5YR 7/6 reddish yellow fabric, 10YR 8/2 white slip on interior and exterior. Grit and some veg. temper. A2/2.

173   Fig. 33. Rim frag., L. 7.7 cm, diam. 12.0 cm. 10YR 8/3 very pale brown. Veg. temper. A3/2.
  Seven similar rim frags.:
  a. Diam. 16.0 cm. 5YR 7/6 reddish yellow. Veg. and some grit temper. A1/2.
  b. Diam. 12.0 cm. 10YR 7/1 light grey. A3/2.
  c. 7.5YR 8/6 reddish yellow. Veg. temper. A3/2.

  d. A3-A4/2.
  e. Diam. 14.0 cm. 5YR 7/3 pink, surface 5Y 8/2 white. Veg. temper. A4/1.
  f. Diam. 11.0 cm. 7.5YR 7/6 reddish yellow. Veg. temper and fine white grits. A4/2.
  g. 10YR 8/6 yellow. Grit temper. A4/2.

174   Fig. 33. Rim frag., L. 4.2 cm, diam. 8.8 cm. 10YR 8/4 very pale brown. Veg. and white grit temper. B3/2.

175   Fig. 33. Rim frag., L. 2.8 cm, diam. 12.0 cm. 5Y 8/3 pale yellow. Veg. and white grit temper. B3/2.

176   Fig. 33. Rim frag., L. 6.1 cm, diam. 12.0 cm. 10YR 8/4 very pale brown. Veg. temper. A3/2.
  A similar rim frag.:
  a. Diam. *c.*10.0 cm. 7.5YR 7/2 pinkish grey. Veg. temper and white grits. A3/2.

177   Fig. 33. Shoulder frag., max. diam. 17.0 cm. 5YR 7/6 reddish yellow. Grit temper. B5/1.
  See also no. 179.

178   Fig. 33. Shoulder frag., max. diam. 23.8 cm. 2.5Y 8/2 white (fabric and interior), wash of same colour on exterior. Grit temper. A1.
  Approx. 109 sherds bear similar ridges round the base of the neck or on the shoulder:
  A1/5; A1-B1 (two); B1/1; B1-C1 (two); C1 (approx. seventeen); A1-A2/2; B1-B2 (four: three of these pale yellow); A2/2 and 3 (eleven: four of these pale yellow); A2-B2/2; B2/1 (three: two red; one pale yellow); B2/2 (two); A3 (ten: four of these pale yellow); A3-B3/1 (pale yellow); A3-B3/2 (seven: one of these pale yellow); A3-B3/3; B3/1 (three: two of these pale yellow); B3/2 (seven: six of these pale yellow); A4-B4/2 (three); B4/2 (four); B3-B4/2; A4/2; A4-A5/2 (three); A5/1 (three); A5/2 (six); A5-B5/1 (three); B5/1 (two); B5/2 (nine: two of these pale yellow).

179   Fig. 33. Shoulder frag., max. diam. 26.9 cm. 5YR 7/4 pink (fabric and interior), slip 10YR 8/3 very pale brown on exterior. Grit and some veg. temper. A1/3b.
  Approx. 92 sherds bear a similar grooved decoration (see also no. 177):
  A1 (seven); A1-B1 (ten: two of these pale yellow); C1 (approx. seventeen); B1-B2 (three); A2/2 and 3 (four: three of these pale yellow); A2-B2/2; B2/1 (red); B2/2 (five); A3 (five: two of these pale yellow); A3-B3/2 (four: one of these pale yellow); A3-B3/3; B3/2 (three pale yellow); B3-B4/1; B3-B4/2 (pale yellow); A4-B4/1; A3-B4/2 (five); B4/2 (six: four of these pale yellow); A5/1 (eight); A5-B5/1 (two); B5/2 (seven: two of these pale yellow).

180   Fig. 33. Rim frag., L. 4.5 cm, diam. 18.0 cm. 10YR 8/2 white. Grit temper. B1/2.

181   Fig. 33. Rim frag., L. 8.0 cm, diam. 20.0 cm. 5Y 8/3 pale yellow. Grit temper. A1.

182   Fig. 33. Rim frag., L. 10.0 cm, diam. 20.0 cm. 7.5YR 8/4 pink fabric, possibly slip or wash 7.5YR 8/2 pinkish white, veg. and grit temper. B2-B3 (removal of stones).
Thirteen rim frags similar to nos 180-82 (see also no. 253):
a. 5Y 8/3 pale yellow. A1-B1.
b-c. A1-B1.
d. Rim and body sherd. B1-C1.
e-h. A2-B2/2.
i-j. A2-A3.
k. B4-B5.
l. Diam. 20.0 cm, rim 3.5 cm thick. B4-B5.
In addition, approx. fifteen sherds bear a similar decoration of ridges and grooves (see also nos 253, 255, 269):
A1-B1; A2/1; B2/2; A3 (four: one of these pale yellow); B3/2 (four pale yellow sherds from one pot; one light red); B3-B4 (pale yellow); B4/1 (red); A3-A5/2 (pale yellow waster).

183   Fig. 34, Pl. Xc; KQ22; MM for study no. 277. Collapsed jar, reconstructed in drawing, orig. H. *c.*15.0 cm, max. diam. 16.4 cm. Fired yellow-green on outside, grey in centre of core. Large white grit inclusions, some veg. temper. Kiln. See also no. 184.

184   Fig. 34, Pl. Xc; KQ21; MM for study no. 271. Collapsed jar, reconstructed in drawing, orig. H. *c.*14.0 cm, max. diam. *c.*15.0 cm. Fabric as no. 183. Kiln.
Also related to no. 184 are:
a-d. Four similar rim frags. Kiln.
e. Part of a pot adhering to no. 183 from the kiln.
f. A completely collapsed pot as reconstructed in nos 183 and 184. Kiln.

185   Fig. 34. Rim frag., L. 4.9 cm, diam. 12.0 cm. 5Y 8/3 pale yellow. Veg. and white grit temper. A5/2. Sample BM 1984-5-12, 53; see Appendix III.
A similar rim frag.:
a. 5YR 8/4 pink. Veg. and white grit temper. A5/2.

186   Fig. 34. Rim frag., L. 3.5 cm, diam. 7.0 cm. 5Y 8/3 pale yellow. Veg. and white grit temper. A5/2.

187   Fig. 34. Rim frag., L. 9.0 cm, diam. 11.0 cm. 5Y 8/3 pale yellow. Veg. and grit temper. A3-A4/2.
Seven similar rim frags of varying sizes and diameters:
B2/2, A3-A4/2 (five); B3-B4/1.

188   Fig. 34. One-third of rim, diam. 10.4 cm. 7.5YR 7/6 reddish yellow. Veg. and grit temper. B2-B3.
Three similar rim frags:
a. Diam. 14.0 cm. 7.5YR 7/6 reddish yellow. Veg. and grit temper. B2-B3.
b-c. A5-B5/2. Sondage KQ1.

189   Fig. 34. Rim frag., L. 6.5 cm, diam. 14.0 cm. 5YR 8/4 pink. Veg. and white grit temper. A5/2.
A similar rim frag.:
a. 5YR 8/4 pink. Grit temper. A3-A4/1.

190   Fig. 34. One-quarter of rim, diam. 11.0 cm. 5YR 8/4 pink. Very gritty fabric. A3/2.
Two similar rim frags:
a. Diam. 14.0 cm. 10YR 7/2 light grey. Some white grit temper. A3/2.
b. Diam. 14.0 cm. 5YR 8/4 pink; slip 10YR 8/3 very pale brown. Veg. and white grit temper. A3/2.

191   Fig. 34. Rim frag., L. 7.8 cm, diam. 13.0 cm. Pinky-brown. Veg. temper. Kiln.

192   Fig. 34. Frag. of rim, diam. 12.8 cm. 2.5YR 6/8 light red fabric, traces of 7.5YR 8/2 pinkish white slip on interior and exterior. Veg., large white grits and micaceous temper. C1.
Four frags from a similar rim: B1-B2.

193   Fig. 34. Quarter of rim, diam. 13.0 cm. 7.5YR 5/4 brown. Veg. and grit temper. A1/4.
Two similar rim frags: A2/1; Sondage KQ2.

194   Fig. 34. Rim frag., L. 6.5 cm, diam. 12.0 cm. 7.5YR 8/4 pink. Veg. and white grit temper. B4/4.
Six similar rim frags:
a. Diam. 16.0 cm. 10YR 8/3 very pale brown. Veg. temper. A3/2.
b-c. 5Y 8/3 pale yellow. Wasters. A3/2.
d. Diam. 11.0 cm. 5Y 8/3 pale yellow. Veg. temper. B3/2.
e. From larger vessel. 5Y 8/3 pale yellow. Veg. and white grit temper. B3/2.
f. Cooking ware. 10YR 5/1 grey. B4/2.

195   Fig. 34. Four rim frags (longest 7.3 cm), diam. 14.0 cm. 10YR 8/3 very pale brown. Veg. and very sparse grit temper. Kiln. Sample BM 1984-5-12, 30; see Appendix III.

196   Fig. 35. Rim frag., L. 3.5 cm, diam. 13.0 cm. 10YR 8/6 yellow. Veg. and sparse white grit temper. A5/1.

197   Fig. 35. Rim frag., L. 5.5 cm, diam. 12.0 cm. 7.5YR 8/4 pink. Grit temper. A1.
A similar rim frag.: A4-A5/2.

198   Fig. 35. Rim frag., L. 6.2 cm, diam. 12.5 cm. 5Y 8/3 pale yellow. Veg. temper. A5/1.

199   Fig. 35. Four rim frags, longest 6.0 cm, diam. 12.0 cm. 5YR 8/4 pink. Grit temper. B5/2.

200   Fig. 35. Rim frag., L. 7.0 cm, diam. 14.0 cm. 5Y 8/3 pale yellow. B4/2.
Four similar rim frags:
a. Diam. 10.0 cm. 10YR 8/3 very pale brown. Veg. temper. A1/2.

b. Diam. 13.0 cm. 5Y 8/3 pale yellow. Veg. temper. B3/2. Sample BM 1984-5-12, 47; see Appendix III.

c. Diam. 14.5 cm. 5Y 8/3 pale yellow. Veg. temper. B3/2.

d. Similar but smaller. B3 (inside large pot).

201   Fig. 35. One-half of rim, diam. 8.0 cm. 5Y 8/3 pale yellow. B4/1 and B4/2.

Five similar rim frags:

a. Diam. 14.0 cm. 5Y 8/3 pale yellow. B4/2.

b. 10YR 8/6 yellow. Grit temper. B4/2.

c. 5Y 8/3 pale yellow. Veg. temper. B4/2.

d. Diam. *c*.11.0 cm. 2.5YR 6/8 light red. White grit temper. B4/2.

e. Diam. *c*.9.0 cm. 10YR 8/3 very pale brown. Veg. and white grit temper. A5/2.

202   Fig. 35. Rim frag., L. 4.5 cm, diam. 16.0 cm. 10YR 8/3 very pale brown. Veg. (?) temper and sparse white grits. B4/2.

203   Fig. 35. Rim frag., L. 8.0 cm, diam. 12.0 cm. 5Y 8/3 pale yellow. Veg. temper. A5/2.

204   Fig. 35. Rim frag., L. 2.0 cm, diam. 16.0 cm. 5Y 8/2 white. Veg. and sparse white grit temper. B4/2.

205   Fig. 35. One-third of rim, diam. 9.0 cm. 10YR 7/4 very pale brown. Fine white and micaceous grit temper. A5/2. Sample BM 1984-5-12, 44; see Appendix III.

206   Fig. 35. Rim frag., diam. 12.0 cm. 10YR 8/6 yellow. Veg. and grit temper. A4-A5/1.

A similar rim frag.:

a. Reddish brown. A4-A5/1.

207   Fig. 35. Rim frag., L. 9.0 cm, diam. 20.0 cm. 10YR 5/6 yellowish brown fabric, 10YR 7/4 very pale brown slip on interior and exterior. Veg. and grit temper. C1/2.

208   Fig. 35. Rim frag., L. 5.0 cm, diam. 11.0 cm. 5Y 6/3 pale olive. Grit temper. A1.

A similar rim frag.:

a. Diam. 11.0 cm. 2.5Y 8/4 pale yellow. Grit temper. B5/1.

209   Fig. 35. Three-quarters of rim, diam. 18.0 cm. 10YR 7/3 very pale brown. Grit temper. B5/2.

A similar rim frag.:

a. Smaller. Diam. 16.0 cm. B2-B3.

210   Fig. 35. Rim frag., L. 4.8 cm, diam. 12.0 cm. 5Y 8/3 pale yellow. Veg. temper. A5/2.

211   Fig. 36. Rim frag., L. 2.0 cm, diam. 18.0 cm. 7.5YR 8/6 pink. Grit temper. A5-B5/1.

212   Fig. 36. One-third of rim, diam. 16.0 cm. 5YR 7/6 reddish yellow. Grit and veg. temper. A3-A4/2.

213   Fig. 36. Rim frag., L. 6.0 cm, diam. 12.0 cm. 5Y 8/3 pale yellow. B4/2. Sample BM 1984-5-12, 55; see Appendix III.

Two similar rim frags:

a. Diam. 10.0 cm. 5Y 8/3 pale yellow. B4-B5.

b. Diam. 10.0 cm. Reddish. B4-B5.

214   Fig. 36. Rim frag., L. 5.5 cm, diam. 12.0 cm. 10YR 8/6 yellow. Veg. and white grit temper. A5/2.

215   Fig. 36. Rim frag., L. 3.0 cm, diam. 16.0 cm. 5Y 8/3 pale yellow. Grit temper. B4-B5.

216   Fig. 36. Rim frag., L. 6.0 cm, diam. 18.0 cm. 5Y 8/3 pale yellow. Veg. and white grit temper. A4/2.

217   Fig. 36. Rim frag., L. 5.5 cm, diam. 12.0 cm. 5Y 7/6 reddish yellow. Veg. and grit temper. A1.

A similar rim frag.:

a. Similar diam. and fabric but slightly more rounded. A1.

218   Fig. 36. Rim frag., L. 3.5 cm, diam. 12.0 cm. 5YR 7/6 reddish yellow. Veg. and grit temper. A1.

Thirteen similar rim frags:
A2-A3-B2-B3 (three); A2/2 and 3 (ten).

219   Fig. 36. Quarter of rim, diam. 13.0 cm. Fabric and interior 2.5YR 6/6 light red, slip 10YR 8/2 white on exterior. Veg. and grit temper. A1/3.

Twenty similar rim frags of varying diameters:
A2/2 and 3 (fifteen); B2/2 (four); A3-B3/2.

220   Fig. 36. Rim frag., L. 5.0 cm, diam. 21.0 cm. 10YR 8/4 very pale brown. B4/2.

A similar rim frag.:

a. From smaller rim. Diam. 22.0 cm. 7.5YR 6/4 light brown. Veg. and white grit temper. A4/2.

221   Fig. 36. Rim frag., L. 6.0 cm, diam. 26.0 cm. 5YR 7/6 reddish yellow fabric, with 5YR 8/2 pinkish white slip on interior and exterior. No visible grit or veg. temper. A1/4.

Seven similar rim frags: A2/1; A3-B3/2 (four); A4-A5/2 (two).

222   Fig. 36. Rim frag., L. 11.0 cm, diam. 26.0 cm. 5YR 7/6 reddish yellow. Grit and some veg. temper. A2/2.

Three similar rim frags.:
A2-B2/2 (one 5Y 8/3 pale yellow).

223   Fig. 36. Rim frag., L. 4.5 cm, diam. 28.0 cm. Fabric 5Y 6/2 light olive grey, interior and exterior 5Y 7/2 light grey. Veg. and grit temper. A1.

224   Fig. 36. Rim frag., L. 4.0 cm, diam. 20.0 cm. 5YR 7/6 reddish yellow with 7.5YR 8/4 pink slip. Veg. temper. B1-B2.

A similar rim frag.:

a. 5Y 8/3 pale yellow. Veg. and white grit temper. B3/2.

225 Fig. 36. Rim frag., L. 5.3 cm, diam. 20.0 cm. 10YR 6/6 brownish yellow. Veg. and white grit temper. B3/2.

226 Fig. 36. Rim frag., L. 11.5 cm, diam. 22.0 cm. 5Y 8/3 pale yellow. Veg. temper. A5/2.

227 Fig. 37. Rim frag., L. 6.0 cm, diam. 11.0 cm. 5Y 8/3 pale yellow. Grit temper. B2/2.
Twenty similar rim frags:
a-h. A2-B2/2; A2-A3 (six); B2-B3.
i. Diam. 11.5 cm. Pinkish. A3-B3/2.
j. Diam. 13.0 cm. Pinkish. A3-B3/2.
k-t. A3-A4/1; A3-A4/2 (four); B3-B4/1 (two); A4-B4/2; A4-A5/2; A4-A5-B4-B5.

228 Fig. 37. Rim frag., L. 9.0 cm, diam. 12.0 cm. 5YR 7/6 reddish yellow fabric, 7.5YR 8/4 pink slip on interior and exterior. A3-A4/1.
Three similar rim frags:
a. A3-A4/2.
b. Diam. 11.0 cm. 2.5Y 8/2 white. Veg. and grit temper. B5/2.
c. Red. Trench WR.

229 Fig. 37. One half of rim preserved, diam. 12.0 cm. 10YR 8/3 very pale brown. Grit temper. B2/2.

230 Fig. 37. Rim frag., L. 6.0 cm, diam. 9.0 cm. 5Y 8/3 pale yellow. B4/1.
Five similar rim frags:
a-c. Diams 11.0-12.0 cm. 5Y 8/3 pale yellow. Veg. temper. A3/2.
d. Waster. 5Y 8/3 pale yellow. Veg. temper. A4/1. Sample BM 1984-5-12, 35; see Appendix III.
e. Diam. 12.0 cm. 7.5YR 7/4 pink. Veg. temper. B4/2.

231 Fig. 37. Two rim frags, longest 4.0 cm, diam. 16.0 cm. 5Y 8/3 pale yellow. B5/2.
Four similar rim frags:
a. Diam. 12.0 cm. Reddish. A3-B3/3.
b-d. A3-A4/2; A4-B4/2; A4-A5-B4-B5.

232 Fig. 37. Rim frag., L. 6.5 cm, diam. 12.0 cm. 10YR 7/3 very pale brown. Veg. temper and sparse white grits. Kiln. Sample BM 1984-5-12, 36; see Appendix III.
Seven similar rim frags:
a. Diam. 12.0 cm. 10YR 7/4 very pale brown. Grit temper. A1.
b. A2-A3-B2-B3.
c. Diam. 10.6 cm. 5Y 8/3 pale yellow. Veg. temper. B3/2.
d. 10YR 8/3 very pale brown. Veg. and white and micaceous grit temper. B3/2.
e. Diam. 14.0 cm. 10YR 7/4 very pale brown. Veg. and white grit temper. B3/2.
f. Diam. 12.0 cm. 10YR 8/4 very pale brown. Veg. temper. Kiln. Sample BM 1984-5-12, 33; see Appendix III.

g. Diam. 11.0 cm. 10YR 8/3 very pale brown. B5/2.

233 Fig. 37. Rim frag., L. 7.3 cm, diam 13.0 cm. 10YR 8/3 very pale brown. Veg. temper. A4/1.
Five similar rim frags:
a-c. Diams 9.0, 11.0, 11.0 cm. 5Y 8/3 pale yellow (one waster?). Veg. temper. A4/2.
d. 10 YR 7/1 light grey, surface 5Y 8/3 pale yellow. Veg. temper with white grits (?). A5/2.
e. 5Y 8/3 pale yellow. Veg. temper. Waster. A5/2. Sample BM 1984-5-12, 48; see Appendix III.

234 Fig. 37. One half of rim preserved, diam. 13.0 cm. 10YR 8/3 very pale brown. Sparse white grit temper. B4/2.
Five similar rim frags:
a-b. Diam. 12.0 cm. 10YR 7/2 light grey. White grit temper. A3/2.
c. 5Y 8/3 pale yellow. Veg. temper. A3/2.
d. Diam. *c.*15.0 cm. 5Y 8/3 pale yellow. Veg. temper. B3/2.
e. Diam. *c.*10.0 cm. 5YR 8/4 pink. Veg. and white grit temper. B4/2.

235 Fig. 37. Rim frag., L. 6.1 cm, diam. 12.0 cm. 10YR 8/3 very pale brown. Veg. temper. A3/2.
Three similar rim frags:
a. Diam. 18.0 cm. 5Y 8/3 pale yellow. Veg. and white grit temper. A3/2.
b. Diam. *c.*10.0 cm. 10YR 8/3 very pale brown. Veg. temper. A3/2.
c. Diam. 11.0 cm. 10YR 6/2 light brownish grey. Veg. and white grit temper. A3/2.

236 Fig. 37. Rim frag., L. 4.5 cm, diam. 13.0 cm. 5YR 7/6 reddish yellow. Grit temper. B5/2.

237 Fig. 37. Rim frag., L. 4.5 cm, diam. 12.0 cm. 10YR 8/3 very pale brown. Veg. (?) and fine white grit temper. B4/2.

238 Fig. 37. Rim frag., L. 4.3 cm, diam. 14.0 cm. 5Y 8/3 pale yellow. Little visible temper. A5/2.

239 Fig. 37. Rim frag., L. 7.0 cm, diam. 12.0 cm. Pale brown. Veg. and grit temper. Kiln.
Seven similar rim frags:
a. L. 5.8 cm, diam. 12.0 cm. 10YR 8/4 very pale brown. Veg. and grit temper. Kiln. Sample BM 1984-5-12, 45; see Appendix III.
b-f. Diams *c.*12.0 cm. One 5Y 8/3 pale yellow and the others pale brown. Kiln.
g. Red. Trench PF.

240 Fig. 37. Three-quarters of rim preserved, diam. 12.5 cm. 5Y 8/2 white. Grit temper. A1.

241 Fig. 38. Rim frag., L. 7.0 cm, diam. 26.0 cm. 5YR 7/6 reddish yellow. Grit temper. A1.

242 Fig. 38. Rim frag., diam. 22.0 cm. 5YR 7/6

reddish yellow. Grit temper. A2-A3.
  A similar rim frag.:
  a. Diam. 46.0 cm. 7.5YR 7/4 pink. Grit temper.
     B2/1.

243 Fig. 38. One-quarter of rim, diam. 21.0 cm.
7.5YR 8/4 pink. Veg. and grit temper. C1/1.
  A similar rim frag.: A3-B3/2.

244 Fig. 38. Rim frag., L. 2.0 cm. 5Y 8/3 pale
yellow. Grit temper. C1/1.
  A similar rim frag.:
  a. Thicker, with groove round the widest part. Diam.
     30.0 cm. Grit temper. A1-B1.

245 Fig. 38. Rim frag., L. 5.8 cm, diam. 30.0 cm.
5YR 7/6 reddish yellow. Veg. temper. B4/2.

246 Fig. 38. Rim frag., diam. 35.0 cm. 5Y 8/2
white. Veg. and grit temper. B3-B4/2.

247 Fig. 38. Rim frag., L. 8.5 cm, diam. 26.0 cm.
7.5YR 7/6 reddish yellow. Grit temper. B2/1.

248 Fig. 38. Rim frag., L. 5.0 cm, diam. 36.0 cm.
5Y 8/3 pale yellow. Veg. and sparse white grit temper.
B3/2.

249 Fig. 38. Rim frag., L. 4.5 cm, diam. 21.0 cm.
Fine fabric, 2.5YR N6/ grey. Fine micaceous grit
temper. B3/2.

250 Fig. 38. Rim frag., L. 12.0 cm, diam. 34.0 cm.
2.5Y 8/2 white. Veg. temper. A2-A3-B2-B3.
  A similar rim frag.:
  a. Smaller. Diam. 14.0 cm. 5Y 8/3 pale yellow. Grit
     temper. A3-A4/2.

251 Fig. 38. Rim frag., L. 4.0 cm, diam. 50.0 cm.
5Y 8/2 white (burnt on interior). Veg. and grit temper.
A1.
  A similar rim frag.:
  a. A3-A4/1.

252 Fig. 39. Rim frag., L. 8.0 cm, diam. 30.0 cm.
10YR 7/3 very pale brown, 2.5Y 8/2 white slip on
interior and exterior. Veg. and grit temper. A1.

253 Fig. 39. Rim frag., L. 15.0 cm, diam. 30.0 cm.
7.5YR 8/4 pink fabric, 10YR 8/4 very pale brown slip
on interior and exterior. Veg. and grit temper. B2-B3
(removal of stones).
  Nine similar rim frags (see also nos 180-82):
  a-c. All large. One 5Y 8/3 pale yellow. A1-B1.
  d. Rim frag. and one body sherd. 5Y 8/3 pale yellow.
     B1-C1.
  e-f. Different sizes. A2-A3.
  g. Diam. *c*.22.0 cm. B2-B3.
  h. Sondage KQ2.

254 Fig. 39. Rim frag., L. 3.0 cm, diam. 28.0 cm.
5Y 8/2 white. A3-A4/2.

255 Fig. 39. Rim frag., L. 20.0 cm, diam. 33.0 cm.
5Y 8/3 pale yellow. Veg. temper. B3/2.
  Three joining shoulder frags with ridge and grooves.
  Max. diam. *c*.24 cm. A2/2 (see also no. 182.).

256 Fig. 39. Rim frag., L. 7.0 cm, diam. 26.0 cm.
5YR 7/6 reddish yellow. Grit temper. A1.
  A similar rim frag.:
  a. 5Y 8/3 pale yellow. Veg. temper. B4.

257 Fig. 39. Rim frag., L. 4.5 cm, diam. 48.0 cm.
5YR 7/4 pink. Grit temper. B2/1.

258 Fig. 39. Rim frag., L. 3.0 cm, diam. 32.0 cm.
5YR 7/6 reddish yellow, with 10YR 8/3 white slip on
exterior. Grit temper. A1.

259 Fig. 40. Rim frag., diam. 7.0 cm. 10YR 7/4
very pale brown fabric, 10YR 8/2 white slip on interior
and exterior. Grit temper. A4-B4/2.

260 Fig. 40. Three-quarters of rim, diam. 8.0 cm.
5YR 7/6 reddish yellow. Grit temper. B2/2.

261 Fig. 40. Shoulder frag., max. diam. 8.0 cm.
7.5YR 7/6 reddish yellow. A2/2.

262 Fig. 40. Wall frag., max. diam. 5.0 cm. 5YR
7/6 reddish yellow. Veg. and grit temper. A2/2.

263 Fig. 40. Rim frag., L. 2.0 cm, diam. 6.0 cm.
5YR 7/4 pink. Grit temper. A3-B3/1.
  A similar rim frag.:
  a. Diam. 22.0 cm. 10YR 8/3 very pale brown. Veg.
     and white grit temper. A5/1.

264 Fig. 40, Pl. VIIa; KQ16; Sulaimaniya
Museum. Complete jar (small part of rim missing), H.
8.3 cm, max. diam. 8.95 cm. 5YR 7/6 reddish yellow.
Coarse fabric with veg. temper and large white grits.
B2-B3/2.

265 Fig. 40. Rim frag., L. 1.5 cm, diam. 3.9 cm.
5YR 7/4 pink. Veg. and sparse white grit temper. B4/2.
  A similar rim frag.: B4-B5.

266 Fig. 40. One-third of rim, diam. 4.5 cm. 5Y
8/2 white. Grit temper. A1-A2/1.

267 Fig. 40. Two rim frags, wasters, diam. 5.0 cm.
10YR 4/1 dark grey, with slip 5Y 5/2 olive grey on
interior and exterior. Fine grit temper. A2/2.
  A similar but burnt rim frag.: A3-A4-B3-B4.

268 Fig. 40; KQ19; Sulaimaniya Museum. Jar
with rim missing, H. 10.2 cm, max. diam. 7.9 cm. 10YR
7/4 very pale brown. Fine grit temper. B1/2.

269 Fig. 40; KQ20; MM for study no. 273. Jar,
part of body missing, half of rim and neck preserved.
H. 24.0 cm, max. diam. 14.0 cm. 5Y 8/3 pale yellow.
Veg. and white and black grit temper. B3. See also no.
182.

270   Fig. 40; KQ18; MM for study no. 272. Footed goblet, 5 cm of rim preserved, H. 12.0 cm, max. diam. 9.1 cm. 5Y 7/3 pale yellow. Veg. and grit temper. Base split in firing, probably a waster. A2/2.

Painted pottery

271   Fig. 40, Pl. VIIIa; KQ17; Sulaimaniya Museum. Jar, small chip missing from rim, H. 7.5 cm, max. diam. 7.1 cm. 10YR 7/4 very pale brown, with three bands of reddish-brown paint, much faded, on shoulder and another on bottom of neck; originally there may have been more. Fine white and black grit temper. B2-B3/2.

272   Fig. 40. Wall frag. of fine ware, max. diam. 8.0 cm. 7.5YR 8/4 pink, 7.5YR 8/2 pinkish white slip on exterior, with three bands of 2.5YR 5/6 red paint on exterior. A3-A4/1.

273   Fig. 40. Rim frag., L. 2.5 cm, diam. 3.45 cm. 7.5YR 7/4 pink, four bands of dark brown/black paint. Very friable; no visible temper. A5-B5. Sample BM 1984-5-12, 67; see Appendix III.

274   Fig. 40. Rim frag., diam. 3.4 cm. 7.5YR 8/6 reddish yellow, with four bands of 7.5YR 3/2 dark brown paint. Grit temper. A5-B5 (just above the stones).

275   Fig. 40. Neck (?) frag., 2.9 cm x 2.3 cm. 7.5YR 7/4 pink, with single band of light red paint. Sparse white and micaceous grit temper. B5/2. Sample BM 1984-5-12, 64; see Appendix III.
   A painted body sherd:
a. 3.9 x 3.7 cm, thickness 1.0 cm. Fabric 10YR 7/3 very pale brown, with three bands of 5YR 5/4 reddish brown paint. Grit temper. B5/2. Sample BM 1984-5-12, 63; see Appendix III.

276   Fig. 40, Pls VIIb, XIa; KQ15; IM. Complete bottle, H. 11.85 cm, max. diam. 5.9 cm. 7.5YR 7/4 pink, with 10YR 8/3 very pale brown slip, with nine bands of 7.5YR 4/2 dark brown paint. Grit temper. The slip has blistered in several places, suggesting that the bottle might be a waster. A2/2.

Cooking wares

277   Fig. 41. Rim frag., L. 5.5 cm, diam. 14.0 cm, with part of handle. Core of fabric 10YR 7/1 light grey, firing to 10YR 7/4 very pale brown on interior and exterior surfaces. White grit temper. A1/4.

278   Fig. 44. Quarter of rim, with handle, diam. 16.0 cm. Large white grit temper. A1/3.

279   Fig. 41. Rim frag., L. 7.0 cm, diam. 18.0 cm, with handle. 10YR 5/4 yellowish brown fabric, fire-blackened on interior. Large white grit temper. A1.

280   Fig. 41. Frag. of wall and handle. 10YR 6/3 pale brown, fire-blackened. Large white grit temper. B2/1.

281   Fig. 41. Part of wall and handle. Wall firing from 5Y 7/2 light grey on interior to 2.5YR 6/6 light red on exterior and handle, 5Y 8/2 white slip on exterior. Veg. and grit temper. A3-B3/2.

282   Fig. 41. Rim frag., L. 8.0 cm, diam. 18.0 cm. 7.5YR 5/4 brown fabric with white grits, fire-blackened on interior, 7.5YR 5/2 brown on exterior. C1.
   A similar rim frag.: B1-B2.

283   Fig. 41. Rim frag., L. 7.5 cm, diam. 24.0 cm. 7.5YR 5/4 brown, fire-blackened on interior and exterior. Grit temper. A2/2.

284   Fig. 41. Rim frag., L. 4.0 cm, diam. 19.0 cm. Outer layer of fabric and exterior 5YR 6/4 light reddish brown, inner layer of fabric and interior 2.5Y N3/ very dark grey, rim blackened. Large white grit temper. A1/2.

285   Fig. 41. Rim frag., L. 3.0 cm, diam. 16.0 cm. 2.5YR 6/6 light red burnt to black. Large white grit temper. B2/2.

286   Fig. 41. Rim frag., L. 8.0 cm, diam. 14.0 cm. 5YR 5/4 reddish brown fabric with 7.5YR 6/4 light brown wash on interior and exterior. White grit temper. A1/4.

287   Fig. 41. Rim frag., L. 9.0 cm, diam. 14.0 cm. 7.5YR 7/4 pink. Abundant grey and white grit temper. A2-B2/2.

288   Fig. 41. Rim frag., L. 6.5 cm, diam. 20.0 cm. 7.5YR 5/4 brown, fire-blackened. White grit temper. B2/1.

289   Fig. 41. Rim frag., L. 11.0 cm, diam. 24.0 cm. 10YR 8/3 very pale brown. Veg. and grit temper. A1.

In addition to nos 277-89, the following fragments of cooking ware deserve special note:
a-b. Rim frags, diams 20.0 and 22.0 cm. 10YR 6/2 light brownish grey, fire-blackened on interior. White and grey grit temper.
c-i. Rim frags, from hole-mouth cooking pots: B1/2; A2/2 and 3(four); A3-B3/2; B4-B5.
j. Plain rim frag. A3-A4/2.
k. Small rim frag., perhaps similar to no. 194. 10YR 5/1 grey. Grit temper. B4/2.
l. Frag. with handle on side of pot. 5YR 5/4 reddish brown, fire-blackened. Grit temper. B5.
m-n. Handle frags, round in section: A1-B1; A2-B2/2.

Pithoi and coffins

290   Fig. 42. Fragments of a coffin, H. 55.2 cm, at top 81.0 cm. x 54.8 cm. 10YR 6/2 light brownish grey fabric, core fired to 10YR 7/3 very pale brown on the surface. In places there is a 5Y 8/3 pale yellow wash or slip and the firing seems to have been uneven because the colour varies. Heavy salt incrustations. Veg. and grit temper. Uneven, fairly coarse manufacture. A2/2.

Three rim frags from similar, flat-sided vessels:
a-b. 5Y 8/3 pale yellow. A4-A5/2.
c. B4/2.
d. Roughly made. 10YR 7/4 very pale brown. B5/2.

291   Fig. 42. Rim frag., L. 10.0 cm, diam. 33.0 cm. 7.5YR 8/6 reddish yellow. White grit temper. B3/2.

292   Fig. 42. Rim frag. 5YR 7/6 reddish yellow, wash 10YR 8/3 very pale brown on exterior. Veg. and grit temper. B5/1.

293   Fig. 42. Rim frag., L. 8.0 cm, diam. 54.0 cm. 5Y 8/3 pale yellow. Veg. temper. B1/1.

294   Fig. 42. Rim frag., L. 12.0 cm, diam. 58.0 cm. 5Y 8/3 pale yellow. Veg. and grit temper. B4/4.

A similar rim frag.:
a. Large and crude. 5Y 8/3 pale yellow. B4.

295   Fig. 42. Wall (?) or shoulder (?) frag. 10YR 7/4 very pale brown, 5Y 8/2 white slip on exterior. Veg. temper with large grit inclusions. A3-B3/2.

296   Fig. 42. Rim frag., L. 10.6 cm. 5YR 7/4 pink. Grit and some veg. temper. A1.

A similar rim frag.: B3 (inside large pot).

297   Fig. 42. Wall frag. 2.5YR 6/8 light red, grit temper. B5/2.

A rim or cordon frag:
a. Very worn, with thumb-nail impressions. A2-A3-B2-B3.

298   Fig. 42. Pithos frag., 2 cm thick. 5Y 8/1 white fabric and slip on interior and exterior. Grit and veg. temper. B2/1.

299   Fig 42. Rim frag., L. 30.0 cm, diam. 65-70 cm. 10YR 7/4 very pale brown, fire-blackened all over. Grit temper. A1/3c.

A similar rim frag.: C1.

300   Fig. 42. Rim frag., L. 31.0 cm, diam. 68.0 cm. 10YR 8/6 yellow. Veg. temper with some white grits. B3/2.

In addition to nos 290-300, the following fragments of pithoi deserve special note:
Five pithos rim frags:
A1-B1 (two: one of these 5Y 8/3 pale yellow); B1-B2; A3-A4/2; A4-A5 (5Y 8/3 pale yellow - waster?).

Three frags with corded decoration:
a. C1.
b. Light brown fabric, cream surface. A4/2.
c. B4/2.

Three frags from the flat bases of two pithoi:
a. Diam. *c.*30.0 cm. 5Y 8/3 pale yellow. B1-B2.
b-c. Flaring sides. 10R 6/8 light red fabric, 10YR 8/3 very pale brown surface. B3/2.

Bases

301   Fig. 43. Base, with carefully made hole in centre. 10YR 8/3 very pale brown. Veg. and grit temper. B4/2.

302   Fig. 43. Base. 10YR 7/3 very pale brown. Grit temper. B5/2.

A similar base frag.:
a. Thick and solid. 2.5Y 8/2 white. Veg. and grit temper. C1/2.

303   Fig. 43. Base. 5YR 8/4 pink. White grit and veg. temper. A3/2.

304   Fig. 43. Frag. of base. 2.5YR 6/8 light red. Grit temper. B4/2.

305   Fig. 43. Half of base. 10YR 8/3 very pale brown. Veg. and white grit temper. B4/1.

306   Fig. 43. Base. 5Y 8/2 white. Grit and some veg. temper. A3-A4/2.

307   Fig. 43. Base. 2.5YR 6/6 light red. Grit temper. B5/2.

A similar base frag.:
a. 5YR 7/6 reddish yellow. Grit and veg. temper. B1/2.

308   Fig. 43. Base. 10YR 7/4 very pale brown. Veg. and white grit temper. B4/1.

Eleven similar base frags:
a-d. B2/2 (three:two of these 5Y 8/3 pale yellow); B2-B3.
e. 7.5YR 8/4 pink. Veg. temper with micaceous grits. B3/2.
f-h. Two pink/light brown; one overfired 5Y 8/3 pale yellow. Kiln.
i. 10YR 6/2 light brownish grey. Grit temper. B4/4.
j. 10YR 8/6 yellow. Coarse veg. temper. A5/2.
k. Light brown. Trench WR.

309   Fig. 43. Three-quarters of base. 5YR 8/4 pink. Veg., white and micaceous grit temper. A3/2.

Three similar base frags.:
a. Closely similar. A3/2.
b. Less bulbous, brownish grey. A3/2.
c. More grit temper.

310   Fig. 43. One-eighth of base preserved. 5Y 8/3 pale yellow. Veg. temper. B4/2.

A similar base frag.:
a. Diam. 3.6 cm. 5YR 7/6 reddish yellow. Grit temper. B5.

311 Fig. 43. One-third of base preserved. 5Y 8/2 white. Grit temper. B2/2. Sample BM 1984-5-12, 46; see Appendix III.
A similar base frag.:
a. Red. A2-A3-B2-B3.

312 Fig. 43. Base. 2.5Y 8/2 white. Grit temper. A1.
Three similar base frags: A3-A4/2 (two); A4-B4/2.

313 Fig. 43. Base. 5Y 7/2 light grey. Grit and veg. temper. B5/2.

314 Fig. 43. One-half of base. 5YR 7/3 pink fabric and interior firing to 10YR 8/2 white on exterior. Veg. temper and a few grits. A1/2.

315 Fig. 43. Base. Fabric 5Y 7/1 light grey firing to 7.5YR 7/4 pink on surfaces. Traces of burning. Veg. and grit temper. A2/2.
A similar base frag.:
a. Light red. Veg. and grit temper. Trench PF.

316 Fig. 43. Three-quarters of base. 7.5YR 5/4 brown. White grit temper. B4/1.

317 Fig. 43. Base. 5Y 8/3 pale yellow. Veg. temper. Clearly a waster. A3/2.

318 Fig. 43. One-half of base. 2.5Y 7/4 pale yellow. Grit temper. B2/1.

319 Fig. 43. One-half of base. 5YR 8/4 pink, with 7.5YR 8/2 pinkish white slip on exterior. A3/2.
A similar base:
a. 7.5YR 7/6 reddish yellow. Soft grit-tempered ware with some veg. A2-B2/1.

320 Fig. 43. One-half of base. 7.5YR 7/6 reddish yellow. Grit and some veg. temper. A2/2. Sample BM 1984-5-12, 39; see Appendix III.

321 Fig. 43. Base. 5YR 8/4 pink. Veg. and white grit temper. B3/2.

322 Fig. 43. One-fifth of base. 5YR 7/6 reddish yellow, grit and veg. temper. B2/2.
A similar base frag. from a smaller vessel: 5Y 8/3 pale yellow. B2-B3.

323 Fig. 43. One-quarter of base, 10YR 7/4 very pale brown. Grit temper. C1.
A frag. of a base with a fairly large nipple: B3 (inside large pot).

324 Fig. 43. Base. 2.5Y 8/2 white. 'Fine ware'. A3-A4/1.

325 Fig. 43. Base. 7.5YR 7/4 pink fabric and interior, 7.5YR 8/2 pinkish white wash or slip on exterior. Grit and veg. temper. C1.

326 Fig. 43. One-quarter of base. 5Y 8/2 white. Grit temper. B2/1.

327 Fig. 43. Frag. of base. 7.5YR 7/4 pink. Veg. and white grit temper. A1/2.
A similar base frag.:
a. 10YR 8/4 very pale brown. Grit temper. A1/3.

328 Fig. 43. Frag. of base. 10YR 8/3 very pale brown. Sparse veg. temper (fine ware). B4/2.

329 Fig. 44. Fragment of base. 5Y 8/3 pale yellow. White grit temper. B3/2.
A base frag. from a steeper-sided vessel. 10YR 7/6 yellow. Veg. temper with some white grits. A4/2.

330 Fig. 44. Frag. of base. 5Y 7/1 light grey firing to 7.5YR 7/4 pink on surfaces. Grit temper. A2/2.

331 Fig. 44. Frag. of base. 5YR 8/4 pink. White grit temper. B3/2.

332 Fig. 44. One-quarter of base. 10YR 8/2 white. Very fine ware with no visible temper. B4/4.
Two similar base frags:
a. Diam. 8.0 cm. 10YR 8/3 very pale brown. Veg. temper with sparse white grits. A5/2.
b. 5Y 8/3 pale yellow. Fine. B4/2.

333 Fig. 44. Frag. of base. 10YR 8/3 very pale brown. White grit temper. B3/2.
A similar base and a body frag., diam. 6.0 cm. 10YR 8/2 white. Sparse white grit temper. A3/2.

334 Fig. 44. One-quarter of base. 10YR 6/1 light grey. Fine grey ware as tripods with no visible temper. B3/2.

335 Fig. 44. Frag. of base. 5YR 6/6 reddish yellow. A1/3.
A similar base frag.:
a. Diam. similar. 5YR 6/6 reddish yellow. A1/3.

336 Fig. 44. One-quarter of base. 5YR 8/3 pink with 10YR 8/1 white slip on interior and exterior. Sparse white grit temper. A3/2.
A similar base frag.:
a. Diam. 10.0 cm. 5YR 7/6 reddish yellow. Grit temper. B1/1.

337 Fig. 44. One-quarter of base. 10YR 8/3 very pale brown, possibly with 7.5YR 8/4 pink slip. Fine white grit temper. B4/2.

338 Fig. 44. Base. 10YR 7/2 light grey firing to 2.5Y 8/4 pale yellow on surface. Grit temper. A2/2.

339 Fig. 44. Base. 10YR 8/3 very pale brown with 10YR 8/2 white slip. Grit temper. B2/1. Sample BM 1984-5-12, 59; see Appendix III.

340   Fig. 44. Frag. of base. Grey fabric possibly with traces of red paint on exterior surface but this could be a result of over-firing. B4. Sample BM 1984-5-12, 65; see Appendix III.

341   Fig. 44. Base. 10YR 6/4 light yellowish brown. White grit temper. B3/2.
   A similar base frag.:
   a. Diam. *c*.8.0 cm. 10YR 7/3 very pale brown. White grit temper. B3/2.

342   Fig. 44. 2.5YR 6/8 light red. Veg. and white grit temper, irregular hole near centre of base, probably accidental, filled with a black substance, probably bitumen. B4/4.

343   Fig. 44. One-third of base. 7.5YR 6/4 light brown fabric and interior, firing to 7.5YR 7/4 pink on exterior. Veg. and grit temper. A1.

344   Fig. 44. Frag. of base. 5YR 7/8 reddish yellow. Veg. temper. A4/2.

345   Fig. 44. Frag. of base. 2.5Y 8/2 white. Veg. and grit temper, clearly a waster. A1/2.

346   Fig. 44. One-third of base. 7.5YR 7/4 pink, possibly a slip on exterior. Grit temper. A3-A4/2.

347   Fig. 44. Base. 5Y 8/3 pale yellow. Grit temper. A2/2.

348   Fig. 44. Frag. of base. 5Y 8/4 pink. Veg. temper B5/2.

349   Fig. 44. One-quarter of base. 10YR 10/1 light grey. Fine black and white grits. Two drilled holes and outline of third in base of wall. Purpose of these holes obscure, but presumably not for ancient repair as no break between the two holes closest together. A4/2.

350   Fig. 44. One-quarter of base. 2.5YR 6/8 light red. White grit and veg. temper. B4/2.
   A base frag.: 5YR 8/4 pink. Veg. temper with white and micaceous grits. A5/2.

In addition to nos 301-50, a number of flat and ring bases were recorded without further details:
   Flat bases (cf. nos 317, 319, 327)
   A1-B1; B1-C1; A1-A2; A2/2 and 3 (three); B2/2 (three); A2-A3 (two); A3-B3/2 (three); A3-A4/2; B3-B4/2; Kiln; B4-B5; A5-B5/1; A5-B5/2; B5/2 (eight or nine).
   Ring bases (cf. nos 341-50)
   a. Diam. 9.0 cm. 5YR 7/4 pink. Grit temper. A1.
   b. 5Y 8/2 white, burnt on interior. Veg. temper with grits. A1/3.
   c. Diam. 13.0 cm. 7.5YR 5/2 brown. Grit temper. A1/4.
   d. Diam. not more than 10.0 cm. 5YR 7/4 pink, surface slipped 10YR 7/3 very pale brown, burning

on interior. Veg. temper. A1/4.
   e. Diam. *c*.7.0 cm. 5Y 8/3 pale yellow. B1/2.
   f. Diam. 8.5 cm. Red. B2-B3.
   g. Diam. 7.4 cm. Red. B2-B3.
   h. Diam. 9.0 cm. Brownish. B2-B3.
   i. Diam. 11.0 cm. 10YR 8/4 very pale brown. Veg. temper. B4/1.
   j. Diam. 10.0 cm. 10YR 8/6 yellow. Veg. temper. B4/2.
   k. 10YR 8/3 very pale brown. Veg. temper. B4/2.
   l. Diam. 10.0 cm. 2.5YR 8/4 very pale yellow. Grit and veg. temper. B4/2.
   m.Diam. 9.0 cm. 5Y 8/3 pale yellow. B4/2.
   Also in A1-B1 (two); B1-C1 (three); B1-B2 (four); C1 (nine); A2/2 and 3 (eight); A2-B2/2; B2/1 (five: one of these pale yellow); B2/2 (two: one of these pale yellow); A2-A3 (six: two of these pale yellow); B2-B3 (two); A3/2 (fourteen); A3-B3/2 (three); A3-A4/2 (eight); B3-B4/1; B3-B4/2 (two); A4-B4/2 (six); Kiln (six); A4-A5/2 (three); A4-A5-B4-B5; B4-B5 (two); A5-B5/1; A5-B5/2 (two); B5/1 (two).

Glazed and incised pottery

351   Fig. 45, Pl. XIb; KQ24; MM for study no. 275. Part of polychrome glazed jar, rim and part of wall missing but base intact, max. diam. 18.2 cm, extant H. 20.2 cm. Pale brown fabric, veg. and white grit temper. Whole jar covered in green (light blue-green) glaze, on which are applied two bands of zigzag pattern, each coloured orange/yellow at bottom and a dirty white at the top. It is possible that some of the colours may be outlined in orange, but these could be vestigial lines from one of the glazes. There are traces of light green glaze on the inside of the jar as well, suggesting the whole vessel was dunked in glaze. B2-B3.
   a. Glazed sherd, 2.5 x 2.4 cm, probably from same type of jar. A5/2. Sample BM 1984-5-12, 66; see Appendix III.
   b. Glazed sherd, 4.8 x 5.7 cm, in poor condition but probably from same type of jar. A2-A3/1. Sample BM 1984-5-12, 62; see Appendix III.

352   Fig. 45. Frag. of glazed jar, 7.6 cm x 3.3 cm, yellow (X-hatched) on white. Possibly a waster, as it looks as if the yellow glaze has run. B2-B3. Sample BM 1984-5-12, 61; see Appendix III.

Four more sherds of glazed ware :
   a. Sherd of glazed ware - yellowish green - from globular pot. A1/2-3.
   b. Sherd which may have been glazed but is possibly highly vitrified. It measures 4.2 x 3.7 cm and was found in A2/2. Sample BM 1984-5-12, 60; see Appendix III.
   c. Small glazed sherd, patches of yellow on green. 2.1 x 2.9 cm. A5/2.
   d. Sherd 10YR 7/3. Grit temper. Greenish-blue glaze

on interior and 5Y 8/2 white on exterior. Sondage KQ1.

353   Fig. 45. Two non-joining wall fragments of jar with incised decoration. 5Y 8/3 pale yellow. Veg. and grit temper. B3/1 and B4/2.

354   Fig. 45. Rim frag., L. 2.5 cm, diam. 16.0 cm. 10YR 8/4 very pale brown. Veg. and fine white grit temper. B4/4.

355   Fig. 45. Wall frag. 5Y 8/3 pale yellow. Veg. and grit temper. B3-B4/2.

356   Fig. 45. Wall frag. 10YR 7/4 very pale brown. Grit temper. B3-B4/2.

357   Fig. 45. Wall frag. 5Y 8/3 pale yellow. Veg. temper. A3/2.

358   Fig. 45. Wall frag. 5Y 8/3 pale yellow. Veg. temper. A3/2.

359   Fig. 45. Wall frag. 5Y 8/3 pale yellow. Veg. temper. A3/2.

Miscellanea

360   Fig. 45; KQ7; MM for study no. 276. Pottery pipe lamp, mostly complete but sides and upper part of bowl missing. Crude light brown fabric, with veg. temper and coarse grit inclusions. L. 17.2 cm. Surface now black, presumably through having been burnt. B2-B3.

361   Fig. 45. Pottery knob or handle, diam. 2.5 cm. 2.5Y 8/2 white. Grit temper. B3/1 (130 cm → W. baulk, 110 cm → S. baulk, *c*.15cm b.s.).

Khirbet Qasrij sherd-count

	Totals	Pale yellow fabric (5Y 8/3, 8/4, 7/3, 7/4)	Fine ware	Cooking	Wasters
A1	1091	?	-	27	1
A1-B1	309	48	4	15	4
B1	218	42	2	1	1
B1-C1	110	19	2	-	-
C1	553	?	?	?	?
A1-A2	145	17	10	-	-
A1-A2-B1-B2	?	?	?	?	?
B1-B2	171	47	6	5	-
A2	734	179	17	31	3
A2-B2	216	19	5	9	1
B2	498	70	15	31	1
A2-A3	382	61	14	-	6
A2-A3-B2-B3	28	3	-	-	-
B2-B3	340	21	7	-	-
A3	1086	239	27	3	23
A3-B3	376	76	36	2	12
B3	592	137	9	16	7
A3-A4	733	151	46	1	6
A3-A4-B3-B4	104	11	1	-	-
B3-B4	232	46	2	-	4
A4	279	59	6	-	6
A4-B4	232	55	13	-	10
B4	683	120	24	2	4
Kiln	753	137	108	-	37
A4-A5	193	62	16	6	1
A4-A5-B4-B5	105	13	-	-	-
B4-B5	281	49	15	5	2
A5	498	95	8	-	1
A5-B5	214	34	6	-	-
B5	626	182	25	15	5
Sondage KQ1	58	12	5	-	-
Sondage KQ2	46	8	-	-	-
Trench PF	31	1	-	-	-
Trench WR	32	1	-	-	-
Totals	11949	2014	429	169	135

NB. These totals represent a combination of unjoined body sherds and diagnostic pieces, listed in the catalogue, that are sometimes counted as single items even when they are made up of a number of sherds.

Fabric types of catalogued pottery from Khirbet Qasrij

Mainly vegetable temper 70
Mixed vegetable and grit temper 198
Mainly grit temper 192
No visible temper 25

Size of sample 485

f. Discussion of pottery from Khirbet Qasrij

Bowls and tripod-bowls

Small bowls with flat bases (9-10)
At Nimrud, comparable bowls have been found in TW 53, the North-West Palace, the upper debris of the ziggurat excavation and Fort Shalmaneser (Joan Oates 1954: pl. XXXVII, 6; 1959: pl. XXXV, 5-6). Various fabrics are recorded at Nimrud.

Carinated bowls with ring-base and everted rim (20-54)
Amongst the Khirbet Qasrij pottery there are many variant forms, but essentially they may all be regarded as belonging to the same broad category. Amongst the Late Assyrian pottery from Nimrud, this sort of bowl was 'by far the most common type' (Joan Oates 1959: 132). The complete bowl profile no. 30 may be compared with Joan Oates 1954: pl. XXXVII, 5; 1959: pl. XXXV, 23-4.

Bowls with ribbed rims (67-78)
These bowls, with a pronounced rib or ribs on the outside of the rim, may be compared with the bowls from Fort Shalmaneser that Joan Oates describes as having 'folded grooved rims' (Joan Oates 1959: pl XXXV, 13-14, 25). The ribbed rim is also a feature of the Khirbet Qasrij tripod-bowls (nos 112-15), as it is of those from Nimrud (Joan Oates 1954: pl. XXXVIII, 1; 1959: pl. XXXV, 15-16). The more elaborate type of bowl with ribbed rim from Khirbet Qasrij, with clusters of three ribs (nos 75-8), is apparently absent from Nimrud.

Bowls with inverted and thickened rim (79-100)
Rims of this kind were common at Khirbet Qasrij. An almost complete example (no. 88) was found in the kiln, but its condition shows that it was (or would have been) a potter's reject. Other pieces come from all over the site, but they are concentrated in the central part of the main excavated area near the kiln, particularly in trenches A3, B3 and the baulk A3-A4. The type does not appear amongst the published pottery from Nimrud, but it should probably be seen as a developed form of the Late Assyrian bowls with 'folded grooved rims' (e.g. Joan Oates 1959: pl. XXXV, 14, 25). [1] However, an unpublished bowl from Nimrud, now in the Institute of Archaeology, is closely comparable. It bears the number ND 675, and according to the register description was found in 'Trench A49, from deep pit of top level'. [2] This bowl has a light brown fabric, with mixed vegetable and grit temper. As it was apparently found in a pit dug from a high level, the implication might be that this bowl-form is post-Assyrian. Bowls with this distinctive sort of rim, however, do not occur amongst the published Hellenistic pottery from Nimrud (Oates and Oates 1958). In southern Mesopotamia, the form can be found in contexts variously ascribed to the Neo-Babylonian or Achaemenid periods, for example at Tell ed-Der (De Meyer 1980: pl. 10, 16) and Nippur (McCown and Haines 1967: pls 97, 18; 100, 11, 13). Both Adams (1965: fig. 13, 9b) and Gibson (1972: fig. 35) use this form as a type fossil of the Neo-Babylonian period. At Warka, bowls of this kind are identified as '*spätbabylonisch*' (Boehmer 1987: 61, pl. 83, 109-14).

At Sultantepe, this form of rim is included among the types from the Late Assyrian level (Lloyd and Gökçe 1953: fig. 7, 14-16, 18-19), but it may be significant that beakers with button bases, sometimes dimpled and usually apparently of 'palace ware', occur 'with great frequency in the levels immediately beneath [the late Assyrian level]' (Lloyd 1954: 107, fig. 7). As Lloyd notes, these beakers are common at Nimrud in a seventh-century context (cf. for example Joan Oates 1959: pl. 37, 60-62) and this raises the question of whether the destruction level at Sultantepe is later than that at Nimrud. Going further afield, it is interesting to note that the shape is well known in the Median level at Nush-i Jan in Iran, both plain and with the addition of one or two horizontal handles (Ruth Stronach 1978: figs 6-7). However, in contrast to the Khirbet Qasrij pottery, these vessels are usually burnished and the fabric generally varies between pink and red, firing on the surface to a reddish or off-white colour. Examples, apparently not burnished, also occur in Level 1 at Baba Jan (Goff 1985: fig. 2, 26-8) and in Level IIIA at Hasanlu (Dyson 1965: fig. 13), demonstrating that the type probably goes on into the Achaemenid period.

Bowls with ring-base, angular carination and flared rim (107-110)
This was an extremely common type of bowl, particularly in the kiln area. Diameters varied between 19.0 and 28.0 cm, but were generally *c.*23.0-26.0 cm. Usually they were very pale brown or pink, although some were reddish or reddish yellow.

These bowls are well known at Nimrud, with examples from Fort Shalmaneser and TW 53 (Joan Oates

---

1. Examples of this type are known, however, from the nearby site of Khirbet Khatuniyeh, excavated by the British Museum expedition in 1984-5. They occur in late seventh-century and earlier Assyrian contexts.

2. Trench A49 was dug in the 1949 season on the north-east corner of the acropolis in squares F3, 4 (Mallowan 1950: pl XXVI); from this trench was recovered the interesting dagger with iron blade and bronze handle terminating in the form of a bone, now in the Ashmolean Museum. Trench A49 is contiguous with the area subsequently known as TW 53.

1954: pl. XXXVII, 3; 1959: pl. XXXVI, 31). The example from TW 53 is described as buff ware with buff slip.

Tripod-bowls (112-115)

No complete tripod-bowls were found at Khirbet Qasrij, but substantial parts of four different bowls were recovered. In addition, we collected nine further fragments of tripods of this type. All these pieces come from the kiln, except the tripod no. 115 and two single fragments that are from trenches A2 and A3 and the A3-B3 baulk respectively. These tripod-bowls are all made in a light grey fabric, sometimes firing to pinkish-grey. The fabric is extremely fine, with either no visible inclusions or very fine grit temper. By contrast, the feet are much coarser, with a large amount of vegetable temper, and are applied to the bowl with vegetable-tempered clay. A number of tripod-bowls of practically identical form were found at Nimrud, both in Fort Shalmaneser and in various locations on the acropolis (Mallowan 1950: pl. XXXII, 1; Joan Oates 1954: pl. XXXVIII, 1; 1959: pl. XXXV, 15-16; Rawson 1954: pl. XLI, 2). These examples from Nimrud are either of grey ware or buff or pinkish clay. In the latter cases the rim and interior of the bowls are generally covered with a brightly burnished red slip.

Fine wares (116-146)

Fine wares were distributed throughout the site, with a high concentration in and around the kiln. No complete vessels or even complete profiles were found at Khirbet Qasrij. This is not suprising, however, as through its very nature fine ware is extremely fragile and only survives complete in exceptional circumstances. Amongst the sherds classified as fine ware there is a wide range of fabric colours and, to a lesser extent, of fabric consistency, ranging from sherds with mixed vegetable and grit inclusions to sherds with grit temper only and finally to very fine fabrics with no visible inclusions. In the last category we are presumably dealing with what is known in the Assyrian period as 'palace ware'. It is worth remarking, though, that these very fine fabrics survive beyond the Late Assyrian period, and in the Achaemenid period they are known as 'eggshell ware'.

Some of the fine-ware rims from Khirbet Qasrij might belong to 'istikans', small drinking-cups resembling in shape modern oriental tea-glasses, which are well represented at Nimrud (e.g. Joan Oates 1959: pl. XXXVI, 37-40), while others, notably nos 117, 122 and related pieces, clearly belong to so-called 'palace ware' beakers. These are vessels with a high flared rim and a bulbous body tapering towards the base, and occur in some quantity at Nimrud (cf. Joan Oates 1959: pl. XXXVII, 64-7). Sometimes these beakers are decorated with dimples on the lower part of the body, and the fragment

no. 132 may be a body-sherd from one of these. It is not necessarily of the Late Assyrian period, however, as there are in the British Museum examples from Ur of eggshell ware with dimples dating from the Achaemenid period. The pointed bases nos 141-2 may also belong to fine-ware beakers, as perhaps also do the more angular forms nos 143-4.

The bowl no. 140, with carinated shoulders and everted rim, may be compared with Assyrian 'palace ware' bowls from Nimrud (Hamilton 1966: fig. 30a, d; Mallowan 1950: pl. XXXII, 2; Joan Oates 1959: pl. XXXVII, 59). Generally, however, in these Late Assyrian pottery bowls - and in their metal counterparts - the shoulder is fuller and sometimes slightly flattened. That is not to say the Qasrij bowl is not Late Assyrian: in any event, it is certainly not as late as the Achaemenid period, for although this type of bowl survives until then the shoulders become less pronounced and the profile less angular (Luschey 1939: *passim;* Moorey 1980: 32-8).

Jars with everted and club-shaped rims (147-226)

The majority of jar rims from Khirbet Qasrij fall into this broad category. Within it, there are many variations of rim-form, colour and fabric. The three complete or semi-complete jars (nos 147, 183-4) all have ring-bases. Nos 183-4 were found in the kiln, and had partially collapsed during firing (Pl. Xb); however, their original form could be easily estimated, and it is this that is reproduced here. Another jar of the same form was also found in the kiln, but this example had completely collapsed. These jars, particularly nos 183-4, are similar to squat ring-based jars from Nimrud that are said to be 'the commonest and most easily recognised late Assyrian jar'; the type apparently occurs frequently in both Late Assyrian and squatter occupation debris (Joan Oates 1959: 134, 145, pl. XXXVIII, 93). The rim form of the illustrated example from Nimrud is not identical to nos 183-4, being slightly more elaborate, but it is clearly related.

Jars with folded rims (227-240)

Jar-rims of this sort form a distinctive category and were well represented at Khirbet Qasrij. They were distributed across the site, with concentrations in trench A3, in the A2-A3 and A3-A4 baulks, and in the kiln, where nine examples were found. Their occurrence in a securely stratified context (the kiln) demonstrates they are not intrusive, and further examples from the outlying trenches PF and WR shows the form was widespread at Khirbet Qasrij.

These rim forms are rare in early Iron Age contexts, but they are not entirely unknown. There is, for example, a jar from Susa with a rim of this form dated to the early part of the Neo-Elamite period (Miroschedji 1978: fig. 52, 2). They do not seem to occur among the published Assyrian pottery from Nimrud, although the rims of the large storage jars from TW 53 are not altogether dissimilar (Joan Oates 1954: pl. XXXIX). Because of their absence from Nimrud, and because rimforms of this general type are sometimes regarded as typical of the Hellenistic period at sites in Palestine and Jordan (cf. for example Lapp 1961: type 11c; McNicoll *et al.* 1981: pl.127, 8), it has been suggested that the Khirbet Qasrij examples are a comparatively late form. Although they do not apparently occur in the Hellenistic levels at Nimrud (Oates and Oates 1958), a similar rim form is attested among the Hellenistic material from three of the sites in the Saddam Dam Salvage Project, namely Tell Mohammed 'Arab, Tell Deir Situn and Grai Darki. Generally, however, these Hellenistic rims are more stubby in form, with the thickened part at the top of the rim shorter and the neck less extended.

In Mesopotamia rim forms related to these, but not precisely comparable, are first attested in the Late Kassite period, with examples from the Warenkomplex B at Warka (Boehmer 1987: pl.50, 433-51) and Tell Zubeidi in the Hamzin (Boehmer and Dämmer 1985: pls 126, 297-300; 127, 307-12). The form, then, is established in Mesopotamia at a relatively early date. Thereafter, there is a dearth of examples until related types are attested in Neo-Babylonian or Achaemenid contexts at sites such as Nippur (McCown and Haines 1967: pl. 28, 15), Isin (Hrouda *et al.* 1981: pl. 31, nos 32-3, pl. 35, Grab 75), and Ur (Woolley 1962: pl. 50, 148, etc.). Also belonging to the same family, but again not very similar, are the rim forms of storage jars with rounded bases from graves at Kamid el- Loz dated to the fifth to fourth centuries BC (Poppa 1978: pls 13, 14, 20, 25). At Pasargadae, rim forms very close in shape, but not in fabric, come from the Tall-i Takht, ranging in date from the Late Achaemenid to early Hellenistic periods (e.g. Stronach 1978: fig. 118, 26-8); the published examples have cores either 'pinkish buff' or 'red'.

Large jars (241-258)

Among the larger jars from Khirbet Qasrij, a number of rim forms occur. Unusual are the vertical rim with external rib no. 249 and the tapering rim no. 258. Occasionally (e.g. nos 242, 250, 258), these larger jars have bands of applied decoration on the neck.

Bottles and small jars (259-269)

The rims nos 259-60 are from bottles of a type known at Nimrud in the Late Assyrian period (Joan Oates 1959: pl. XXXVIII, 86). The fabric of no. 259 is rather unusual, in that it is very pale brown with a white slip on the interior and exterior surfaces. Bottles with necks of the same sort of shape survive into the Hellenistic period; an example from Nimrud (Oates and Oates 1958: pl. XXVIII, 3) is made of salmon-coloured clay with a buff slip.

The small jar with a rounded base, no. 264, is broadly comparable with a series of jars from Nimrud (Joan Oates 1959: pl. XXXVIII, 83-4), although it is slightly squatter in profile. Small jars of this general form continue long after the Late Assyrian period, witness an example of the Hellenistic period from Nimrud (Oates and Oates 1958: pl. XXIV, 20). The small jar with pointed base, no. 268, lacking a rim, is like Joan Oates 1959: pl. XXXVII, 80.

Vase (269)

This vessel again finds a parallel at Nimrud (Joan Oates 1959: pl. XXXVIII, 97), but the Nimrud example is flattened at the base instead of being completely rounded. Some of the rim forms classified above as jars may of course belong to vases of this sort.

Goblet (270)

A number of footed goblets similar to no. 270 have been found in Fort Shalmaneser at Nimrud (Joan Oates 1959: pl. XXXVII, 55-7). They sometimes come from comparatively late contexts ('second destruction level') and are generally of 'dark buff clay'. The fabric of the Khirbet Qasrij example is pale yellow, and its split base and distorted shape suggest that it may have been a waster.

Painted pottery (271-276)

In this category there are two complete vessels, a small jar (no. 271) and a bottle (no. 276), two rim fragments from bottles (nos 273-4) and two body-sherds (nos 272, 275). The miniature bottle (no. 276) has a pinkish fabric with light brown slip, and is decorated with bands of dark brown paint. It bears some resemblance to a type of small bottle known from Nimrud (Joan Oates 1959: pl. XXXVIII, 90), which is also decorated with bands of dark brown paint, but the Nimrud bottles are pointed at the base ('carrot-shaped'), whereas the Khirbet Qasrij example has a flat base. It is interesting, though, that the painted cosmetic bottles from Nimrud are invariably badly fired (Joan Oates 1959: 137), and the surface of the Khirbet Qasrij bottle is blistered in several places, which suggested to us at the time of excavation that it might be a waster. The small jar no. 271 is again decorated with bands of paint, this time of a reddish hue, on a light brown background; this type does not seem to be paralleled at Nimrud. The two rim fragments nos

273-4, both decorated with bands of dark brown or black paint, come from bottles with a quite different character to no. 276, being much finer and thinner-walled, and are possibly imported. At Nimrud, painted decoration is said to be rare in the Assyrian period (Joan Oates 1959: 137) and this would seem to be the case also at Khirbet Qasrij.

Cooking wares (277-289)

These were found predominantly in square A1 and in the A1-B1 baulk, in the vicinity of the oven. There was another group in A2 and in the A2-B2 baulk. It is remarkable how the cooking-ware sherds were clustered in the east part of the excavation and comparatively scarce in the central and western parts (see Figs 46-7).

Pithoi and coffins (290-300)

There were four separate concentrations of pithos-type sherds: in C1 where there were remains of at least five different pithoi, in A2 which also contained a coffin, and in A3 and B5. Deserving of special mention is the terracotta coffin no. 290, fragments of which were found strewn over much of trench A2. Strommenger has shown that terracotta coffins with one end rounded and the other squared-off (*Hockersarkophage*) occur at Ashur in the Middle and Late Assyrian periods. From Assyria the form spread to Babylonia, and at Babylon examples are found dating between the early eighth century BC and the mid-fourth century BC (Strommenger 1964: 170-71, fig. 1). There are many examples from Ur dating from the Neo-Babylonian and Achaemenid periods (Woolley 1962: 67), and in the Late Assyrian period the type is also found in bronze (Curtis 1983). A coffin from Warka with a band of cable ornament around the side, very similar to the Khirbet Qasrij example, has been published by Boehmer (1987: pl. 19a-c). It is dated to the Late Babylonian or Achaemenid period. It may be thought that the Khirbet Qasrij example, with a length of only 81 cm, is too small to be a coffin, but an example from Babylon, found with skeleton and grave-goods inside (Strommenger 1964: fig. 3, 6) is only about 95 cm long. An interesting feature about the Khirbet Qasrij coffin is that it has a hole in the front near the base. This is presumably to allow liquids to run out, and could be taken to imply that such receptacles had a domestic function. I have argued elsewhere that they were in fact coffins (Curtis 1983: 86-7), but this need not have excluded a dual function for some of them.

Glazed pottery (351-352)

The main find from Khirbet Qasrij in this category was a polychrome glazed jar with globular body and narrow, convex base (no. 351). It is mostly complete, save for the neck and rim which are entirely missing. The jar is covered with a light blue-green glaze, on which are two bands of conjoined triangles. These triangles are orange or yellow in colour, on a background that is now off-white but may originally have been yellow. Two more sherds, probably from the same type of polychrome glazed jar, were also recovered.

Very similar to no. 351 is a polychrome glazed jar from Nimrud (Oates and Oates 1958: pl. XXVIII, 15). It is of similar shape, and apparently of about the same size - the Nimrud jar, complete, has a height of 26.0 cm, whereas the Qasrij example, with neck and rim missing, has an extant height of 20.2 cm. Also, the form of decoration and the colour scheme appear to be almost identical. The Nimrud jar, ND 5005, was found in an inhumation grave in the Nabu Temple, together with a pottery bowl and a bronze ladle (David Oates 1957: 37). This grave was initially dated to *c*.500 BC on the basis of the glazed jar, about which David Oates commented, 'the chevron bands on the glazed jar are a common motif of neo-Babylonian potters, which may continue into Achaemenian times'. Subsequently, however, it was recognised that this jar must have been older than the grave, which was probably dug in the period *c*.180-140 BC (Oates and Oates 1958: 123); this late date is indicated by the pottery bowl which has dog-tooth decoration around the shoulder (*ibid.*: pl. XXIV, 8), and probably also the bronze ladle. The evidence of the Nimrud jar, then, is not helpful for the dating of the Qasrij jar: it cannot, as we shall see, be as late as the second century BC, and must be appreciably earlier. In this connection it is interesting to note that also found at Nimrud were a few polychrome sherds 'with chevron and triangular ornament in orange, white, and blue', as well as fragments of a large jar apparently inscribed with a king's name (Joan Oates 1959: 138). These were all found in Fort Shalmaneser, and therefore presumably all date from the Late Assyrian period.

At Ashur there are a number of examples of glazed jars of this general type, with bands of 'yellow' triangles appearing once, twice or three times (Andrae 1925: 46). Amongst the published examples, a jar from grave 928 is particularly close to the Nimrud and Qasrij examples, both in terms of size and scheme and colour of decoration (Andrae 1925: pl. 18a). This grave is unfortunately undated (Haller 1954: 84). Another comparable jar, slightly smaller, again with two bands of triangles but now with the addition of a 'strip of squares' between them (Andrae 1925: 42, pl. 186), does come from a dated grave, no. 791, which Haller (1954: 67-8) attributes to the Late Assyrian period. The same sort of decoration and colour scheme also occurs at Ashur on small polychrome glazed jars or bottles with rounded bases of the sort found at Khirbet Khatuniyeh (Curtis and Green 1987: 75, pl. 5); one example (Andrae 1925: pl. 17d) was found in a grave that Andrae (1925: 41) describes as Late Assyrian; this grave was not listed by Haller. Another example is possibly a flask from grave 54 (Haller 1954: 14, pl. 3aw) that is classified as Late Assyrian.

The evidence from Ashur, then, seems to suggest that the polychrome glazed jars of this sort belong in the Late Assyrian period, but we should not exclude the possibility that some of the graves may be post-Assyrian - the graves at Ashur are not particularly well dated and the evidence from them should be treated with caution. There is a large glazed jar from Khorsabad, presumably Late Assyrian in date, but the form of the design is not clear from the published photograph (Loud and Altman 1938: pl. 63, 231).

A number of polychrome glazed vessels have been found at Babylon, but none that are exactly comparable with the Qasrij and Nimrud jars. At least some of these appear to be earlier than the sixth century BC (Strommenger 1964: *passim*). Generally, then, it seems that the heyday of polychrome glazed vessels was in the second half of the eighth and the seventh centuries BC (Peltenburg 1969). But the tradition probably continued into the Late Babylonian period. Glazed vessels do not appear to go on much into the Achaemenid period (Stern 1982: *passim*, where they are quite absent), even though there was still a thriving tradition of polychrome glazing at this period, witness the brick panels from Susa.

A handful of other glazed sherds was found at Khirbet Qasrij, but they merit little comment; at least one of them was probably intrusive.

Lamp (360)

Pipe lamps of this kind with a circular bowl (missing on the Khirbet Qasrij example) were the most common form of pottery lamp in the Late Assyrian period (Joan Oates 1959: 135, 146, pl. XXXIX, 103). The type continues into the Late Babylonian period (Koldewey 1914: 253, fig. 170) and is also attested in Hellenistic times (Oates and Oates 1958: 153, pl. XXVIII, 21).

Pottery knob (361)

Such knobs are often called 'turban handles', and come from the handles of elaborate Islamic jars. They are used by Adams as a period type-indicator for the 'Late Abbasid' period, about tenth to twelfth centuries AD, in the Diyala (Adams 1965: 133-4, fig. 15, no. 15B). I am indebted for this information to Mr St John Simpson, who also suggests that as the spread of Sasanian-Islamic pottery at Babneet village extended almost as far as Tell Mohammed 'Arab, the sherd from Khirbet Qasrij was possibly a stray from that scatter. This pottery knob was the only clearly Islamic sherd noted at Khirbet Qasrij, and was found in the topsoil just 15 cm below the surface.

g. Conclusions

Khirbet Qasrij is a relatively large site, probably nearly 0.5 km across at its greatest extent. Excavations were concentrated on an area in the east part of the site, but outlying trenches (PF and WR) produced material identical to that from the main excavation and show that the site measured at least 375 m from east to west. The sherd scatter, however, was greater than this and covered the area between the two wadis. The settlement may also have been a place of some substance, to judge from the finding of a few terracotta wall-nails of the sort usually associated with important administrative or religious buildings. In all the areas dug, the ancient remains were close to the surface and there was evidence of only one period of settlement. Everywhere the stone pavements and walls were lying on virgin soil. Nor was there any evidence of alteration or rebuilding such as would have been found if the settlement had been of any duration. There was no sign of destruction, though, and it seems that the site was peaceably abandoned after a relatively short time, probably no longer than a single generation or about thirty years.

In the main excavated area, part of an industrial complex was found centred on a kiln for firing pottery. Around this kiln were pavements and work surfaces, presumably for use by the potters. To the east of this industrial complex were the remains of a building or buildings that were more domestic in character. In the excavations a large amount of pottery was found - more than 12,000 sherds were 'processed' - and there were a few interesting small finds, outstanding among them a stone duck-weight (Pl. XII).

As we have said, Khirbet Qasrij is a single-period site and all the pottery found ought to be more or less contemporary. In spite of the fact that the remains were all close to the surface, and in most cases the pottery could not really be said to have come from sealed deposits, a check was possible because many of the types were found in a securely stratified context in the fire-pit of the kiln. It seems sure, then, that the pottery is a homogeneous group and it ought to provide good dating evidence for the site of Khirbet Qasrij.

As has been noted in the discussion of the pottery above, many of the forms, notably a large proportion of the bowls, the tripods, the goblet, some of the fine wares, a number of the jars and in particular the glazed jar, all find close parallels with Late Assyrian pottery of the late seventh century BC, particularly at Nimrud. However, there are two types of vessel, both well represented at Khirbet Qasrij and both assuredly contemporary with the other material, which, as I have argued above, appear to be post-Assyrian. These are the bowls with inverted and thickened rims (nos 79-100) and the jars with folded rims (nos 227-40). This would seem to indicate, then, that the whole corpus should be placed in the post-Assyrian period, and such a conclusion is also suggested by the duck-weight, which finds its closest parallels in the sixth or even fifth century BC. Given, then, that Khirbet Qasrij should be dated after the destruction of Assyria in the late seventh century BC, how much later is it?

As we have said, many of the pottery types from Khirbet Qasrij are similar to those from the destruction levels at Nimrud. This is particularly the case with the tripods, which in appearance are identical to those from Nimrud. The Khirbet Qasrij corpus, then, cannot be very much later than the latest pottery at Nimrud, but what date is this? It has long been recognised that there was some Assyrian occupation at Nimrud after 612 BC, but it is impossible to determine exactly how long it continued. David Oates writes that three levels of post-Assyrian occupation were identified within the walls of Fort Shalmaneser, and he says that they 'all produced pottery identical with that of the latest Assyrian occupation from when they cannot have been far removed in time' (Oates 1968:58-9). If this is so, it would seem unlikely that occupation continued long into the sixth century, if at all. In any event, our corpus must be later than about 600 BC; there is no good reason to suppose, however, as I originally thought, that it is as late as the Achaemenid period, that is, 539 BC. This seems certain because the tripod-bowls in particular cannot be too far removed in time from those at Nimrud. Probably, then, Khirbet Qasrij belongs in the first half of the sixth century BC, but this date might need revision in the light of future discoveries. Samples for carbon 14 analysis were taken from the kiln fire-pit and submitted to the British Museum Research Laboratory, but they were found to contain insufficient carbon for the usual sort of test.

A post-Assyrian date for Khirbet Qasrij is also indicated by a comparison of the pottery with that from the Late Assyrian site of Qasrij Cliff. As we noted above, a conspicuous feature of the Qasrij Cliff pottery was the high proportion of vegetable-tempered wares. At Khirbet Qasrij the situation was completely different, in that grit-tempered wares and wares with mixed grit and vegetable temper predominated (see table of fabric types of catalogued pottery from Khirbet Qasrij). Another characteristic feature of the Khirbet Qasrij pottery that distinguished it from the Qasrij Cliff collection was the relatively high proportion (nearly 20%) of sherds of pale yellow fabric (see Khirbet Qasrij sherd-count). At the time of excavation this seemed so remarkable that we called such pottery 'sherbet ware', because the colour was so similar to that of the sherbet powder sold in packets in Britain and elsewhere. In fact, the colour corresponds to the Munsell codes 5Y 8/3, 5Y 7/3, 5Y 8/4 and 5Y 7/4, all of which are described as pale yellow. Fabric of this colour was hardly noticed at Qasrij Cliff, and given that in addition the sort of ware was so

markedly different, the two collections certainly cannot be contemporary and must be separated from each other by a relatively substantial period of time.

Assuming that Khirbet Qasrij does indeed belong to the post-Assyrian period, into what sort of political and cultural context should it be fitted? Unfortunately, the history of Northern Iraq between the sack of Nineveh by the Medes and the Babylonians in 612 BC and the imposition of Achaemenid rule in Iraq, culminating in the capture of Babylon in 539 BC, is particularly obscure. For the nineteenth-century historians, though, there was no difficulty. Thus Canon George Rawlinson felt able to write of the situation following the collapse of Assyria as follows: 'While Cyaxares took to his own share the land of the conquered people, Assyria Proper, and the countries dependent on Assyria towards the north and north-west, Nabopolassar was allowed, not merely Babylonia, Chaldaea and Susiana, but the valley of the Euphrates and the countries to which that valley conducted' (Rawlinson 1871: II, 397-8). At the time, this view was perfectly valid, given that the classical sources seem to imply that Assyria was under Median control. This is suggested not only by Herodotus (I, 103, 106) but also by Xenophon, who refers to both Nineveh (Mespila) and Nimrud (Larisa) as having once been inhabited by the Medes (*Anabasis* III, IV, 7, 10). With the subsequent availability of Babylonian sources, however, some modern scholars have seen in them grounds for believing that in fact the Babylonians had hegemony over the Assyrian heartland (e.g. David Oates 1968: 59; Wiseman 1961: 19-20). By contrast, scholars writing on the history of Iran have tended to follow the traditional view that Assyria belonged to the Medes (e.g. Olmstead 1948: 32-3; Diakonoff 1985: 125; Dandamaev and Grantovskii 1987: 815).

What, in fact, do the Babylonian sources tell us? From the Chronicle recording the fall of Nineveh we learn that for the final assault on the city the armies of the Medes and the Babylonians, commanded by Cyaxares and Nabopolassar respectively, met each other and 'marched along the bank of the Tigris' before camping outside Nineveh (Grayson 1975: 94, lines 38-41). After a siege of three months the city fell, and the remnants of the Assyrian court fled westwards to Harran where they managed to hang on for another two years. In the month after the sack of Nineveh, Cyaxares and his army returned to Media, while the Babylonian army marched to Nisibin; subsequently, plunder and exiles from that area were brought to the king at Nineveh (Grayson 1975: 94, lines 47-9). It would certainly seem, then, that immediately after the capture of Nineveh, Nabopolassar held sway there, but this does not necessarily mean that he had exclusive rights over the conquered territory. In both the next years, 611 and 610 BC, the Babylonian army 'marched about victoriously in Assyria' (Grayson 1975: 95, lines 53-5, 58-9), but

Wiseman deduces from the context of the passages in question that the term 'Assyria' here refers to the district of Harran that had once formed a part of the Assyrian kingdom (Wiseman 1961: 18). The Medes reappeared on the scene later in 610 BC, when they joined the Babylonians for an assault on Harran, which was abandoned by Ashuruballit II and his Egyptian allies (Grayson 1975: 95, lines 59-61). Thereafter the Medes are not mentioned in the Babylonian chronicles, and we know of their activities largely from classical sources. Much significance has been attached to the fact that, according to another Neo-Babylonian chronicle, in 608 BC Nabopolassar followed the bank of the Tigris and 'went up to the mountain of Bit-Hanunya in the district of Urartu. He set fire to the cities (and) plundered them extensively' (Grayson 1975: 97, lines 1-4).[1] If Nabopolassar really did follow the Tigris all the way, then Bit-Hanunya must have been a western outpost of Urartu, and Wiseman locates it about 80 km north-west of Nisibin (Wiseman 1961: 22, map 2). But for our purposes the relevance of this passage is that it seems to show Nabopolassar had a right of way through the very heart of Assyria. But is this enough to show that it had become a dependency of Babylonia? What are the reasons for supposing the Medes might have had a claim to the area?

It is generally agreed that much of the eastern part of Anatolia was brought under Median control, and it was this that brought them into direct confrontation with Lydia. Five years of warfare, from 590 BC onwards (Herodotus I, 74), culminated in the famous battle marked by a solar eclipse in 585 BC. The frontier between the Medes and the Lydians was then established on the River Halys, and the king of Babylon acted as one of the mediators. We may suppose, then, that in the years 590-585 BC the Medes were campaigning, probably annually, in the area to the east of the River Halys. Of crucial importance, here, is how they got to this area. If they did not go through Northern Iraq, it would have to be supposed that they took a northern route through Urartu. The modern road goes from Tabriz to Khoi, crosses the Iran-Turkey frontier at Bazargan, passes to the south of Mount Ararat and leads eventually to Erzerum and points west. Such a route is perfectly feasible, but it passes through mountainous country and if there were other, more direct ways of reaching the River Halys one might expect the Medes to have taken them, and it would, of course, have been much easier for them to go through Assyria.

Thus, from Nineveh there are two options. One is to follow the east bank of the Tigris and cross the river at Cizre, and the other is to proceed to Nisibin, following the line of the later Persian Royal Road. Both routes lead

to Mardin, and from there one can turn northwards to Diyarbakir. In this way, the Medes would have avoided the upper Euphrates valley and Cilicia, which are assumed to have been under Babylonian control (Wiseman 1961: 39).

There are some other indications that the Medes may have had a free run of Assyria. After Cyrus had deposed Astyages and proclaimed himself king of Persia, Croesus of Lydia saw an opportunity to extend his dominions and violated the Halys boundary. This resulted in an attack on Lydia in 547 BC, and to get there we are told in the Nabonidus Chronicle that Cyrus 'mustered his army and crossed the Tigris below Arbail (Erbil)' before marching on to Lydia (Grayson 1975: 107, lines 15-16). There is no suggestion in the chronicle that in crossing Assyria Cyrus came into conflict with Babylonia, and the implication must be that at this time the Babylonians did not have any proprietorial interests in the area. Secondly, Diakonoff has argued that the Medes settled the Sagartians, a tribe of Iranian nomads, in the district of Erbil (Diakonoff 1985: 125, n. 2). He infers this from a passage in Darius' inscription at Bisitun in which it is stated that the rebel Cissantakhma, a Sagartian, was put to death at Erbil (Kent 1950: 124, S33). According to Diakonoff, it was the custom to execute a rebel in the centre of his province. On the other hand, however, contemporary texts indicate that Arrapkha (Kirkuk) belonged to the Neo-Babylonian kingdom at least from the reign of Nebuchadnezzar onwards (Unger 1932).

What does all this add up to? It has to be admitted that the situation is confused, and the picture by no means clear. Initially, at least until 608 BC when they sacked Bit-Hanunya, the Babylonians seem to have been able to travel through Assyria and perhaps even exercised some authority there. But this is possibly due to the fact, as some commentators believe, that the Medes had suffered a reverse at the hands of the Scythians (cf. Wiseman 1961: 17), and this would explain their temporary disappearance from the scene. At least from 590 BC onwards, however, they may have considered Northern Iraq as their own preserve. It would be strange indeed if this were not the case, for is it likely that the Medes, who had probably played the major part in the downfall of Assyria, would have relinquished Syria, Cilicia *and* Assyria to the Babylonians and contented themselves with Armenia (never a part of Assyria) and Cappadocia? It may also be significant that in the Assyrian homeland not a single Late Babylonian tablet has been found, which would be a strange omission if the Babylonians had attempted to impose any sort of administration on the area.

But how can this postulated Median domination of Assyria be reconciled with the fact that the Babylonians held Kirkuk? It would have to be supposed that the approximate boundary between the two powers ran along the Lesser Zab, with Erbil belonging to the Medes

---

1. This does not imply that from 608 BC Urartu became a province of Babylonia, as suggested by Barnett (1982: 364, chronological table 1).

and Kirkuk to the Babylonians. Just such a division was proposed by Goosens in a perceptive paper more than thirty-five years ago. He wrote: 'Il semblerait donc que la frontière entre l'empire babylonien et l'empire mède, pour autant qu'il en ait une, suit le Tigre et le Petit Zab, excluant le coeur de l'Assyrie de l'empire babylonien' (Goosens 1954: 90). Further support for this theory may perhaps be found in the statement that, en route for Lydia, Cyrus crossed the Tigris below Erbil. This could imply that he had entered Mesopotamia by the mountain passes that link Sanandaj with Sulaimaniya, via Marivan, thus avoiding the Great Khorassan Road further to the south. It could well be that this route was regularly used by the Medes, for it is the most direct road between Hamadan and Erbil and Mosul.

Even if the Medes were masters in Assyria, though, and then perhaps only for part of the period under discussion, it would be a mistake to assume that it was a province in any meaningful sense of the word. There is no evidence whatsoever that they attempted to impose any sort of administration on Assyria, nor indeed that it was incorporated as part of 'Media'. Most likely they saw it as a convenient thoroughfare to Turkey, and as a means of curbing Babylonian aspirations in the north and north-east. It could also have been a useful source of revenue, but it is doubtful whether this was collected in any sort of organised way. Perhaps - but this is pure speculation - they rode through at irregular intervals, terrorising the inhabitants and burning the odd township or village if the requisite amount of tribute was not forthcoming. In any event, the indications are that Assyria was an impoverished country at this time. Settlement at the major centres such as Nineveh and Nimrud was greatly reduced, if it did not stop altogether, and, to judge from the Cyrus Cylinder, Ashur seems to have been in ruins (Pritchard 1950: 316). Again, we may concur with Goosens when he says (1954: 90): 'En réalité personne ne se soit soucié de revendiquer un pays aussi ravagé que l'Assyrie; le pays a dû être abandonné à lui-même.' With the absence of a strong central authority there is likely to have been a complete breakdown in law and order, and to avoid disturbance from marauding bands settlement would probably have been away from the major urban centres. Economic and trade links, such as there were, are likely to have been with Babylonia rather than with Media, if only for reasons of geographical proximity.

It is into this sort of context, then, that Khirbet Qasrij should be fitted, that is if we are right about the date of the pottery, namely that it belongs somewhere in the first half of the sixth century BC. As we have seen, the pottery is close to Late Assyrian types, in some cases (e.g. the tripods) even identical, and it may not be stretching the imagination too far to suggest that Khirbet Qasrij represents a settlement of Assyrians who had been forced to leave their erstwhile homes and were attempting to establish themselves anew in this area far from the major Assyrian cities. It could even be that the potters had come from one of those cities. The brief duration of the settlement could well reflect the general insecurity at this time, with the site being abandoned, for unknown reasons, only a relatively short time after it had been founded. In any event, it is interesting to note that the site is, to all intents and purposes, Assyrian. It seems likely, then, that after the collapse of Assyria in the late seventh century BC, Assyrian culture continued, albeit perhaps in a debased form, probably until the area was incorporated in the Achaemenid empire. It is noteworthy that neither at Khirbet Qasrij, nor so far as I am aware at any other site in Northern Iraq, is there any trace of the Medes, showing that they made little impression on this area.

Concordance of BM Sample Numbers and Pottery Catalogue Numbers

Sample number	Pottery catalogue	Sample number	Pottery catalogue
BM 1984-5-12, 1	QC7	BM 1984-5-12, 35	KQ230d
BM 1984-5-12, 2	QC3	BM 1984-5-12, 36	KQ232
BM 1984-5-12, 3	QC17	BM 1984-5-12, 37	KQ92
BM 1984-5-12, 4	QC30	BM 1984-5-12, 38	KQ142
BM 1984-5-12, 5	QC52	BM 1984-5-12, 39	KQ320
BM 1984-5-12, 6	QC40	BM 1984-5-12, 40	KQ132a
BM 1984-5-12, 7	QC63	BM 1984-5-12, 41	KQ107a
BM 1984-5-12, 8	QC42	BM 1984-5-12, 42	KQ117d
BM 1984-5-12, 9	QC24	BM 1984-5-12, 43	KQ120
BM 1984-5-12, 10	QC72	BM 1984-5-12, 44	KQ205
BM 1984-5-12, 11	QC98	BM 1984-5-12, 45	KQ239a
BM 1984-5-12, 12	QC51	BM 1984-5-12, 46	KQ311
BM 1984-5-12, 13	QC36	BM 1984-5-12, 47	KQ200b
BM 1984-5-12, 14	QC29	BM 1984-5-12, 48	KQ233e
BM 1984-5-12, 15	QC67	BM 1984-5-12, 49	KQ143
BM 1984-5-12, 16	QC30d	BM 1984-5-12, 50	KQ121
BM 1984-5-12, 17	QC15	BM 1984-5-12, 51	KQ97a
BM 1984-5-12, 18	QC35a	BM 1984-5-12, 52	KQ117c
BM 1984-5-12, 19	QC20	BM 1984-5-12, 53	KQ185
BM 1984-5-12, 20	QC81	BM 1984-5-12, 54	KQ154
BM 1984-5-12, 21	QC53	BM 1984-5-12, 55	KQ213
BM 1984-5-12, 22	QC64	BM 1984-5-12, 56	KQ151
BM 1984-5-12, 23	QC87	BM 1984-5-12, 57	KQ14
BM 1984-5-12, 24	QC27	BM 1984-5-12, 58	KQ7
BM 1984-5-12, 25	KQ27	BM 1984-5-12, 59	KQ339
BM 1984-5-12, 26	KQ115	BM 1984-5-12, 60	KQ352b
BM 1984-5-12, 27	KQ117	BM 1984-5-12, 61	KQ352
BM 1984-5-12, 28	KQ41	BM 1984-5-12, 62	KQ351b
BM 1984-5-12, 29	KQ109a	BM 1984-5-12, 63	KQ275a
BM 1984-5-12, 30	KQ195	BM 1984-5-12, 64	KQ275
BM 1984-5-12, 31	KQ132b	BM 1984-5-12, 65	KQ340
BM 1984-5-12, 32	KQ114	BM 1984-5-12, 66	KQ351a
BM 1984-5-12, 33	KQ232f	BM 1984-5-12, 67	KQ273
BM 1984-5-12, 34	KQ84		

BIBLIOGRAPHY

Adams, R.McC., 1965. *Land behind Baghdad*, Chicago.

Al-Tekriti, A.Q., 1960. 'The excavation at Tell ed-Daim (Dokan)', *Sumer* 16: 93-109 (in Arabic).

Alizadeh, A., 1985. 'A protoliterate kiln from Chogha Mish', *Iran* 23:39-50.

Andrae, W., 1913. *Die Festungswerke von Assur*, text and plates, Leipzig.

————, 1925. *Coloured ceramics from Assur*, London.

Barnett, R.D., 1982. 'Urartu', *Cambridge Ancient History* III, 1: 314-71.

Beck, H.C., 1931. 'Beads from Nineveh', *Antiquity* 5: 427-37.

Boehmer, R.M., and Dämmer, H.-W., 1985. *Tell Imlihiye, Tell Zubeidi, Tell Abbas*, Baghdader Forschungen 7, Mainz am Rhein.

Boehmer, R.M., 1987. *Uruk, Kampagne 38: Ausgrabungen in Uruk-Warka, Endberichte I*, Mainz am Rhein.

Carter, T.H., 1964. 'Early Assyrians in the Sanjar', *Expedition* 7: 34-44.

Childe, V.G., 1955. 'Rotary motion', in Singer, C., Holmyard, E.J., and Hall, A.R. (eds), *A History of Technology* 1: 376-412.

Crane, E., 1983. *The Archaeology of Beekeeping*, London.

Curtis, J.E., 1979. *An Examination of Late Assyrian Metalwork*, 2 vols, unpublished Ph.D. thesis, University of London.

————, 1983. 'Late Assyrian bronze coffins', *Anatolian Studies* 33: 85-95.

————, 1985. 'Industrial interlude in the dark ages in Iraq', *British Museum Society Bulletin* 48: 12-15.

Curtis, J.E., and Green, A.R., 1987. 'Preliminary report on excavations at Khirbet Khatuniyeh, 1985', *Researches on the Antiquities of the Saddam Dam Salvage Project and other Researches*, Baghdad: 73-7.

Damdamayev, M., and Grantovskii, E., 1987. 'The Kingdom of Assyria and its relations with Iran', *Encyclopaedia Iranica* 2: 806-5.

Delcroix, G. and Huot, J.-L., 1972. 'Les fours dit "de potier" dans l'orient ancien', *Syria* 49: 35-95.

De Meyer, L., (ed.), 1980. *Tell ed-Der* 3, Louvain.

Diakonoff, I.M., 1985. 'Media', *Cambridge History of Iran* 2: 36-148.

Dyson, R.H., 1965. 'Problems of protohistoric Iran as seen from Hasanlu', *Journal of Near Eastern Studies* 24: 193-217.

Fiey, J.M., 1958. 'Identification of Qasr Serej', *Sumer* 14: 125-7.

Gibson, M., 1972. *The City and Area of Kish*, Coconut Grove.

Gibson, M. *et al.*, 1978. *Excavations at Nippur: Twelfth Season*, Oriental Institute Communication no. 23, Chicago.

Goff, C., 1985. 'Excavations at Baba Jan: the architecture and pottery of Level 1', *Iran* 23: 1-20.

Goosens, G., 1954. 'L'Assyrie après l'Empire', *Compte Rendu de la Troisième Rencontre Assyriologique Internationale*, Leiden: 84-100.

Grayson, A.K., 1975. *Assyrian and Babylonian Chronicles*, Texts from Cuneiform Sources 5, Locust Valley, New York.

Haller, A., 1954. *Die Gräber und Grüfte von Assur*, Berlin.

Hamilton, R.W., 1966. 'A silver bowl in the Ashmolean Museum', *Iraq* 28:1-17.

Herzfeld, E., 1938. *Altpersische Inschriften*, Berlin.

Hodges, H., 1964. *Artifacts*, London.

————, 1970. *Technology in the Ancient World*, Harmondsworth.

Hrouda, B., *et al.*, 1981. *Isin-Isan Bahriyat* 2, Munich.

Kent, R.J., 1950. *Old Persian Grammar, Texts, Lexicon*, New Haven.

Killick, R., and Black, J., 1985. 'Excavations in Iraq, 1983-84', *Iraq* 47: 215-39.

Koldewey, R., 1914. *The Excavations at Babylon*, London.

Lamberg-Karlovsky, C.C., 1976. 'The third millennium of Tappeh Yahya: a preliminary statement', *Proceedings of the IVth Annual Symposium on Archaeological Research in Iran*, Teheran: 71-84.

Lapp, P.W., 1961. *Palestinian Ceramic Chronology 200 B.C.-A.D. 70*, New Haven.

Layard, A.H., 1849a. *Nineveh and its Remains*, 2 vols, London.

————, 1849b. *The Monuments of Nineveh*, London.

————, 1853. *Discoveries in the Ruins of Nineveh and Babylon*, London.

Lloyd, S., and Safar, F., 1945. 'Tell Hassuna: excavations by the Iraq Government Directorate General of Antiquities in 1943 and 1944', *Journal of Near Eastern Studies* 4: 255-89.

Lloyd, S., and Gökçe, N., 1953. 'Sultantepe', *Anatolian Studies* 3:27-51.

Lloyd, S., 1954. 'Sultantepe, part II', *Anatolian Studies* 4: 101-10.

Loud, G., and Altman, C.B., 1938. *Khorsabad* 2, Chicago.

Luschey, H., 1939. *Die Phiale*, Bleicherode am Harz.

Majidzadeh, Y., 1977. 'The development of the pottery kiln in Iran from prehistoric to historical periods', *Paléorient* 3: 207-20.

Mallowan, M.E.L., 1950. 'Excavations at Nimrud, 1949-1950', *Iraq* 12: 147-83.

————, 1966. *Nimrud and its Remains*, 2 vols, London.

McCown, D.E., and Haines, R.C., 1967. *Nippur* 1, Chicago.

McNicoll, A., *et al.*, 1982. *Pella in Jordan*. Canberra.

Mellaart, J., 1967. *Çatal Hüyük: a neolithic town in Anatolia*, London.

Moorey, P.R.S., 1980. *Cemeteries of the first millennium B.C. at Deve Hüyük*, Oxford.

Neufeld, E., 1978, 'Apiculture in Ancient Palestine (Early and Middle Iron Age) within the framework of the Ancient Near East', *Ugarit-Forschungen* 10: 219-47.

Oates, D., 1957. 'Ezida: the temple of Nabu', *Iraq* 19: 26-39.

————, 1968. *Studies in the history of Northern Iraq*, London.

Oates, D. and J., 1958. 'Nimrud 1957: the Hellenistic settlement', *Iraq* 20: 114-57.

Oates (Lines), J., 1954. 'Late Assyrian pottery from Nimrud', *Iraq* 16: 164-7.

Oates, J., 1959. 'Late Assyrian pottery from Fort Shalmaneser', *Iraq* 21: 130-46.

Olmstead, A.T., 1948. *History of the Persian Empire*, Chicago.

Oppenheim, A.L., 1956. *The Interpretation of Dreams in the Ancient Near East*, Transactions of the American Philosophical Society 46, part 3, Philadelphia.

Peltenburg, E.J., 1969. 'Al Mina glazed pottery and its relations', *Levant* 1: 73-96.

Pillet, M., 1962. *Un pionnier de l'Assyriologie: Victor Place*, Paris.

Poppa, R., 1978. *Kamid el-Loz 2: Der eisenzeitliche Friedhof*, Bonn.

Pritchard, J.B. (ed), 1950. *Ancient Near Eastern Texts*, Princeton.

————, 1954. *The Ancient Near East in Pictures*, Princeton.

————, 1985. *Tell es Sa'idiyeh: Excavations on the Tell, 1964-1966*, Philadelphia.

Rawlinson, G., 1871. *The Five Great Monarchies of the Ancient Eastern World*, 3 vols, 2nd edition, London.

Rawson, P.S., 1954. 'Palace wares from Nimrud: technical observations on selected examples', *Iraq* 16: 168-72.

Roaf, M.D., 1983. 'A report on the work of the British Archaeological Expedition in the Eski Mosul Dam Salvage Project from November 1982 to June 1983', *Sumer* 39: 68-82.

————, 1984. 'Excavations at Tell Mohammad 'Arab in the Eski Mosul Dam Salvage Project', *Iraq* 46: 141-56.

Salonen, A., 1964. 'Die Öfen der alten Mesopotamier', *Baghdader Mitteilungen* 3: 100-124.

Schmidt, E.F., 1957. *Persepolis* 2, Chicago.

Starr, R.F.S., 1937-3. *Nuzi*, 2 vols, Cambridge, Mass.

Stern, E., 1982. *Material Culture of the Land of the Bible in the Persian Period 538-332 B.C.*, Warminster.

Strommenger, E., 1964. 'Grabformen in Babylon', *Baghdader Mitteilungen* 3: 157-73.

Stronach, D., 1978. *Pasargadae*, Oxford.

Stronach, R., 1978. 'Median pottery from the fallen floor in the fort [at Nush-i Jan]', *Iran* 16: 11-24.

Thompson, R.C., and Mallowan, M.E.L., 1933. 'The British Museum Excavations at Nineveh, 1931-32', *Liverpool Annals of Archaeology and Anthropology* 20: 71-186.

Unger, E., 1928. 'Arrapha', *Reallexikon der Assyriologie I*: 154.

Watkins, T., and Campbell, S., 1986. *Excavations at Kharabeh Shattani* 1, University of Edinburgh, Department of Archaeology, Occasional Paper no. 14.

Watson, P.J., 1979. *Archaeological Ethnography in Western Iran*, Tucson.

Weissbach, F.H., 1907. 'Über die babylonischen, assyrischen und altpersischen Gewichte', *Zeitschrift der Deutschen Morgenländischen Gesellschaft* 61: 379-402.

Wiseman, D.J., 1961. *Chronicles of Chaldaean Kings (626-556 B.C.) in the British Museum*, London.

Woolley, C.L., 1962. *Ur Excavations 9: The Neo-Babylonian and Persian Periods*, London.

Yusif, Kerim Toma, 1987. 'Excavations at Tulul al-Baqaq 2', *Researches on the Antiquities of the Saddam Dam Salvage Project and other Researches*, Baghdad: 40-49 (in Arabic).

APPENDIX I

Notes on Conservation

R.K. Uprichard

The following notes are a description of the methods used in the conservation of materials excavated at Khirbet Qasrij.

Pottery

Most of the sherds and vessels had, to a greater or lesser degree, an encrustation of salts[1] and dirt which proved to be insoluble in the river water which was being used for pot washing. Prolonged soaking, for five days, had no noticeable effect on the encrustation.

A 2.5% solution of nitric acid[2] was found to be effective in loosening[3] the encrustation. Limited supplies of concentrated nitric acid restricted the use of this treatment to complete vessels and diagnostic sherds.

The sherds and vessels were soaked in water prior to treatment with a 2.5% solution of nitric acid which was dropped on to a small area of the surface using a rubber-teated glass pipette. When the resulting effervescence had abated, the objects were immersed in water to reduce the possibility of etching the surface of the ceramic (Dowman 1970: 117-19). The action of the acid loosened the encrustation sufficiently to allow its removal by scalpel and brushing. The possible presence of fragile surface decoration required careful observation of the cleaned areas to ensure that damage was not occurring. In the event, no damage was observed on any of the sherds and vessels being treated and so the treatment was continued until the whole of the surface was cleaned in all cases.

The objects were then soaked in daily changes of water for four days to remove any traces of acid and, as far as possible, to remove any soluble salts present. They were then dried in air.

Where reconstruction was possible, HMG cellulose nitrate adhesive was used.

Stone

The stone duck-weight, KQ1, had an encrustation similar to that found on the pottery. It was cleaned by the same method as that used on the pottery, a small area of the base having first been tested to check for any damage which might have resulted from such treatment.

Iron

The ironwork displayed no visible signs of instability and was not treated in any way.

Reference

Dowman, E.A., 1970. *Conservation in Field Archaeology*, London.

1. Analysis by Dr V. Daniels (British Museum, Department of Conservation) using X-ray diffraction showed these salts to be mainly calcium sulphate with a lesser quantity of a carbonate, probably calcium carbonate.

2. Nitric acid is a hazardous liquid and care must be taken when handling it. Acid-resistant gloves and eye protection must be worn and the treatment should be carried out in a well-ventilated area.

3. It is possible that the loosening effect was due to the reaction of the carbonate portion of the encrustation with the nitric acid.

APPENDIX II

Examination of a Fragment
of Egyptian Blue from Khirbet Qasrij

M.S. Tite

A small fragment of Egyptian blue from Khirbet Qasrij was examined in order to obtain information on the method used in its production.

The SEM examination of a polished section through the fragment showed that it consisted of small crystals of the Egyptian blue mineral (i.e. calcium-copper tetrasilicate $CaCuSi_4O_{10}$) which were uniformly interspersed between un-reacted quartz grains (Plate 13). No obvious glass phase was visible, which is consistent with the fact that no alkalis (i.e. sodium and potassium oxides) were detected with the X-ray spectrometer attached to the SEM.

The microstructure, as well as the hardness ($\sim$1 Moh) and colour (light blue), of the Khirbet Qasrij fragment is very similar to those observed for the majority of the Egyptian blue samples from Nimrud and Nineveh dating to the ninth to seventh century BC. It therefore seems probable that, as proposed for the Nimrud and Nineveh Egyptian blue (Tite *et al*. 1984), the Khirbet Qasrij fragment was made using a two-stage firing cycle in which the coarse-textured Egyptian blue produced in the first firing was finely ground, moulded into the required shape and then refired.

Reference

Tite, M.S., Bimson, M., and Cowell, M.R., 1984. 'Technological examination of Egyptian blue', in Lambert, J.B. (ed.), *Archaeological Chemistry* III, Washington, American Chemical Society: 215-42.

APPENDIX III

Examination of Ceramics from Qasrij Cliff and Khirbet Qasrij

I.C. Freestone and M.J. Hughes

Introduction

Some 24 sherds of pottery from the Late Assyrian site of Qasrij Cliff, and 43 sherds from Khirbet Qasrij, a post-Assyrian site a few hundred metres away, were submitted to the British Museum Research Laboratory. At Khirbet Qasrij, a kiln has been excavated and, in addition to the pottery, a fragment of vitrified lining from the fire-pit as well as possible clay and stone raw materials were provided. The samples were examined macroscopically, with a x10 hand lens, in thin section in the petrological microscope and a selection has been analysed by instrumental neutron activation analysis (NAA). The aim of this study has been to establish as far as possible the nature of the production of the pottery assemblages. We begin by establishing the sources of the raw materials of the pottery using NAA, then petrology and the occurrence of any non-local types. We then move on to discuss the processing of these raw materials to form the pottery, and the degree of control exercised by the potters upon their final products.

Neutron activation analysis of a selection of the pottery

Background

When pottery is analysed for the concentrations of the elements which it contains, the pattern of results can be used as a 'fingerprint' of the clay source used to make the pottery. This approach is known as ceramic provenance studies. Thus pottery made in different places, or by different clay preparation techniques at the same place, can be identified by its elemental composition. The most widely used technique for elemental analysis is neutron activation analysis, which is now used in many laboratories throughout the world (Perlman and Asaro 1969; Harbottle 1976): its particular advantages are the sensitivity of the technique for measuring trace elements in clay; the fact that it provides measurements for more than twenty different elements in a single sample; the accuracy of the results; and its widespread use, which means that exchange of data between laboratories can supplement the efforts of a single laboratory, so that it is not necessary to repeat the analyses of material which may already have been analysed in another laboratory.

The British Museum Research Laboratory has been using neutron activation analysis since 1978 and details of the technique and some of the completed projects have been published: for example Main and Hughes 1983, on technique; Hughes, Leese and Smith 1988, on pottery lamps from Greece and Turkey; Hughes and Vince 1986, on Spanish medieval lustre ceramics.

The aim of the present investigation was to see if neutron activation could suggest which of the ceramics recovered during the excavation were made locally at Khirbet Qasrij, which were made by different clay-processing techniques, and which were imported from elsewhere, either from another local site or more distantly. It was also intended to integrate as far as possible the results of the neutron activation analyses with the petrological analyses: our previous experience at the British Museum Research Laboratory (e.g. on English medieval floor tiles, see Hughes *et al.* 1982) in integrating the results of these two techniques has been very encouraging. Because the techniques are looking at different aspects of the pottery, the results complement each other and provide a more accurate picture of the pottery-making process than either method used alone. Thus petrology gives most information about the inclusions present, whether naturally or deliberately added to the clay, and the firing conditions, while neutron activation analysis provides most information on the clay body itself (i.e. the fine clay minerals).

Neutron activation analysis: sampling and analysis

A representative group of pottery from the excavation at Khirbet Qasrij and a smaller group from Qasrij Cliff were selected for analysis. The samples were prepared as powders: a broken edge on each sherd was drilled using an artificial sapphire drill or a 2mm diameter tungsten carbide twist drill, mounted in the handpiece of a flexible-shaft drill with variable speed. The first few millimetres of drilled-out powder were discarded to avoid surface contamination or leached areas on the sherd, and then the sample powder was collected on greaseproof paper, drilling sufficiently into the sherd to obtain a sample of about 200 milligrams. The powder was stored in glass specimen tubes and dried at 100°C for several hours to remove any remaining moisture. Portions of about 40-70 milligrams were weighed into short lengths of pure silica tubing (very high purity grade) and sealed in. These tubes were packed in batches of about 50-55 samples together with six samples of a standard pottery (British Museum Standard

Pottery) for calibration. This standard has been measured against a range of similar standards and is principally calibrated against Perlman and Asaro's Standard Pottery (1969): measurements made to date show that it is equivalent to the latter except for europium, and an inter-standard correction factor has been established for this one element.

The samples and standards were packaged in a 3″ x 1″ aluminium can and sent for irradiation at the commercial irradiation facilities at Harwell (Amersham International plc), where they were irradiated with thermal neutrons for 20 hours and then returned for counting to the Laboratory four days after the irradiation. The counting equipment consisted of a Canberra Instruments hyperpure germanium detector, multichannel analyser and automatic 20-position sample changer for unattended operation. The equipment runs under the control of the Laboratory's Hewlett Packard 21MX series computer, on which the spectra from the multichannel analyser are stored, processed using the program HYPERMET to calculate the concentrations of the elements in the samples, and the subsequent statistical study carried out. The samples were counted twice to detect the radioactive isotopes which have been produced in the clay samples. They were counted immediately on arrival at the Laboratory for 2000 seconds to obtain results on the short-lived isotopes (with half-lives of 0.5 to 6 days) and again about 16 days after irradiation for 6000 seconds for long-lived isotopes (greater than 10 days). The short-lived isotopes are sodium (Na), potassium (K), lanthanum (La), calcium (Ca), arsenic (As), antimony (Sb), lutetium (Lu), uranium (U) and ytterbium (Yb) and the long-lived isotopes are cerium (Ce), terbium (Tb), thorium (Th), chromium (Cr), hafnium (Hf), barium (Ba), caesium (Cs), rubidium (Rb), scandium (Sc), tantalum (Ta), iron (Fe), cobalt (Co) and europium (Eu) (= 23 elements in total). These are virtually all the detectable elements present in the spectra, given the irradiation conditions, and the time lapse between irradiation and measurement resulting from the distance between the reactor and the counting equipment. The method adopted in this Laboratory therefore gives the concentrations of 23 elements in each sample of pottery. Further technical details and applications have been published elsewhere (Main and Hughes 1983; Hughes and Vince 1986).

The analytical results are listed in Table 1. They include 38 samples of pottery (31 from Khirbet Qasrij, 7 from Qasrij Cliff) and 4 samples of locally collected clays. All the samples are made of calcareous (calcium-rich) clays, and at first inspection the compositions all look fairly similar to one another. Two element plots were made as a preliminary step in investigating the results. These showed, for example, that calcium was inversely correlated with many of the elements (the samples with higher calcium have lower amounts of other elements): this is a straightforward dilution effect where the presence of calcite in the clay simply dilutes the clay percentage and therefore lowers the concentrations of all the clay-associated elements. The four local clays contain notably more calcite than the average for the pottery, indicating some clay-refining before use.

Multivariate statistical analysis

To study the elemental analyses in detail it is necessary to use computer-based statistical techniques to look for structure in the results. The main technique used was the Cluster Analysis program CLUSTAN (Wishart 1978 and 1982). The program looks at all the elemental concentrations in each sample and uses them to cluster together samples (items) of similar composition; each cluster then represents a group of pottery made from the same original clay source using the same clay-preparation technique. Very often these clusters represent a single batch of pottery made at the same time. Batches made at different times often show slight chemical differences because either the clay was not dug from exactly the same place or not prepared in the same way (e.g. use of settling tanks): such pottery may therefore fall into a different composition cluster because of subtle chemical differences to the first. Items with different compositions are assigned to different clusters, and outliers can be identified (items which do not match any other pieces in chemical composition, often indicating imported items).

The initial cluster analysis was carried out using 16 elements, *viz.* sodium, caesium, potassium, rubidium, scandium, lanthanum, cerium, europium, lutetium, terbium, ytterbium, hafnium, thorium, chromium, iron and calcium. These were the elements remaining after elements with occasional missing values in Table 1 (or those which are generally considered unreliable for provenance studies because they are too volatile, e.g. arsenic and antimony) were omitted. Ward's method was used (error sum of squares option), followed by the Relocate procedure (to reassign samples which became 'stuck' in the wrong cluster at an earlier stage). The details of how the program works are given in Wishart's manual describing the CLUSTAN program; we followed the procedures recommended in the manual and by Everitt (1980).

An initial run of CLUSTAN was carried out with 42 samples (all those in Table 1) using the results for sixteen elements (as listed above, and in Fig. 48 plus calcium and sodium). The 5-k linkage lists were printed out (the lists of the 5 nearest samples in composition terms, for each sample in turn): samples KQ92, KQ114, KQ340 and QC81 were outliers, i.e., they were distant from any other samples and from each other, indicating that they have unusual compositions. Everitt (1980) and others have stressed that outliers can distort the other clusters obtained, so the program was re-run with these four omitted. Also a principal components analysis (see below) had shown that the elements sodium and calcium had very much higher scatter in their concentrations than any others, so to prevent them unduly biasing the cluster analysis, these two elements were omitted and CLUSTAN re-run with fourteen elements. Different starting options were tried (cf. Everitt), and in each case there was seen to be a significant increase in the dissimilarity coefficient when reducing from 9 to 8 clusters, while the same cluster identities were obtained at 9 clusters from different starting options. This pointed to the 9 cluster 'solution' as being the optimum number of clusters (to best represent the relationships between the 42 samples). The memberships of these clusters are listed in Table 2 and the average concentrations of the elements in each cluster are given in Table 3. These clusters have quite narrow concentration ranges for many elements, often having a spread of no more than 2-4% about the average. Numerous provenance studies using analysis have concluded that spreads of 5-10% are the norm, so the Qasrij clusters do represent quite fine distinctions. It might be quite acceptable to combine a number of the clusters which the CLUSTAN program indicated were quite close to one another in composition: pairs of clusters nearest to each other (in descending order of similarity) are 2 nearest to 3, 1 nearest 2 and 6 nearest 3 (also indicated in Table 2). The dendrogram from the Ward's method is shown in Fig. 47: this does not quite correspond to the clusters of Table 2 because the Relocate option has moved a very few samples around. (The figure was prepared when only 27 samples had been analysed; in the next section we have described the tests on all 42 samples, however.) Table 3 and Fig. 47 give an indication of which clusters are nearest each other in terms of concentration. Another way of seeing the relationship between the clusters is in the isometric principal components plot (Fig. 48), where the clusters have been identified: this attempts to give a three-dimensional picture of how the clusters (and the samples) relate to one another in composition terms. One of the difficulties of cluster analysis is finding a means of adequately presenting the computer output so that the significance of the clusters can be readily appreciated, and for this principal components analysis was employed as described below.

Principal components analysis

This is a statistical technique which is often used in archaeometric studies (Hope 1978) since it is multivariate like cluster analysis, i.e. it takes into account the concentrations of all the elements submitted to it and summarises the data in a digestible form. Principal components analysis looks for those elements which have the greatest concentration spread across all the samples, and reduces most of the information contained in these to a relatively small number (usually up to three is sufficient) of measurements (or principal components). Whereas the results on the original (say) sixteen elements represent sixteen dimensions, condensing the data to (say) three components allows one to make an isometric three-dimensional drawing to illustrate the results, as in Fig. 48, which shows them in terms of the clusters of Table 2. (Fig. 48 was prepared, like Fig. 47, when only 27 results were available.)

For the Qasrij neutron activation analysis results, several principal components analyses were run: initially the measurements for sixteen elements (listed in Fig. 48) were used for 27 samples, and the concentrations were first transformed to logs (as is conventionally done). This showed that calcium dominated the first principal component (indicative of the major significance of its concentration in these samples); as this was undesirable, the same 27 were run again with calcium omitted (fifteen elements). This again showed a dominating element, sodium, so the program was re-run with fourteen elements (calcium and sodium omitted), and the program output now showed a reasonable balance such that a number of elements contributed to the principal components. (If one had not removed these two elements then the resulting principal components plot would have been virtually equivalent to a plot of calcium against sodium: this is undesirable since the point of multivariate statistics is to summarise the results from many elements in each sample.) The first three principal components (which contained 34.5, 25.5 and 15.9% of the variance respectively = 75.9% total for PC1-3) have been

plotted in the isometric drawing in Fig. 48: the cluster memberships of the cluster analysis (Table 2) have been indicated, and this gives a reasonable graphical expression of the relationship between the clusters. The program was rerun with all 42 samples, and this produced a plot very like Fig. 48 but with the extra samples fitted into the established pattern.

Principal components analysis is here being used mainly as a means of visualising which clusters are near to each other and vice versa. Thus clusters 1, 2, 3, 4, and 6 occupy an arc from the back left swinging round the right to the lower centre (cluster 3). Sample 27 (KQ275a) is off to the left, while cluster 7 is a rather 'high' cluster (above the plane of the top of the 'box') near cluster 5, which is in the front right foreground. The outliers nos 6 and 10 can be clearly seen to be remote from the other samples and from each other. Cluster 9 (not shown on Fig. 48) fits between the 'local' clusters 1-6. To anticipate the discussion below, the interpretation of Fig. 48 is that cluster 7 is composed predominantly of sherds which are unlikely to be products of the Khirbet Qasrij kiln, whereas all the other clusters grouped at the back of Fig. 48 are products of the kiln.

Comparison with other published neutron activation analysis studies

There have been relatively few neutron activation analysis studies on pottery from this region and none apparently before the present study has concentrated on pottery of the Assyrian period. Fig. 49b shows the location of the sites to be discussed. Davidson and McKerrell (1976) analysed prehistoric Halaf pottery from a number of sites in the Khabur Headwaters region of north-east Syria which showed local manufacture of this pottery in the Khabur region and an extensive trade in Halaf painted ware between different sites. A further study by Davidson (1981) of sherds from one of the sites, Tell Aqab, confirmed local production of many wares and trade in others. Of relevance to the present study, Davidson found that a series of clay samples taken at intervals along 2 km of the course of a wadi all had the same general clay composition, which differed somewhat from clay samples around the site but away from the wadi. One can conclude that local environmental (depositional) factors may produce a similar clay chemical composition over some distance (e.g. along a wadi or river's course) but differences may arise as one moves away from the wadi/river area.

In a continuation of their analytical program, Davidson and McKerrell (1980) analysed Halaf and Ubaid period pottery from Tell Arpachiyeh and Tepe Gawra. This demonstrated the export of Halaf painted pottery from Arpachiyeh to Gawra, and trade between the sites of Ubaid pottery. Additionally, the analyses showed the change in clay composition accompanying the changes in pottery production at Arpachiyeh, which seems to be linked to phases in occupation of the Tell and is definitely linked to the different styles of painted pottery. Related to these authors' studies has been an attempt to locate the site of the 'lost' city of Wassukanni in Mesopotamia, by the analysis of cuneiform clay tablets written in the city and found at Tell El-Amarna (Dobel, Asaro and Michel 1977). Their results however suggested that Fakhariyeh was not Wassukanni, and comparison with Davidson and McKerrell's data for the Khabur triangle appeared to rule out that area also.

Table 1   List of samples and full list of neutron activation analysis results

All results in parts per million, except Na, K, Fe and Ca in percent

Rec.	Pottery Catalogue No.	BMRL	Na	K	Rb	Cs	Ba	Sc	La	Ce	Eu
1	QC7	22895X	.699	1.11	112.	4.57	529	20.3	21.3	51.7	1.15
2	KQ27	22896V	.286	1.85	96.4	4.68	800	20.9	22.5	54.0	1.20
3	KQ115	22898R	.561	1.88	92.1	3.69	1006	17.5	24.3	54.9	1.24
4	KQ41	22900V	.557	1.72	76.9	4.08	631	12.6	24.7	54.5	1.19
5	KQ195	22871R	.472	1.71	69.8	3.61	737	16.2	21.6	46.9	1.07
6	KQ114	22902S	.220	1.33	71.2	4.12	324	15.3	17.6	45.3	.996
7	KQ232f	22903Q	.512	1.34	79.2	5.09	414	15.1	22.5	50.1	1.15
8	KQ84	22904Z	.410	2.51	81.3	4.06	811	15.3	24.7	53.0	1.16
9	KQ232	22906V	.878	1.27	93.6	5.62	464	16.6	24.4	55.6	1.26
10	KQ92	22907T	.472	1.61	53.7	2.77	366	12.0	19.9	46.9	.977
11	KQ142	22908R	.460	1.52	68.4	3.56	846	18.1	22.5	46.1	1.16
12	KQ320	22909P	.307	1.31	63.3	3.31	622	11.4	26.8	55.5	1.23
13	KQ107a	22911Q	.462	1.73	73.3	3.29	1475	19.9	21.0	49.5	1.14
14	KQ311	22916R	.799	1.30	68.3	3.68	1191	14.6	23.9	52.8	1.19
15	KQ200b	22917P	.845	1.20	90.4	5.37	752	15.8	25.2	55.3	1.31
16	KQ143	22919W	.357	2.27	102.	5.59	738	21.7	22.4	48.3	1.10
17	KQ97a	22921X	.465	2.05	69.0	3.66	852	17.5	20.5	42.7	1.00
18	KQ185	22923T	.760	1.62	69.0	3.55	667	15.5	22.8	50.9	1.19
19	KQ154	22924R	.430	1.27	67.5	3.42	836	14.5	24.0	52.7	1.18
20	KQ213	22925P	.782	1.23	75.9	4.00	490	14.5	25.6	56.6	1.24
21	KQ151	22926Y	.789	1.45	89.3	4.03	656	17.2	26.7	58.8	1.32
22	KQ14	22927W	.439	1.45	83.8	2.82	804	17.7	22.8	48.4	1.08
23	KQ339	22929S	.675	2.11	93.2	4.65	770	21.6	24.2	56.7	1.22
24	KQ352b	22930V	1.26	1.46	87.9	5.27	560	17.8	22.3	52.2	1.14
25	KQ352	22931T	1.26	1.20	81.2	4.59	549	15.3	22.9	52.1	1.13
26	KQ351b	22932R	.828	1.30	83.5	5.17	440	20.1	23.7	51.5	1.21
27	KQ275a	22933P	.864	1.82	63.6	2.56	1167	12.0	22.8	50.1	1.10
28	KQ132b	22901U	.674	1.08	87.9	4.59	344	21.6	20.4	42.0	1.15
29	KQ230d	22905X	.586	1.52	71.3	3.65	371	15.0	21.9	43.6	1.12
30	KQ233e	22918Y	.703	1.30	81.6	4.12	497	14.0	24.7	46.8	1.24
31	QC81	22890W	.462	1.25	43.3	1.98	271	9.07	14.5	27.4	.776
32	KQ205	22914V	.635	2.02	92.1	4.14	739	17.1	24.0	47.5	1.28
33	KQ340	22935W	.199	1.82	90.1	5.32	358	22.8	65.0	135.	2.84
34	QC63	22877Q	.875	2.46	80.5	3.62	573	19.9	24.9	52.3	1.29
35	QC72	22880P	.946	1.45	67.0	4.73	709	18.4	22.8	45.0	1.16
36	QC29	22884S	1.29	1.29	76.2	4.26	403	19.1	23.5	50.7	1.17
37	QC20	22889T	.562	2.60	73.8	3.24	505	16.6	20.8	44.0	1.11
38	QC87	22893Q	.684	1.87	73.0	2.72	612	12.1	20.3	40.6	1.02
39	KC1	30689Q	.480	2.00	98.3	5.43	178	16.6	19.2	39.8	1.03
40	KC2	30690T	.729	1.56	74.0	3.62	334	13.8	26.0	53.8	1.29
41	KC5	30691R	.611	2.67	102.	5.62	222	18.5	21.0	44.0	1.08
42	KC6	30692P	.688	2.55	80.1	4.35	491	14.7	17.4	37.0	.921

Key to element symbols: Na sodium, K potassium, Rb rubidium, Cs caesium, Ba barium, Sc scandium, La lanthanum, Ce cerium, Eu europium, Lu lutetium, Hf hafnium, Th thorium, Ta tantalum, Cr chromium, Fe iron, Co cobalt, Sb antimony, U uranium, Ca calcium, As arsenic, Sm samarium, Yb ytterbium, Tb terbium.

Rec.: Sample record number used in this Appendix in Tables and Figures.

BMRL: British Museum Research Laboratory identity number for Laboratory records scheme.

Lu	Hf	Th	Ta	Cr	Fe	Co	Sb	U	Ca	As	Sm	Yb	Tb
.392	3.60	8.02	.92	412.	5.57	37.3	.64	1.6	12.9	5.4	4.50	2.10	.70
.382	3.82	8.04	.94	339.	5.84	34.2	.65	1.6	8.4	12.1	5.21	2.29	.67
.351	3.97	8.44	.81	303.	4.92	26.5	.62	2.6	8.0	8.4	5.09	2.32	.73
.374	4.86	8.29	.89	450.	4.55	26.3	.66	1.6	11.8	10.7	5.14	2.32	.71
.326	3.88	7.57	.83	323.	4.63	25.7	.77	2.2	10.1	24.2	4.62	2.06	.61
.251	3.17	7.33	4.59	291.	4.96	170.	.41		10.7	7.6	3.25	1.60	.61
.352	4.02	7.54	.96	286.	4.27	26.0	.48	2.2	14.7	8.5	4.88	2.17	.74
.380	3.92	8.70	.92	227.	4.68	27.3	.69	2.1	12.7	12.0	5.37	2.35	.71
.423	4.43	8.81	1.09	314.	4.72	27.0	.46	2.0	12.2	6.8	5.32	2.24	.76
.315	3.58	6.70	.72	316.	3.44	20.6	.54	1.3	15.6	7.7	4.32	1.96	.60
.335	3.35	7.57	.92	533.	5.06	34.2	.57	1.8	9.8	10.4	4.92	2.21	.59
.362	5.05	8.88	.94	297.	4.03	23.0	.60	1.5	14.3	9.5	5.89	2.69	.79
.333	3.46	7.16	.76	415.	5.43	33.8	.56	1.3	10.7	6.8	4.78	2.18	.66
.362	4.69	7.74	.96	343.	4.22	23.6	.61	2.1	12.2	6.6	5.16	2.32	.69
.400	4.88	8.46	.99	407.	4.74	29.0	.59	2.3	11.2	4.7	5.45	2.56	.80
.352	3.48	8.33	.77	427.	5.87	36.3	.63	1.9	7.9	5.7	4.69	2.16	.65
.334	3.25	6.20	.59	408.	4.79	30.7	.55	1.3	10.9	9.9		2.03	.57
.342	4.15	7.28	.88	615.	4.94	28.7	.66	1.6	8.9	6.4	4.85	2.21	.69
.352	4.64	8.20	.90	361.	4.10	23.6	.68	1.5	14.6	8.1	5.25	2.34	.72
.387	4.53	8.55	.97	365.	4.75	27.4	.82	2.0	12.5	7.9	5.45	2.48	.75
.411	5.38	8.92	.94	420.	4.89	28.4	.64	2.0	10.2	3.5	5.60	2.65	.80
.349	3.48	7.30	.85	426.	4.95	34.2	.59	1.7	7.4	7.5	4.83	2.25	.66
.376	4.25	8.43	.97	459.	5.81	36.8	.58	1.5	8.8	7.7	5.13	2.42	.73
.384	4.01	7.90	.87	386.	4.79	28.9	3.27	1.8	8.7	4.2	4.72	2.14	.71
.413	4.01	7.73	.83	383.	4.87	29.1	3.28	1.5	10.0	5.5	4.57	2.24	.69
.368	3.75	7.98	.92	429.	5.55	34.2	2.13	1.6	9.2	9.5	4.92	2.19	.72
.428	4.82	7.27	.75	395.	3.68	22.9	.83	2.0	11.2	8.7	5.11	2.30	.68
.355	3.57	7.45	.81	482.	5.91	40.3	.72	1.5	14.6	2.6	4.66	2.04	.60
.346	3.64	7.23	1.08	349.	4.25	41.3	.55	1.5	20.9	8.4	4.87	2.04	.69
.380	4.67	7.74	.95	330.	4.07	23.6	.43	2.2	21.0	7.4	5.46	2.32	.70
.230	3.05	4.50	.44	424.	2.39	13.6	.47	1.3	12.3	8.3	3.16	1.38	.42
.397	4.70	7.89	.84	600.	5.05	36.0	.85	1.9	10.8	4.9	5.13	2.34	.72
.739	12.8	19.0	3.07	191.	7.14	34.3	.49	3.4	2.3	12.3	12.6	4.59	1.65
.395	4.25	8.31	.88	473.	5.49	34.1	.73	1.8	9.6	21.9	5.69	2.43	.79
.356	3.72	7.75	.64	378.	4.94	29.8	.52	1.6	15.1	8.0	4.99	2.12	.69
.336	4.17	7.99	.86	437.	5.31	32.0	.76	1.9	13.5	26.4	5.32	2.09	.68
.337	3.49	6.80	.80	384.	4.70	28.0	.74	1.5	14.5	17.6	4.66	1.99	.62
.323	3.89	6.46	.73	297.	3.52	18.6	.65	1.5	17.8	10.4	4.39	1.91	.55
.310	3.49	7.04	.65	390.	4.63	26.2	.57	2.0	17.5	4.8	4.17	1.88	.53
.404	5.77	8.15	.91	578.	4.03	24.8	.73	1.8	17.7	10.7	5.69	2.56	.79
.298	3.46	7.78	.78	493.	4.64	40.4	.72	1.9	15.8	10.4	4.44	1.87	.59
.290	3.11	6.05	.59	407.	4.08	25.7	.85	2.8	19.8	14.1	3.99	1.71	.54

The Arpachiyeh and Gawra analyses are of interest to the present study since the sites are within about twenty-five miles of Qasrij, and one would therefore expect some general similarities in the clay composition, given both the short distances involved and the Tigris river as a dominant influence upon the distribution of sedimentary deposits, further homogenising the clay over large distances. A general comparison of the results does show a similarity between the two sets of data, but for a more specific comparison it is necessary to take into account the slight differences between the methods of standardisation used in the two laboratories. Davidson and McKerrell used the Edinburgh Standard Pottery E4, whereas in this work the British Museum BMSP standard was used. Measurements made in this Laboratory of samples of E4 are given in Table 4, as well as the 'quoted' values used by Davidson and McKerrell for E4. While a detailed discussion of inter-laboratory exchange of data is beyond the scope of this report, the simplest approach (pending further investigation) is to use the ratio of the BM and Edinburgh values of E4 to correct Davidson and McKerrell's data to be compatible with the Qasrij analyses. Davidson and McKerrell's data have been calculated using their original data (their Table 1) for the four groups of pottery listed in their Figures 1 and 6, namely Tell Arpachiyeh early, middle and late Halaf, and Tepe Gawra Halaf and Ubaid together. When these calculations are done (Table 4) and comparisons made with the Qasrij cluster means of Table 3, only Qasrij cluster 7 looks similar to any of the corrected data, namely late Halaf Arpachiyeh pottery. Since Qasrij cluster 7 is thought on the basis of this present study to be produced elsewhere than Qasrij, this similarity with the Arpachiyeh pottery (even though separated chronologically by millennia) suggests that the Qasrij cluster 7 pottery may have been produced further east than Qasrij, towards Arpachiyeh/Mosul. This suggestion must be regarded as a hypothesis based entirely on the similarity in composition of the pottery, but the inference drawn from the analyses does seem worthwhile pointing out.

Recently, Campbell (1987) has published neutron activation analyses of Halaf ceramics from Kharabeh Shattani, a site which is within about 1 km of Khirbet Qasrij. This study is therefore potentially of more significance to the present work than that at Gawra and Arpachiyeh. However, Campbell states that it has not been possible to relate his analyses to the earlier analyses of the Edinburgh group because a different standardisation procedure was used. The implication for the present study is that it is therefore not possible either to compare the Shattani data accurately with that from Qasrij. A summary of Campbell's data is quoted in Table 4: he analysed 26 sherds, four soils and three Arpachiyeh sherds and used cluster analysis on the results. He found two major clusters (called Groups 1 and 2), and the mean concentrations for these two groups are quoted in Table 4. Given the inter-laboratory differences in standardisation, one can only compare these with the Qasrij results with caution. However, Campbell's Group 1 appears on inspection to be not too different from the concentrations in Qasrij cluster 2. This is encouraging, since he regards Group 1 as being locally produced at Shattani, and Qasrij cluster 2 also falls within the presumed local series of clusters for Qasrij. Campbell's Group 2, which he regards as either non-local or of clay prepared by different methods, has no parallels at Qasrij. In conclusion, one may cautiously note

an agreement between the Shattani and Qasrij studies over what is locally produced pottery.

Ceramic petrology

Method

The colours of sherds were recorded from cut or broken edges using a Munsell soil colour chart. Slices were removed from the edges of sherds and thin sections prepared for optical microscopy. The principles of the thin section analysis of ancient ceramics are identical to those used in the study of rocks by geologists, a sub-discipline known as petrology. An overview of ceramic petrology and its application may be obtained from Peacock 1970, Williams 1983, and from papers in Peacock 1977 and Freestone *et al.* 1982. The thin sections of pottery, only 0.03 mm thick, are viewed in transmitted light in a manner analogous to the more familiar cross-sections of biological materials. The ceramic is seen to consist of three basic components: (1) a fine-grained clay matrix; (2) coarse mineral or rock particles embedded in the clay: these are known as inclusions or, if added deliberately by the potter, as temper; (3) holes or pores which open up due to shrinkage effects during drying and firing and which may also be formed by the burning out of organic material during firing or by the dissolution of soluble minerals (e.g. calcite) after burial. The inclusions are usually the most useful component archaeologically, as they may give a direct indication of geological source due to the presence of some special mineral or rock type. Alternatively it may be possible to distinguish between the products of different workshops by the amount, shape and size of a particular inclusion type which varies according to clay source and manufacturing technology (so-called 'textural' analysis). Finally, the microscopy of the sherd can indicate aspects of technology such as paste preparation, firing temperature and application of a slip or other surface coating.

Macroscopic examination

In hand specimen, most sherds are in a fairly hard, fine fabric with few inclusions greater than 0.2 mm or so, except for the occasional calcite grain. Many sherds contain voids which, from their morphology, were originally particles of vegetal matter which has burnt out during firing. The amount of vegetal matter was apparently controlled by the potters (see below). Vegetal matter was less common in ceramics from Khirbet Qasrij than in those from Qasrij Cliff, where nineteen out of twenty sherds contain such voids. It is difficult to estimate precisely the number of sherds with such voids from Khirbet Qasrij, because the density of the voids is often low and it is then sometimes unclear if the voids really do represent burning out of vegetal matter or are due to some other process (e.g. drying) and if they are due to a deliberate addition or are accidental. One sherd from Qasrij Cliff (QC81) shows abundant coarse quartz particles in the fabric; it has a heavily sooted outer surface and probably represents a cooking pot.

Colours of sherds from both sites were similar. Reddish yellows (7.5YR 7/6 and 5YR 7/6) were common, through pinks (7.5YR 7/4) to pale yellow (5Y 8/3) and whites and light greys (2.5Y 8/2 and 2.5Y 7/2).

Table 2   Comparison of NAA clusters, petrographic features and lime content

Cluster Number	Analysis Number	Pottery Catalogue No.	Petrographic Features	Weight percent Calcium
Cluster 1	7	KQ232f	B	12.7
	24	KQ352b	B glazed	8.7
	25	KQ352	B glazed	10.0
	26	KQ351b	B glazed	9.2
	35	QC72	Bv	15.1
	36	QC29	Bv	13.5
Cluster 2	1	QC7	Av	10.1
	2	KQ27	B	12.9
	23	KQ339	Bv	12.2
	28	KQ132b	B (w)	14.6
Cluster 3	3	KQ115	B	8.4
	8	KQ84	A	12.7
Cluster 4	4	KQ41	A	8.0
	12	KQ320	Ai	14.3
	14	KQ311	Bv	12.2
	19	KQ154	B	14.6
	27	KQ275a	Bii	11.2
	30	KQ233e	B (w)	21.0
	40	KC2	clay	17.7
Cluster 5	5	KQ195	Bv	11.8
	17	KQ97a	Ai	10.9
	29	KQ230d	B (w)	20.9
	37	QC20	Av	14.5
	38	QC87	Av	17.8
Cluster 6	9	KQ232	Bv	12.2
	15	KQ200b	Bv	11.2
	20	KQ213	Bv	12.5
	21	KQ151	Bv	10.2
Cluster 8	23	KQ339	Bv	12.2
	32	KQ205	Bii	10.8
	34	QC63	Av	9.6
Cluster 9	39	KC1	clay	17.5
	41	KC5	clay	15.8
	42	KC6	clay	19.8
Cluster 7	11	KQ142	Aiii	7.9
	13	KQ107a	B	10.7
	18	KQ185	Bii	9.2
	22	KQ14	Ai	7.4
Outliers	6	KQ114	B	10.7
	10	KQ92	A	15.6
	31	QC81	cooking pot	12.3
	33	KQ340	iv	2.3

Key: A/B = low/high fired matrix type; i-iii are petrological subgroups; v = vegetal matter additive to clay; w = waster. Clay samples labelled KC1 etc.

Table 3   Average concentrations of the elements in each cluster from the 8 cluster solution using CLUSTAN

Cluster No.		n	Na	K	Rb	Cs	Ba	Sc	La	Ce	Eu	Lu
Qasrij clusters:												
1	(mean=)	6	1.01	1.34	79	4.93	512	17.7	22.5	50.2	1.16	.368
	(standard deviation=)		.33	.10	7	.33	117	2.0	.6	2.7	.03	.023
2		4	.50	1.57	97	4.89	602	21.3	21.6	49.0	1.15	.373
			.21	.58	10	.46	207	.6	.9	5.1	.05	.019
3		2	.49	2.19	86	3.88	908	16.4	24.5	54.0	1.20	.366
			.11	.44	8	.27	137	1.6	.3	1.3	.06	.021
4		7	.62	1.46	72	3.54	750	13.3	24.9	52.3	1.20	.380
			.19	.21	6	.52	320	1.3	1.3	3.0	.06	.026
5		5	.55	1.95	69	3.33	615	15.5	21.1	43.8	1.03	.330
			.09	.41	2	.40	188	2.1	.8	3.0	.05	.006
6		4	.82	1.29	87	4.75	590	16.0	25.5	56.5	1.28	.406
			.05	.11	8	.86	137	1.2	.9	1.5	.04	.015
8		3	.73	2.19	89	4.13	693	19.5	24.4	52.2	1.26	.389
			.12	.23	7	.51	105	2.3	.5	4.6	.04	.012
9		3	.59	2.41	93	5.13	296	16.6	19.2	40.2	1.01	.300
			.10	.35	12	.68	169	1.9	1.8	3.5	0.08	.010
Non-Qasrij cluster:												
7		4	.53	1.58	74	3.30	947	17.8	22.3	48.7	1.15	.340
			.15	.12	7	.35	359	1.8	.9	2.0	.05	.007
Outliers:												
6 = KQ114			.22	1.33	71	4.12	324	15.3	17.6	45.3	.99	.251
10, = KQ92			.47	1.61	54	2.77	366	12.0	19.9	46.9	.98	.315
31 = QC81			.46	1.25	43	1.98	271	9.1	14.5	27.4	.78	.230
33 = KQ340			.20	1.82	90	5.32	358	22.8	65.0	135.0	2.84	.739
For comparison: Halaf period ceramics from Kharabeh Shattani*												
Group 1			.48	1.48	70	5.09		22.5	21.5	46.0	1.25	.405
			.09	.30	16	1.03		2.2	1.0	4.2	.16	.038
Group 2			.31	1.12	62	3.97		18.5	18.4	40.0	1.10	.340
			.10	.34	29	1.02		1.4	1.2	1.9	.16	.030

*Analysed by the University of Edinburgh (Watkins and Campbell, 1987): data taken from Table C.2, p70; Group 1 = their samples 1, 3, 5-7, 11, 12, 16-19, 21-23; Group 2 = 2, 8-10, 13, 15, 24-26; means and standard deviations calculated by the present authors from the published data. No interlaboratory correction factors have been applied.

Hf	Th	Ta	Cr	Fe	Co	Sb	U	Ca	As	Sm	Yb	Tb
3.88	7.83	.90	379	5.01	30.0	1.9	1.74	11.8	10.3	4.89	2.17	.71
.19	.20	.05	55	.44	2.8	1.4	.25	2.6	8.0	.25	.05	.02
3.64	7.96	.86	415	5.83	37.0	.63	1.65	10.9	6.5	4.76	2.15	.66
.14	.37	.09	61	.15	2.5	.03	.19	3.3	4.0	.25	.10	.03
3.84	8.21	.91	5.83	35.4	.63	1.65	8.4	9.4	5.06	2.29	.68	
.04	.18	.08	53	.17	.5	.05	.40	3.3	2.5	.20	.02	.01
4.91	8.04	.92	393	4.10	24.1	.64	1.83	14.7	8.7	5.36	2.42	.73
.40	.47	.07	95	.23	1.5	.12	.30	3.3	1.6	.31	.18	.05
3.57	6.89	.81	352	4.38	28.2	.66	1.59	14.8	14.1	4.62	2.05	.59
.26	.55	.17	45	.52	8.2	.11	.33	4.6	6.7	.20	.06	.06
4.81	8.68	1.00	376	4.78	28.0	.63	2.10	11.5	5.7	5.45	2.48	.78
.43	.22	.06	47	.08	.9	.15	.14	1.0	2.0	.11	.18	.03
4.40	8.21	.89	511	5.45	35.6	.72	1.75	9.7	11.5	5.32	2.40	.75
.25	.28	.07	78	.38	1.4	.14	.19	1.0	9.1	.32	.05	.04
3.36	6.96	.67	430	4.45	30.8	.72	2.26	17.7	9.8	4.20	1.82	.55
.21	.86	.10	55	.32	8.4	.14	.50	2.0	4.7	.22	.09	.04
3.61	7.32	.85	497	5.09	32.7	.60	1.58	9.2	7.7	4.85	2.21	.65
.36	.17	.07	97	.23	2.7	.05	.21	1.4	1.8	.06	.03	.04
3.17	7.33	4.59	291	4.96	170	.41		10.7	7.6	3.25	1.60	.61
3.58	6.70	.72	316	3.44	20.6	.54	1.30	15.6	7.7	4.32	1.96	.60
3.05	4.50	.44	424	2.39	13.6	.47	1.30	12.3	8.3	3.16	1.38	.42
12.8	19.0	3.07	191	7.14	34.3	.49	3.40	2.3	12.3	12.6	4.59	1.65
3.95	8.81		490	6.27	33.9					4.21		
.52	.75		76	.71	4.9					.30		
2.97	7.59		433	5.10	28.8					3.48		
.44	.42		90	.45	4.4					.40		

Table 4   Analyses of ceramics by Davidson and McKerrell: comparison with Khirbet Qasrij samples

		Th	Cr	Hf	Cs	Sc	Fe	Co	Eu
Tell Arpachiyeh									
Early Halaf (16 samples)	original mean	9.90	316	4.41	5.91	20.8	5.48	25.8	1.26
(Davidson and McKerrell,	standard deviation	1.1	89	.51	.84	1.0	.26	2.7	.17
fig. 1)	corrected mean	9.3	308	3.84	5.49	17.6	5.01	23.3	1.22
Middle Halaf (18 samples)	original mean	8.29	415	4.04	3.89	17.0	4.58	24.1	1.19
(Davidson and McKerrell,	standard deviation	1.20	115	1.37	1.12	1.5	.34	2.5	.16
fig. 1)	corrected mean	7.83	405	3.51	3.62	14.4	4.19	21.8	1.15
Late Halaf (26 samples)	original mean	7.50	523	3.51	4.21	21.4	5.61	35.4	1.11
(Davidson and McKerrell,	standard deviation	1.82	97	.55	.89	2.3	.59	5.5	.12
fig. 1)	corrected mean	7.08	510	3.05	3.91	18.1	5.13	32.0	1.08
compare: Khirbet Qasrij	mean	7.32	497	3.61	3.30	17.8	5.09	32.7	1.15
(4 samples) cluster 7	standard deviation	.17	97	.36	.35	1.8	.23	2.7	.05
Tepe Gawra									
Halaf and Ubaid	original mean	8.43	424	4.63	3.15	16.8	4.44	23.6	1.35
(Davidson and McKerrell,	standard deviation	1.43	69	.63	1.29	1.1	.23	1.9	.14
fig. 6)	corrected mean	7.96	414	4.03	2.93	14.2	4.06	21.4	1.31
Edinburgh Standard Pottery E4 (Davidson and McKerrell): quoted concentration used by D. and M.		14.3	110	7.49	8.14	27.3	5.15	18.9	1.97
Analysis of E4 by BM	mean	13.5	107.4	6.52	7.56	23.1	4.71	17.1	1.91
Research Laboratory	standard deviation	.48	3.3	.21	.65	.4	.20	.4	.16
(5 samples)									
E4: ratio of results BMRL / D. and M. value (used to adjust 'original mean' (D. and M.) to obtain 'corrected mean' in this Table)		.944	.976	.870	.929	.846	.915	.905	.970

Thin section examination

In thin section, the bulk of sherds from Khirbet Qasrij are not readily distinguishable from those from Qasrij Cliff. They typically show a fine-grained fired clay matrix which contains sparse to common silt grade (less than 0.1 mm) quartz, sparse fine sand grade quartz and sparse to abundant fine calcite. Fine mica flakes and brown to opaque iron oxide and ferruginous clay grains may be present but, as with the fine calcite, their apparent concentrations are strongly dependent on firing conditions. Thus in the kiln wasters from Khirbet Qasrij no visible mica is present and the calcite content is very low, because at high temperatures these components react to form glass together with very fine-grained silicates. The clay matrices may be subdivided into two types. Type A matrices contain small birefringent domains of clay minerals and fine micas, less than 0.02 mm across. In addition these fabrics show a strong general anisotropy parallel to the surfaces of the sherd when the gypsum plate is inserted between crossed polars. Matrices of type B, on the other hand, show no clay mineral domains or fine micas and do not show preferred orientation. The birefringence in type B originates only from quartz and calcite; the matrix in addition exhibits a diffuse milky glow when viewed in conoscopic light. Type A and type B matrices occur in pottery from both sites.

Petrographic sub-groups of the Khirbet Qasrij material were tentatively established by visual comparison of 35 mm photomicrograph transparencies on a light box. Most were based on minor textural differences of limited significance and also were not supported by the NAA, so are not detailed here. However, a number of sherds were sufficiently different from the majority to suggest that they may represent different clay sources:

i. A group distinguished by the presence of common coarse calcite grains (KQ320, KQ97a, KQ14).

ii. An internally variable group characterised by common to abundant fine quartz sand (KQ205, KQ185, KQ275a; the latter is a painted sherd).

iii. A fabric characterised by a fine-grained matrix containing common fine to medium grade sand grains which include quartz, feldspars, calcite, amphiboles, clinopyroxenes and mica. This sherd, KQ142, is a vessel base with an inner coating of black bituminous material, possibly added as a sealant.

iv. A fabric poor in calcite and with abundant quartz silt and which contains coarse opaque argillaceous inclusions up to at least 1 mm diameter (KQ340).

A single sherd from Qasrij Cliff is distinctive: this is the cooking pot QC81, mentioned above. In thin section, this sherd shows abundant coarse angular to subangular poorly sorted monocrystalline quartz grains and polycrystalline quartz grains with crenulate internal grain boundaries. These range up to sizes in excess of 1 mm. Also present are common calcite grains, typically 0.1 mm and up to 0.5 mm.

Ceramic sources

When attempting to classify a group of relatively homogeneous and undifferentiated pottery, both NAA and thin section analysis suffer from disadvantages. While either technique can establish sub-groups of the assemblage, the significance of these groups is not always clear. Groupings may reflect natural variations in a single raw material or variations due to the production methods of the potters. Using the techniques in tandem, however, allows a much more positive result and where good correspondence is obtained, then firm conclusions on origin may be made.

It is encouraging to observe that there is quite a good correspondence between the NAA and the petrology for the samples analysed using both techniques. Referring to Table 2, the multivariate analysis of the elemental data causes most of the pottery to fall into clusters 1-6. These include the three wasters (KQ132b in cluster 2, KQ275a in cluster 4 and KQ230d in cluster 5) and one of the local clays, KC2 in cluster 4. These clusters are believed to represent a local Qasrij compositional group, including the production of the Khirbet Qasrij kiln and the bulk of the Qasrij Cliff production. Five examples of Qasrij Cliff pottery are spread among clusters 1-6, so that the material from the two sites cannot be distinguished compositionally. The predominant fabrics from the two sites were also indistinguishable petrographically. Within the local grouping, cluster 1 includes all three glazed sherds, nos KQ 351b, 352 and 352b. Table 1 shows that these are characterised by relatively high sodium (Na) and antimony (Sb), elements which are contaminants from the glazing process; however, these elements were not included in the multivariate statistical analysis, so should not affect the formation of this cluster. Cluster 6 includes four of the six sherds from Khirbet Qasrij with heavy vegetal tempering ('v' in third column of Table 2). Thus the individual clusters in the local group may to some extent represent technological processes. It is unclear, however, whether this is because the technology modified the ceramic elemental composition or because different processes (glazing, tempering) were carried out at different times on distinctive batches of clay.

A number of sherds which were assigned to petrographical group i, characterised by the presence of coarse calcite, and group ii, with common quartz, are spread through local clusters 1-6 (Table 2). Petrographically these two groups are ambiguous with respect to origin, and also they are internally heterogeneous. Thus some of them probably represent local products with pastes which are extreme in terms of non-plastics content. On the other hand, KQ275a, a quartz-rich sherd which occurs in local cluster 4, is painted, and this, coupled with its somewhat disparate petrography, leads us to suspect a non-local origin. In fact an increase in the number of clusters from nine to ten causes this sherd to fall out as a singleton, indicating that it does not sit comfortably in cluster 4 and is indeed likely to be non-local.

Cluster 8 (Table 2) merges with cluster 2 if the number of clusters is reduced from nine to eight and therefore is probably local. Cluster 7, however, is a stable cluster which is compositionally distinct from the others. Furthermore this cluster contains three petrographically distinctive sherds including KQ142 which, in petrographic group iii, has a clear non-local mineralogy. Thus cluster 7 can be seen to represent non-local products, imported to the site. Sherd KQ142 is of particular interest as it has a carbonaceous internal surface, possibly reflecting the use of a sealant or the residue of some organic contents. Thus this vessel may have been a container used to transport some liquid product.

Of the four outliers which were removed from the cluster analysis at an early stage, two are highly distinctive petrographically. QC81 is the coarse-tempered cooking pot from Qasrij Cliff, while KQ340 contains coarse argillaceous inclusions and also has very low calcite (reflected in its low Ca content; Table 2). These vessels are clearly imports. Of the other two outliers KQ114 was contaminated with tantalum (Ta) and cobalt (Co) when sampling (Table 1) and although these elements were omitted from the cluster analysis the fact that contamination demonstrably occurred leads us to treat the isolation of this sherd with some circumspection. The final outlier (KQ92) has no special petrographic characteristics but this serves to remind us that clays which appear similar in thin section to the Khirbet Qasrij products occur over a very large geographical area.

The generally good correspondence between the NAA and the petrography on the core groups analysed by both techniques allows us to extend our findings to the rest of the Khirbet Qasrij ceramics and those from Qasrij Cliff, which have been analysed only petrographically.

The bulk of the sherds from both sites are compositionally homogeneous and represent the exploitation of what, analytically, appears a single clay source. In reality, several closely located clay sources would give a similar result. Both assemblages include non-local products. At Khirbet Qasrij these include the painted sherds KQ275a and KQ340 and the container, KQ142. At Qasrij Cliff, the cooking pot, QC81, appears to be the non-local product. The NAA data suggest that sources for the non-local pottery are most likely to lie to the south.

Technological observations

Paste preparation and forming techniques

Most of the clays are very fine, with few inclusions greater than 0.1mm. Calcite is abundant in lower-fired wares and it was originally present in virtually all clays as indicated by their present lime contents (10-20% Ca0). This use of calcareous clays for pottery manufacture is typical of the ancient Near East and Mediterranean areas. With one exception, the cooking pot from Qasrij Cliff (QC81), there is no evidence for the addition of inorganic mineral fragments as temper. One or two of the non-local fabrics are ambiguous in this respect, but certainly there were no such additions to the bulk of the local wares. Thus the large flaggy sandstone block associated with the kiln at Khirbet Qasrij is not a source of tempering material. More likely, it represents a work surface, probably for the wedging of the clay to remove air and inhomogeneities before throwing.

While it is relatively straightforward in many cases to suggest that a temper has been added to a clay, it is more difficult to infer that a clay has been refined by levigation in water to remove coarse particles. However, some of the local clays contain quite coarse particles of calcite, which would have introduced difficulties in firing the pots due to spalling, and it would have made sense to refine the clays to remove any coarse calcite. This would account for the very fine-grained nature of the bodies.

There is little doubt that the voids in the pottery bodies represent the deliberate addition of an organic temper which has burnt out during firing. This is confirmed by the legs of the tripod-bowls at Khirbet Qasrij, which have a very high concentration of the voids relative to the bodies of the vessels. The bowls were wheel-thrown, allowed to dry to the leather hard state, then turned on the wheel before the legs were added as wet clay. The vegetal temper was added to the legs to reduce their drying shrinkage so that they would 'fit' the body which was already part-dried. The fine particle size and mixture of ragged stalk-like and irregular impressions left by the vegetal temper strongly suggests that this was added as dung, a practice well known ethnographically and which has been postulated for a range of pottery from the archaeological record (London 1981: note, however, that the coarser vegetal temper in pottery from the neolithic and chalcolithic 'software' horizons of the Zagros and Iranian plateau is unlikely to be dung, according to Vandiver 1985, in press). As well as controlling shrinkage, dung can be added to improve the workability of clay and perhaps to facilitate throwing. Furthermore, the addition of any temper opens the fabric and facilitates the escape of gases during firing. It has already been noted that dung additions are less common at Khirbet Qasrij than at Qasrij Cliff. Given the similarity in clay types and petrographies, it would seem likely that the Khirbet potters were in general able to exercise better control over some aspects of their production procedures than the potters who produced the Qasrij Cliff material, so that dung additions were needed less frequently.

Many sherds show clear evidence of wheel-throwing, such as corrugations on the interior of the body sherds and spiral patterns in the bases, defined by voids. Some vessels were turned down on the wheel while in the leather hard state, using a sharp tool, to produce footrings and crisply defined rims. There is little evidence for any major differences in forming technology between the sites, but the rims on the Khirbet Qasrij vessels are more precisely turned and sharply defined. The 'cooking pot' from Qasrij Cliff (QC81) appears to have been hand-formed.

Firing

The temperatures attained in a simple updraft kiln such as that excavated at Khirbet Qasrij are typically 800-1000°C. Calcareous clays such as those used are well suited to such kilns, as they develop a very stable microstructure in this temperature range which does not normally bloat or slump until about 1150°C (Maniatis and Tite 1981). Thus it was relatively straightforward to achieve sufficient control to ensure a high proportion of successfully fired products.

In thin section, the pottery has been divided into two types, A and B, on the basis of the ceramic matrix, type A containing relict clay minerals and type B containing none (see above). According to the published data of Jornet (1982), Peters and Iberg (1978), Letsch and Noll (1983), Maggetti (1982) and Cooper and Bowman (1986), illitic clay minerals remain in diminishing amounts in calcareous clays at firing temperatures up to about 900°C but disappear by about 950°C. Thus the A type fabrics typically represent firing temperatures up to 900°C, while the B type fabrics typically represent higher temperatures. This cannot be a precise estimate, however.

Some sherds show zoning of A and B type fabrics in the body, due to varying oxidation conditions during firing (cf. Letsch and Noll, *op. cit.*). In addition the composition may affect the breakdown of the clay minerals, and in Fig. 49a a preponderance of A type fabrics at low calcium contents is observed, suggesting that some control may be exercised by lime content in the present case. Furthermore, two of the three wasters (KQ 230d, KQ233e) have exceptionally high calcium (greater than 20% Ca; Table 2), suggesting that apparent overfiring may in fact represent as much the inability to control precisely the raw materials as failure to control the kiln temperature. Even so, A and B fabrics occur over the full range of calcium contents and we can assume that some of the sherds were fired at temperatures well below 900°C. On the other hand, some of the kiln wasters which warped during firing were probably fired at around 1100°C. The highly slagged wall fragment from the fire-pit of the kiln suggests that temperatures at least this high were attained there. Detailed temperature measurements taken in a simple updraft kiln by Mr A. Tubb of Bristol Polytechnic (pers. comm.) show a range of temperatures of 100-150°C in a single firing, depending on the position of a pot in the kiln; while dramatic variations in the kiln regime between firings are not required to account for the range of wares examined, the maximum kiln temperature must have varied by at least 100°C between firings and probably more. The colour of the pottery varies widely from greys through whites and yellows to pinks and reds. Tables 5a and 5b show that for those sherds for which colours were measured using the Munsell charts (the dark grey and painted sherds were excluded) there is a strong correlation between colour and microstructure, the 'reddish' sherds (Munsell chroma = 6) typically corresponding to A type fabrics and the white, yellows, browns etc., without the 'reddish' descriptive term (Munsell chroma = 2-4) correspond to B type fabrics. Sherds with colours described as 'pink' have microstructures which may fall into either category and may be regarded as intermediate. Thus colour is dependent on firing temperature, kiln atmosphere and composition, a phenomenon which has been discussed in detail by Matson (1971) for clays and ceramics from Seleucia. However, as has been seen, it was probably not possible for the potters to control any one of these parameters sufficiently precisely to be able to predetermine the fired colour of a pot, and a wide range of colours is likely to have resulted from a single firing.

Surface coats

Some sherds have a thin surface 'skin' which is paler than the body. Often such a skin is termed a 'slip', implying that it was deliberately added. However, this is not the case. It is now well established by Matson (1971) and more recently by Peacock (Fulford and Peacock 1984) that these white 'skins' form on calcareous clay bodies when some salt is present in the drying process. In the present case the 'skins' are often not marked and may result from a little salt being naturally present in the clay rather than being deliberately added, as has been recorded from ethnographic studies (Rye 1976; Fulford and Peacock 1984).

The 'glazes' on sherds KQ351b, 352 and 352b are quite poorly preserved. They appear to be of two types. On sherd KQ352b the glaze takes the form of a smooth iridescent weathered layer. On sherds KQ351b and 352 on the other hand the 'glazes' occur as yellowish-green vesiculated ('bubbly') patches. These two types do not appear to represent the same phenomenon. In particular there is some suspicion regarding the yellow-green 'glazes' because these sometimes occur in

Table 5   Comparison of Munsell ceramic body colours with petrographic matrix types

(a) Qasrij Cliff

	Type A Matrix	Type B Matrix	Row Total
Reddish	6	?1	7
Pink	2	2	4
Other Colours	1/2	7	9
Column Total	10	10	20

(b) Khirbet Qasrij

	Type A Matrix	Type B Matrix	Row Total
Reddish	10/12	-	12
Pink	2/3	2	5
Other Colours	?1	20/21	22
Column Total	16	23	39

Notes: Type A matrix, low fired; type B, high fired. Munsell Chroma values for reds = 6, pinks = 4, others = 2-4.

Uncertainties indicated by a slash or a query are in the thin section determination of matrix type.

spalled or damaged areas of the ceramic surface, suggesting that they were applied to an already damaged vessel, not the best of surfaces to decorate.

In order to determine the precise nature of these glazes, they were examined using the scanning electron microscope at the Conservation Analytical Laboratory of the Smithsonian Institution by Dr P. B. Vandiver, who kindly offered to help when our own machine was out of action due to building works. The results indicate that the iridescent layer is a soda-lime-silica glaze, coloured with copper. The yellowish-green vesicular deposits on the other sherds are less characteristic of glazes. They contain undissolved quartz grains and phases rich in copper and are not simple glasses. Their vesicular nature, coupled with the inclusions, suggests that these were not fully molten glazes. Thus they may be seen as less successful (? failed) attempts at glazing, or perhaps they represent the pots in which the glaze raw materials were fritted together before use.

Conclusions

Neutron activation analysis and petrology indicate that pottery was produced on or near site at Khirbet Qasrij and Qasrij Cliff. Local calcareous clays were used and these may have been refined by sieving or washing to produce the very fine bodies of the ceramics. Inorganic temper was not added, but vegetal temper, probably dung, was added to modify the shrinkage and workability of the clay. Pottery was wheel-thrown, dried and turned down on the wheel using a sharp tool. Legs were added to the dried, turned body in the wet plastic state, heavily tempered with dung to ensure that they did not part from the body due to differential shrinkage as they dried.

Glazed sherds group compositionally with local wares and are probably themselves local products. Some may represent vessels used to frit the raw glaze materials. Glazes were of the alkali-lime-silica variety, coloured by copper (probably originally green).

Firing temperatures ranging from below 900°C to in excess of 1000°C were typical for the body and kiln types and for ancient Near Eastern pottery in general. The variation in vessel colour was neither predictable nor controllable by the potters.

The clays used at Qasrij Cliff and Khirbet Qasrij were analytically indistinguishable, suggesting that the same or very closely related clay beds were exploited. At Khirbet Qasrij, there is less pottery tempered with dung, perhaps implying somewhat improved control over the drying or firing processes, or better clay preparation to improve workability (e.g. longer ageing of the clay). Also the rims and bases from Khirbet Qasrij are in some cases more sharply defined, again perhaps implying a little more skill and understanding of the manufacturing process. There are more high-fired type B fabrics from Khirbet Qasrij, but this is to be expected as the assemblage was obtained from an area adjacent to a kiln, where over-fired sherds might be expected, and indeed several clear wasters are included. Thus there is no clear difference in firing conditions used to produce the pottery from the two sites. However, taking into account the features noted above, and the production of glazed sherds at Khirbet Qasrij, it is probably reasonable to say that the potter's craft is more developed in the assemblage from this site.

NAA and petrology indicate that non-local pottery is present at both sites. At Qasrij Cliff this is represented by a single hand-made cooking pot, coarsely tempered with quartz. The preference for coarse hand-made cooking wares is well established in the Mediterranean area, and these were traded over long distances, often in contrast to finer wares which were made locally (Riley 1981). The possibility that the cooking pot is simply a local product which is petrographically distinctive due to the use of a distinctive 'cooking pot technology' may be dismissed in view of the NAA results, which show that the clay composition is also well removed from the local products. At Khirbet Qasrij, non-local pottery includes fine painted wares and a vessel with a bituminous (?) internal coating which may have been a liquid container, implying transport of its contents. The NAA indicates that the local pottery from Arpachiyeh, Gawra and Kharabeh Shattani (though earlier in date) is not very different from the Qasrij pottery in clay composition, showing the same general features, although different sites may be distinguished. Particular similarities between the non-local Qasrij pottery (cluster 7) and the Arpachiyeh material leads us to suggest that the non-local wares may have originated towards the east.

Acknowledgements

We are grateful to Mark Gillings for his assistance in the photomicrography and initial sorting of the sections, and to Pamela Vandiver for discussion and analysis of the glazed wares. Michael Tite kindly commented on a draft of this paper.

References

Bailey, D.M., 1975. *A Catalogue of Lamps in the British Museum*, I, *Greek, Hellenistic and Early Roman pottery lamps*, London.

Campbell, S., 1987?, *Excavations at Kharabeh Shattani*, vol. 1, ch. 3: 'Halaf culture pottery from the 1983 season'; University of Edinburgh, Dept of Archaeology, Occasional paper no. 14: 56-62.

Cooper, N., and Bowman, J., 1986. 'Studying the effect of heat on clay using X-ray diffraction analysis: the role of firing duration in the assessment of ancient firing temperatures'. *Bulletin Experimental Firing Group* 4:37-48.

Davidson, T.E., and McKerrell, H., 1976, 'Pottery analysis and Halaf Period trade in the Khabur Headwaters region', *Iraq* 38:45-56.

———, 1980. 'The neutron activation analysis of Halaf and 'Ubaid pottery from Tell Arpachiyeh and Tepe Gawra', *Iraq* 42:155-67.

Davidson, T.E., 1981. 'The neutron activation analysis of prehistoric pottery from Tell Aqab, Northeast Syria', in Hughes, M.J. (ed.), *Scientific Studies in Ancient Ceramics*, British Museum Occasional Paper 19:21-32; also printed as: 'Pottery manufacture and trade at the prehistoric site of Tell Aqab, Syria,

1981', *Journal of Field Archaeology* 8 (1): 65-77.

Dobel, A., Asaro, F., and Michel, H.V., 1977. Neutron activation analysis and the location of Wassukani, *Orientalia* 46 (3): 375-82.

Everitt, B., 1980. *Cluster Analysis*, 2nd edn, Aldershot.

Fillières, D., Harbottle, G., and Sayre, E.D., 1983. 'Neutron activation study of figurines and pottery from the Athenian Agora', *Journal of Field Archaeology* 10: 55-69.

Freestone, I., Potter, T., and Johns, C., 1982. *Current research in ceramics: thin-section studies*, British Museum Occasional Paper 32.

Fulford, M.G., and Peacock, D.P.S., 1974. *Excavations at Carthage: The British Mission*, vol. I, 2, University of Sheffield.

Harbottle, G., 1976. 'Activation analysis in archaeology', in Newton, G.W.A. (ed.), *Radiochemistry*, vol. 3, Specialist Periodical Reports, The Chemical Society, London: 33-72.

Hope, K., 1978. *Methods of Multivariate Analysis*, London.

Hughes, M.J., Cherry, J., Freestone, I.C., and Leese, M.N., 1982. 'Neutron activation analysis and petrology of Medieval English decorated floor tiles from the Midlands', in Freestone, Potter and Johns, *op.cit.*

Hughes, M.J., Leese, M.N., and Smith, R.J., 1988. 'The analysis of pottery lamps mainly from Western Anatolia, including Ephesus, by neutron activation analysis', appendix in Bailey, D.M., *A Catalogue of Lamps in the British Museum*, III, *Roman Provincial Lamps*, London: 461-85.

Hughes, M.J., and Vince, A., 1986. 'Neutron activation analysis and petrology of Hispano-Moresque pottery', in Olin, J.S., and Blackman, M.J. (eds), *Proceedings of the 24th International Archaeometry Symposium (14-18 May 1984)*, Smithsonian Institution, Washington: 353-67.

Hughes, M.J., Leese, M., and Bailey, D.M., 1983. 'Neutron activation analysis of pottery lamps from Ephesus dating from the Archaic to the Late Roman period', in S.E. Warren and A. Aspinall (eds), *Proceedings of the 22nd Symposium on Archaeometry, University of Bradford 1982*, Bradford: 368-76.

Jornet, A., 1982. 'Analyse minéralogique et chimique de la céramique romaine suisse à enduit brillant'. Thesis, University of Fribourg, Institut de Minéralogie et pétrographie, Switzerland. University Microfilms reprint no. 846.

Kaplan, M.F., Harbottle, G., and Sayre, E.D., 1982. Multi-disciplinary analysis of Tell el Yahudiyeh ware, *Archaeometry* 24: 127-42.

Letsch, J., and Noll, W., 1983. 'Phase formation in several ceramic subsystems at 600°C-1000°C as a function of oxygen fugacity'. *Ceramic Forum International/ Berichte der DKG* (Wiesbaden) 60: 259-67.

London, G., 1981. 'Dung tempered clay', *Journal of Field Archaeology* 8: 189-95.

Maggetti, M., 1982. 'Phase analysis and its significance for technology and origin', in Olin, J.S., and Franklin, A.D. (eds), *Archaeological Ceramics*', Smithsonian Institution Press, Washington: 121-33.

Main, P.L., and Hughes, M.J., 1983. 'Using a Hewlett-Packard minicomputer for the processing of gamma-ray spectra from neutron activation analysis', *Computer Enhanced Spectroscopy* 1 (1): 17-24.

Maniatis, Y., and Tite, M.S., 1981. 'Technological examination of Neolithic-Bronze Age pottery from Central and Southeast Europe and from the Near East', *Journal of Archaeological Science* 8:59-76.

Matson, F.R., 1971. 'A study of temperatures used in firing ancient Mesopotamian pottery', in Brill, R.H. (ed.), *Science and Archaeology*, Cambridge, Mass.: 65-79.

Munsell 1975. *Soil Colour Charts*, Baltimore.

Peacock, D.P.S, 1970. 'The scientific analysis of ceramics: a review', *World Archaeology* 1:375-89.

__________, 1977. *Pottery and Early Commerce*, London and New York.

Perlman, I., and Asaro., F., 1969. 'Pottery analysis by neutron activation', *Archaeometry* 11:21-52.

Peters, T., and Iberg, R., 1978. 'Mineralogical changes during firing of calcium-rich brick clays', *Ceramic Bulletin* 57:503-9.

Riley J., 1981. 'The Late Bronze Age Aegean and the Roman Mediterranean: a case for comparison', in Howard, H., and E.L. Morris (eds), *Production and Distribution; a ceramic viewpoint*, British Archaeological Reports, International Series, vol. 120: 133-43.

Rye, O.S., 1976. 'Keeping your temper under control: materials and the manufacture of Papuan pottery', *Archaeology and Physical Anthropology in Oceania* xi: 106-37.

Slusallek, K., Burmester, A., and Borker, Chr., 1983. Neutronenaktivierungsanalytische Untersuchungen an gestempelten greichischen Amphorenhenkeln: Erste Ergebnisse', *Berliner Beitrage zur Archäometrie* 8: 261-76.

Vandiver, P.B., 1985. 'Sequential Slab Construction: A Near Eastern Pottery Production Technology, 8000-3000 B.C.', PhD Thesis, Massachusetts Institute of Technology.

__________ (in press). 'Sequential slab construction: A conservative southwest Asiatic ceramic tradition, ca.6500-3000 BC.' Submitted to *Paléorient*.

Williams, D., 1983. 'Petrology of Ceramics', in Kempe, D.R.C., and Harvey, A.P. (eds), *The Petrology of Archaeological Artefacts*, Oxford: 301-9.

Wishart, D., 1978. *CLUSTAN User Manual, Version 1C, Release 2*, 3rd edn, Program Library Unit, University of Edinburgh, and 1982: *Supplement to CLUSTAN Manual*.

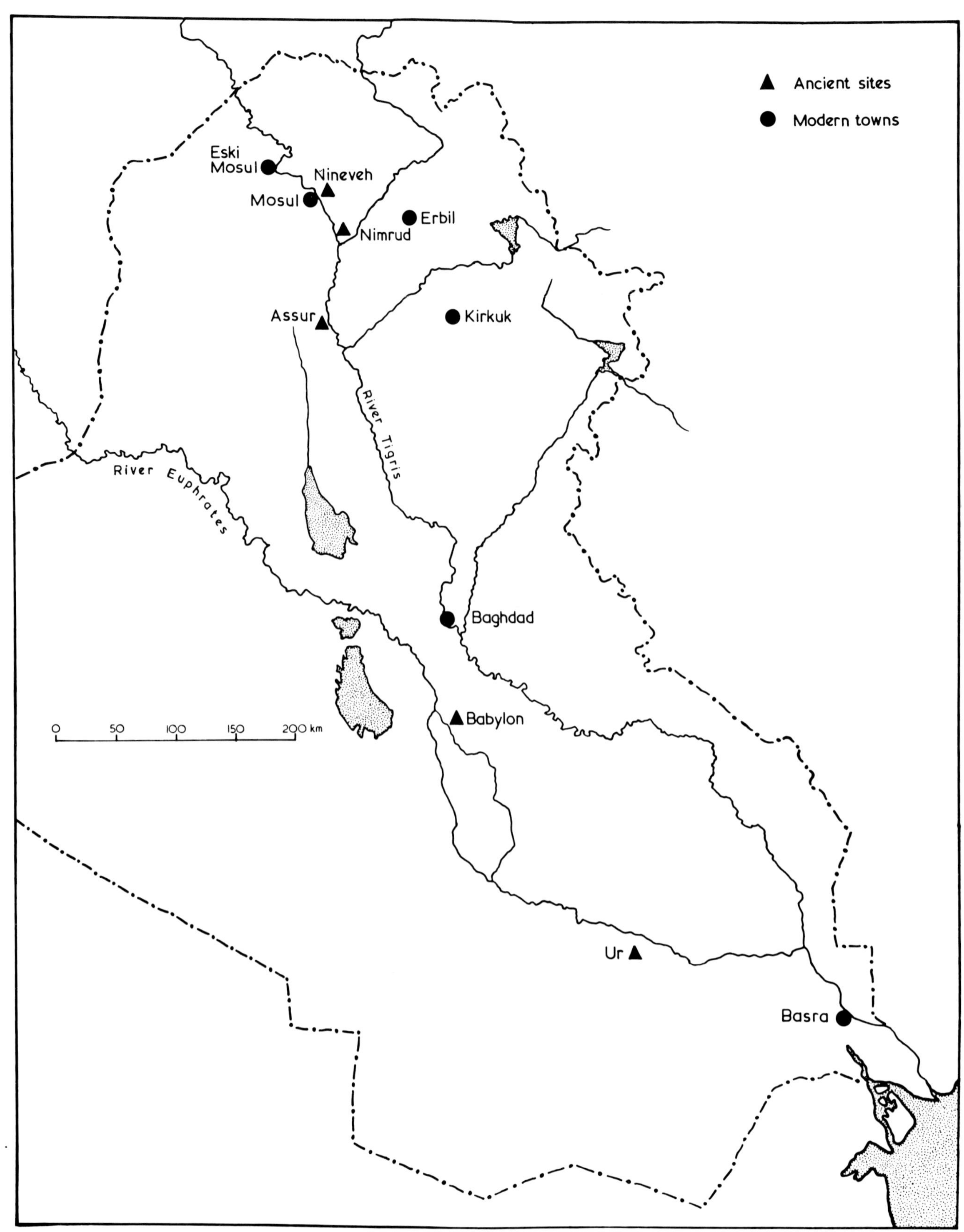

Fig. 1. Map of Iraq

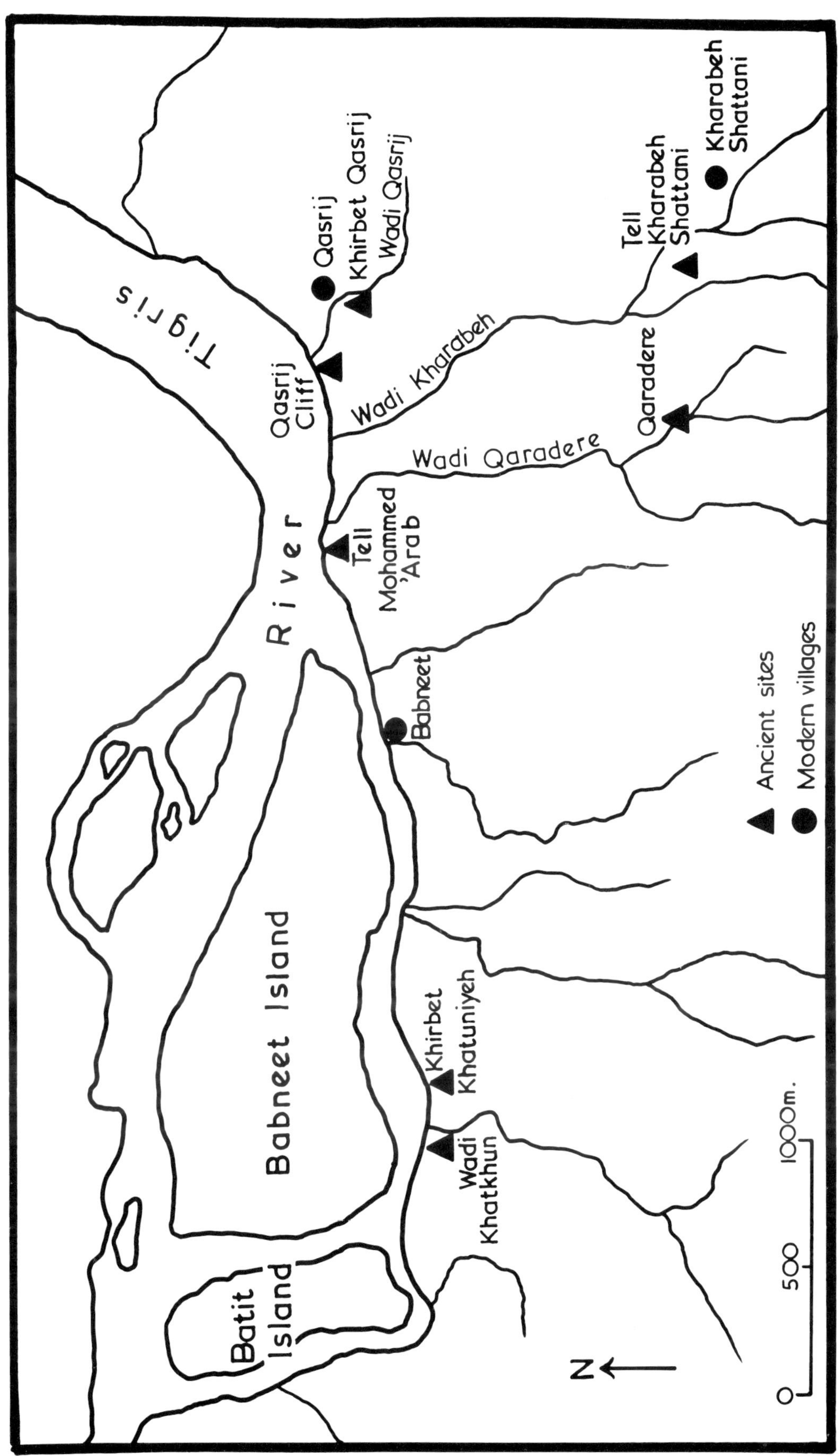

Fig. 2. Ancient sites in the vicinity of Babneet

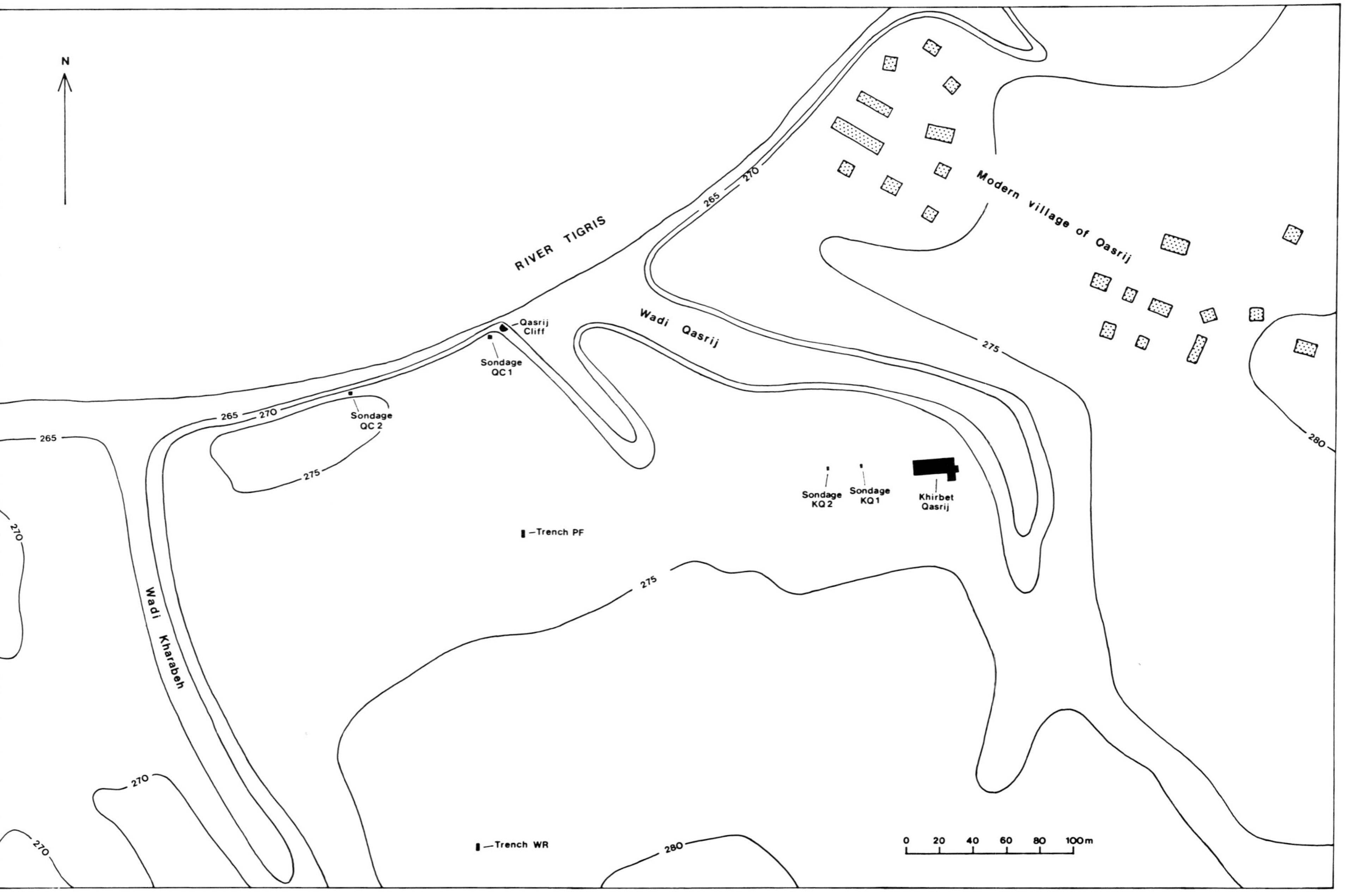

Fig. 3. The sites of Qasrij Cliff and Khirbet Qasrij

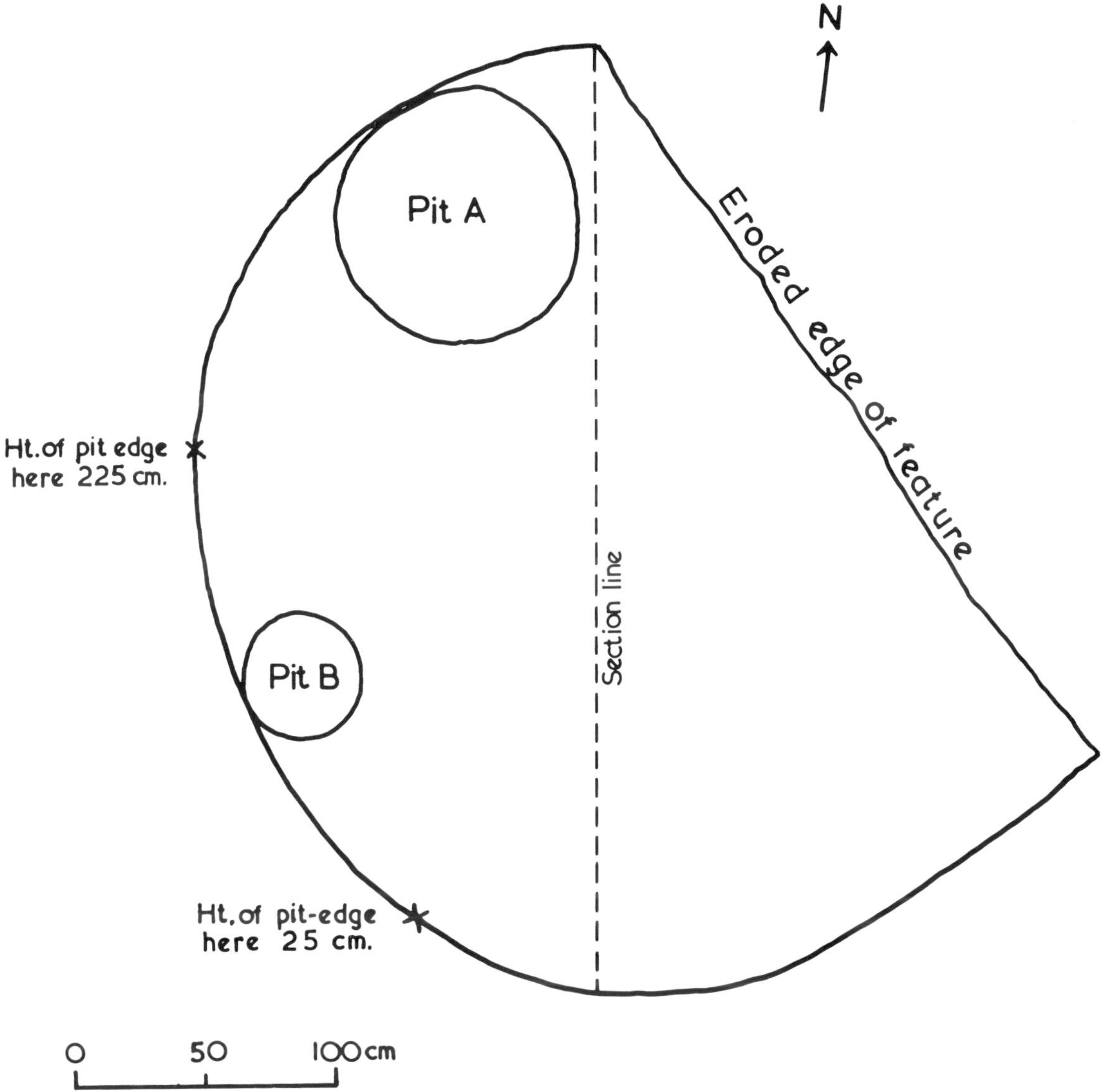

Fig. 4. Ground-plan of pit at Qasrij Cliff

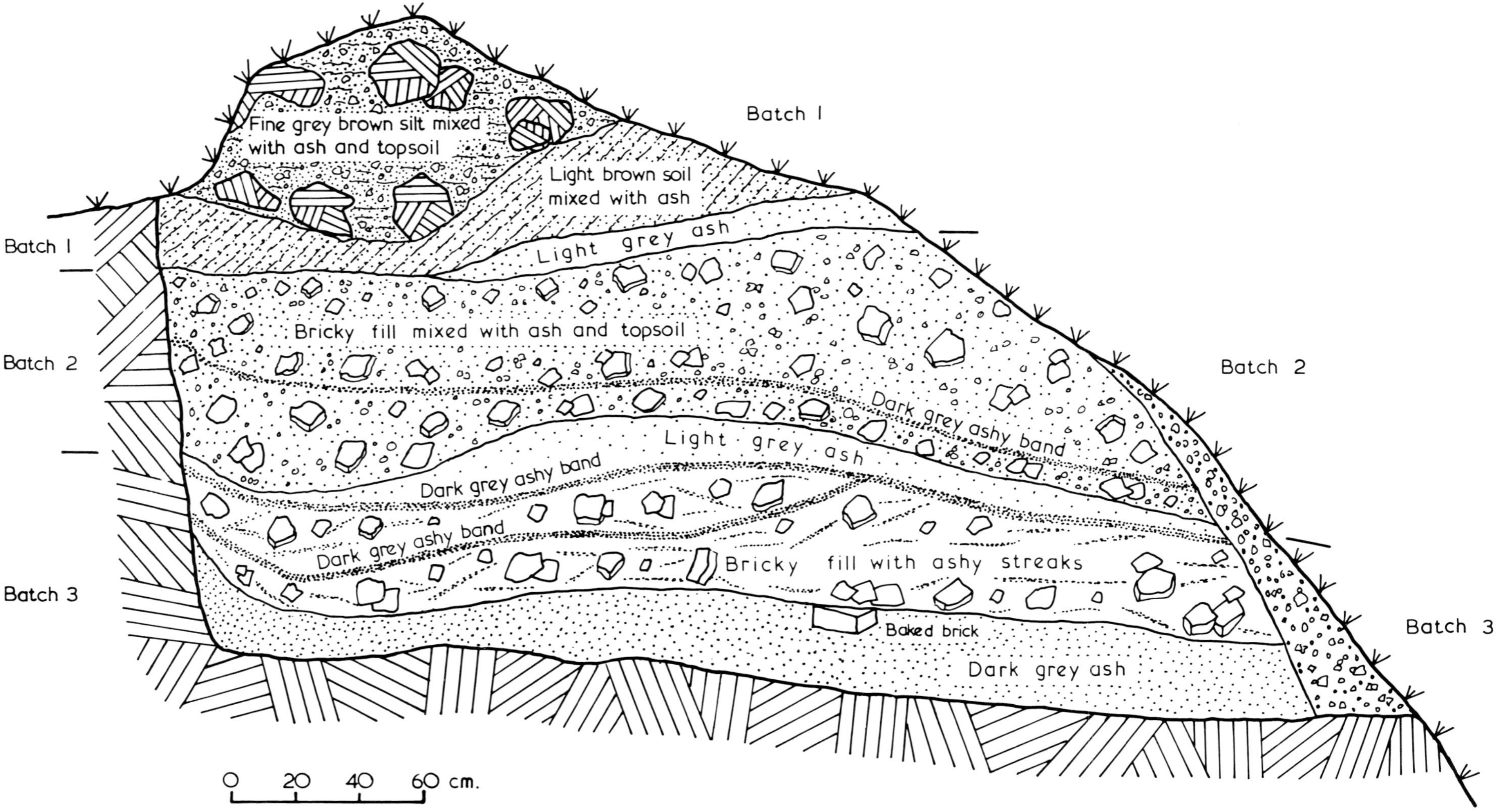

Fig. 5. Section through pit at Qasrij Cliff

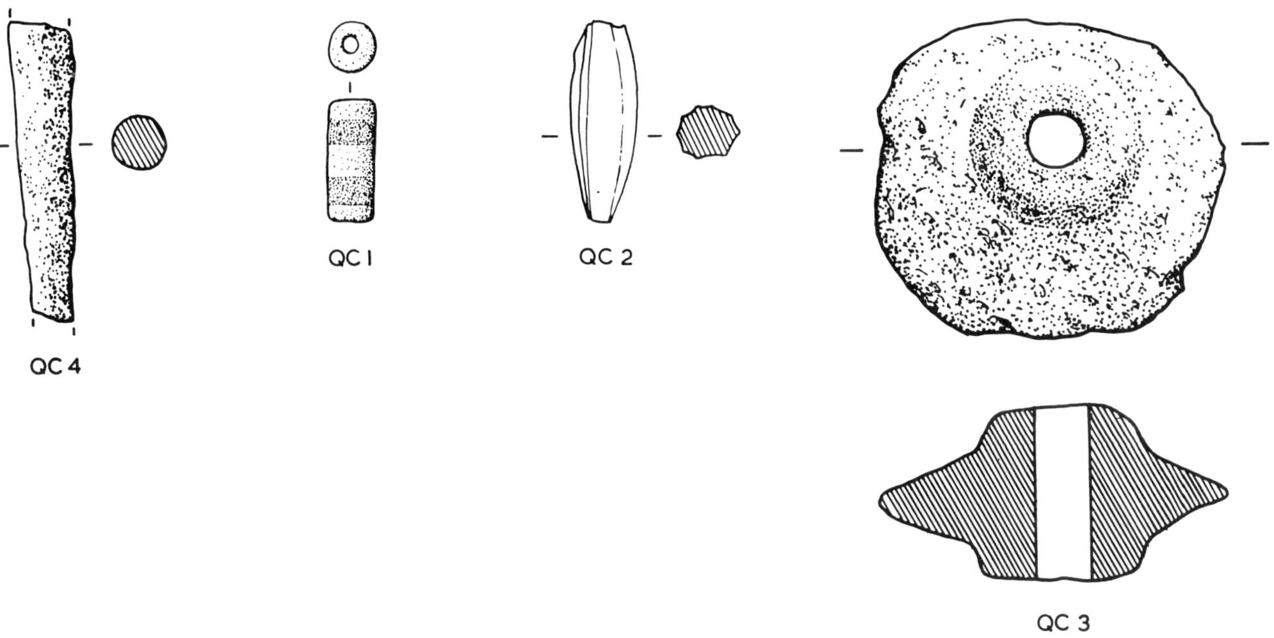

Fig. 6a. Small finds from Qasrij Cliff

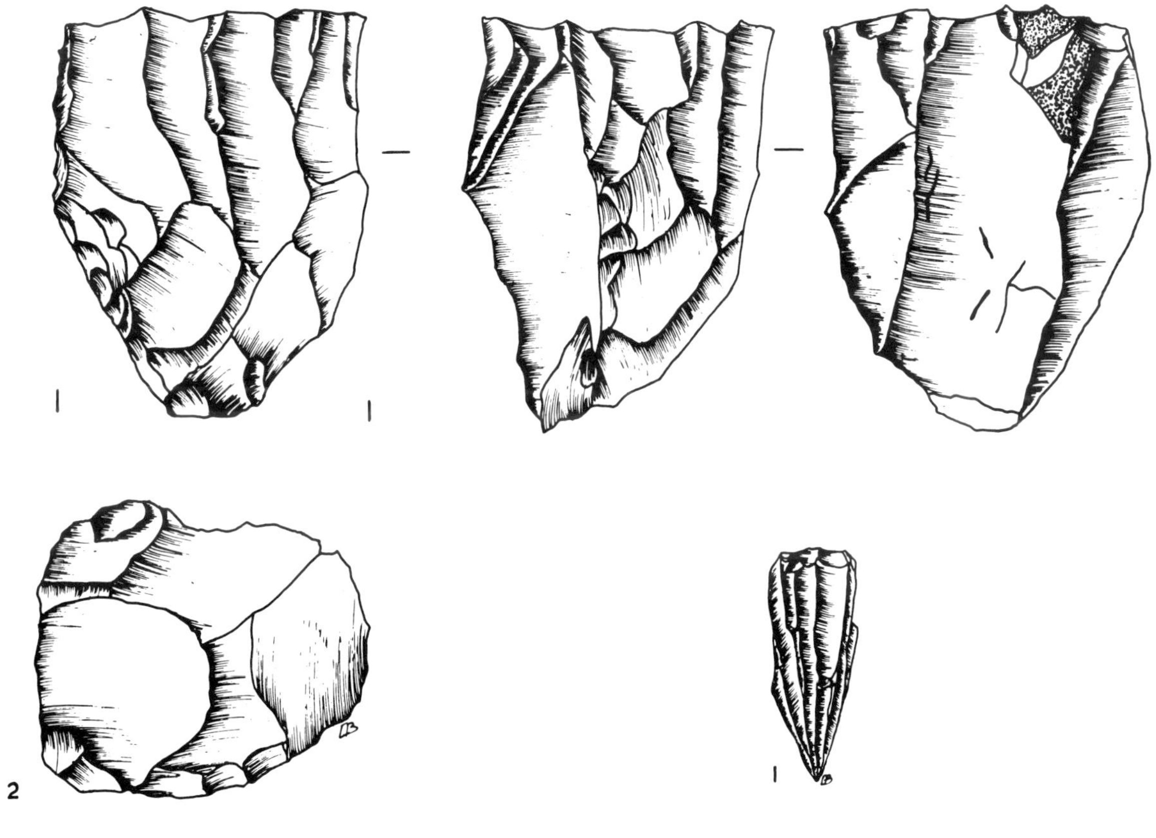

Fig. 6b. Flint cores from the vicinity of Qasrij Cliff

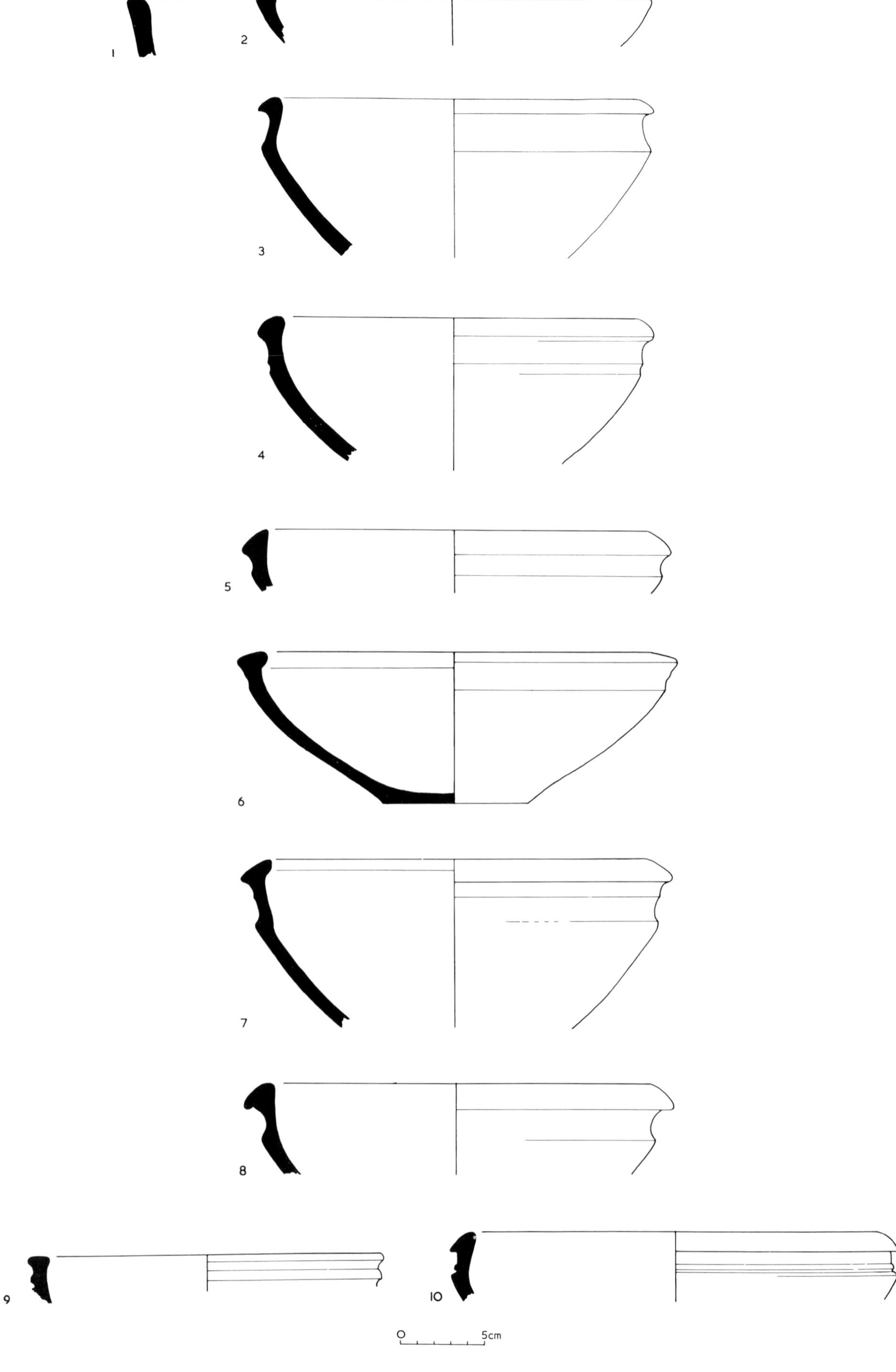

Fig. 7. Pottery from Qasrij Cliff. Scale 1:3

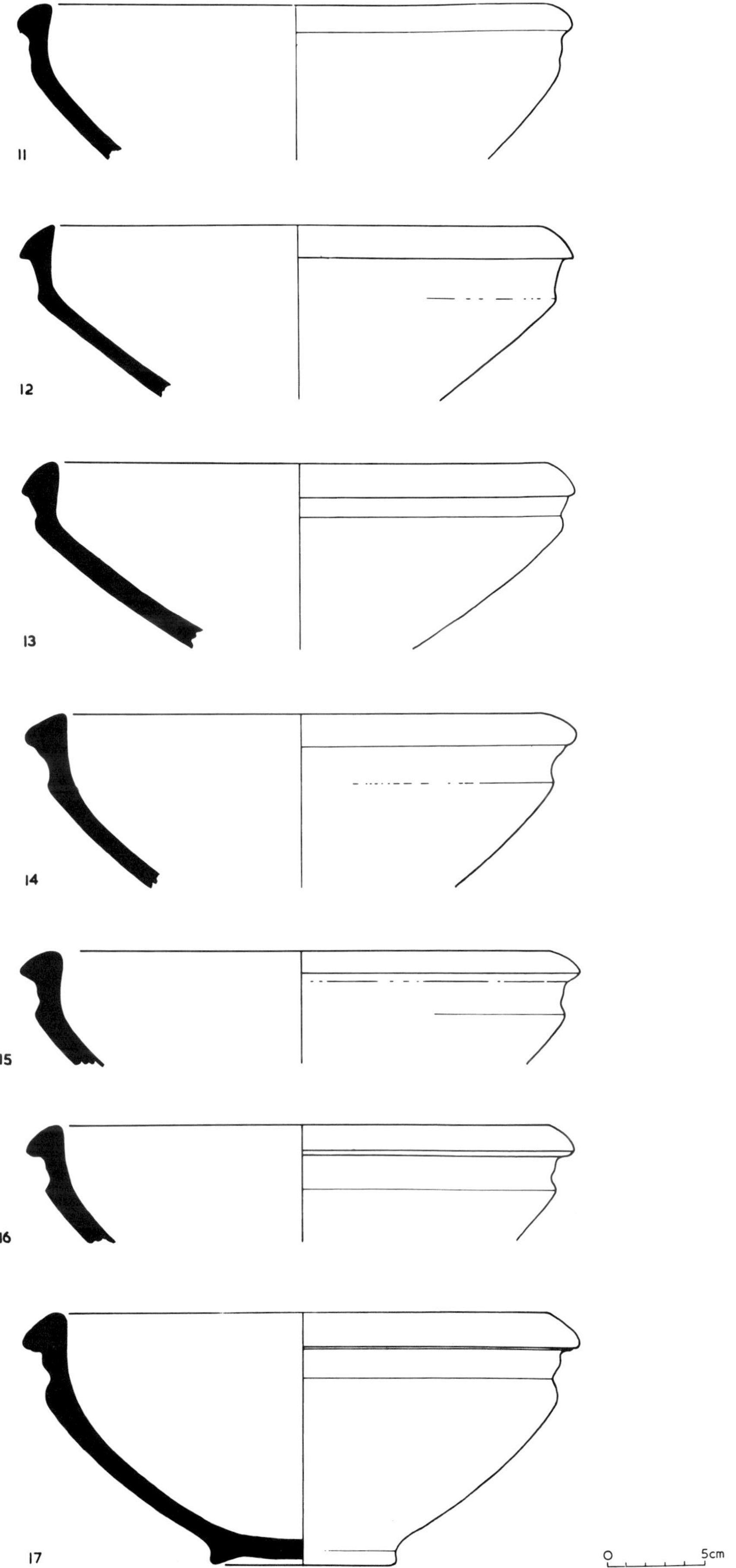

Fig. 8. Pottery from Qasrij Cliff. Scale 1:3

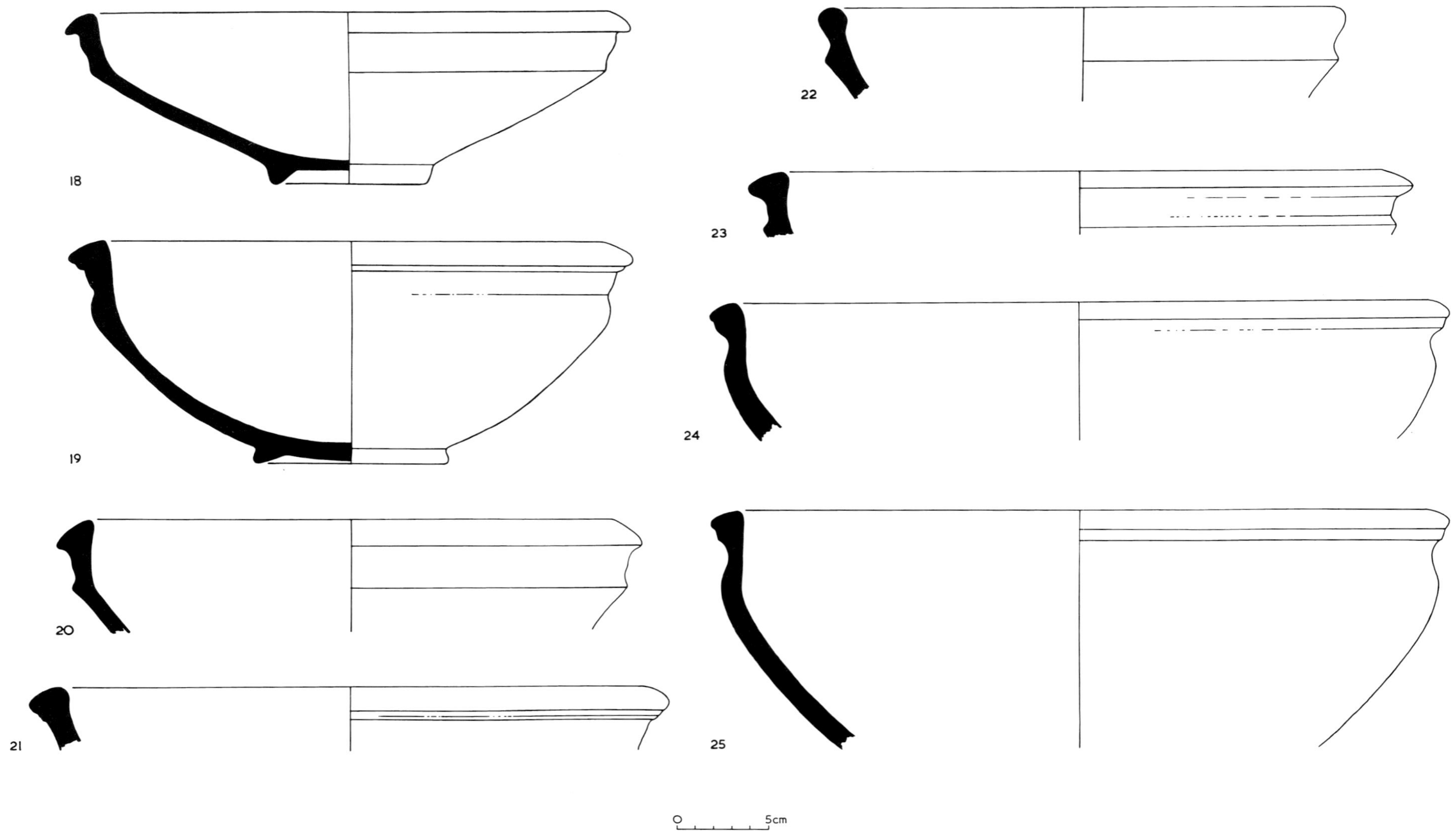

Fig. 9. Pottery from Qasrij Cliff. Scale 1:3

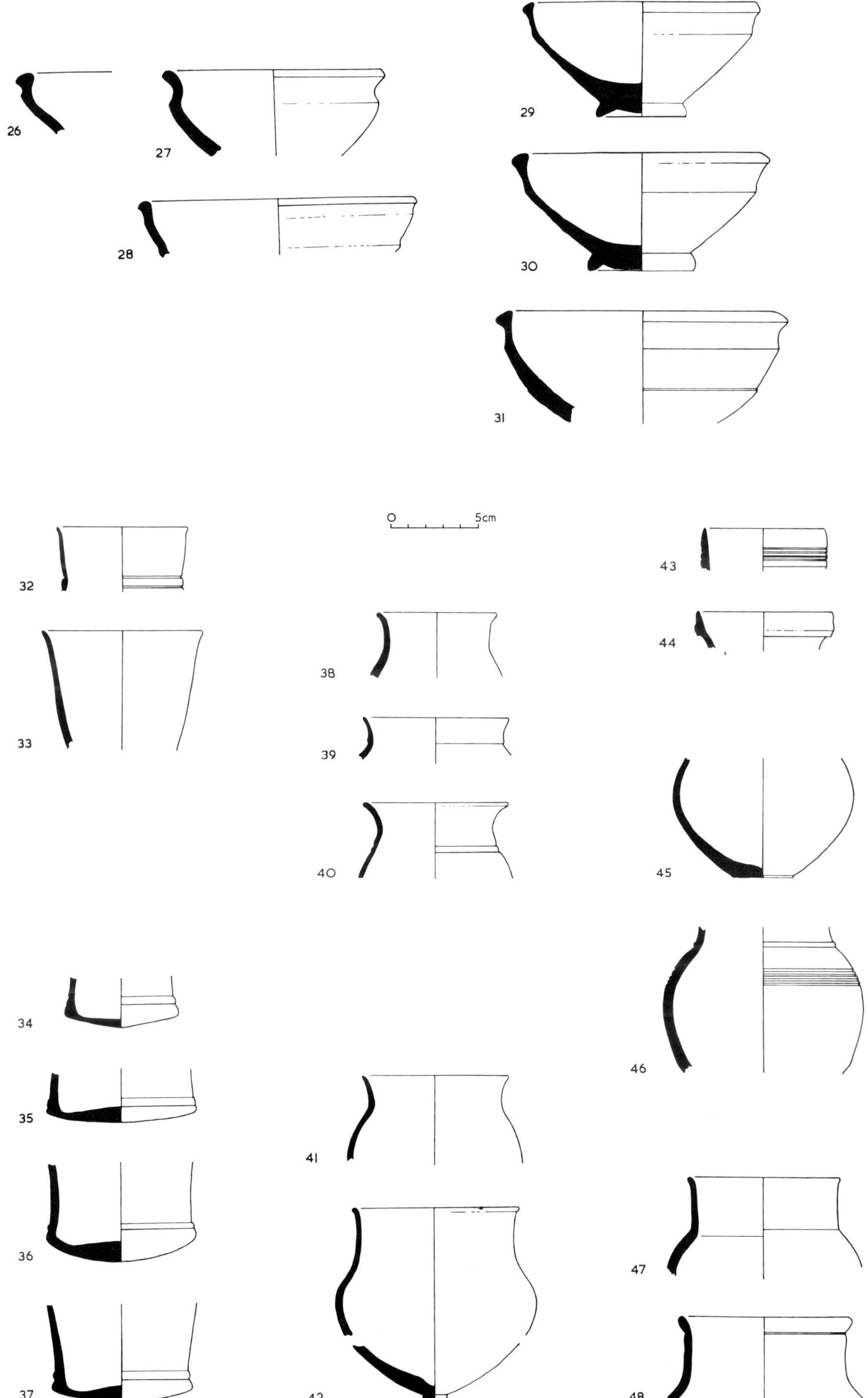

Fig. 10. Pottery from Qasrij Cliff. Scale 1:3

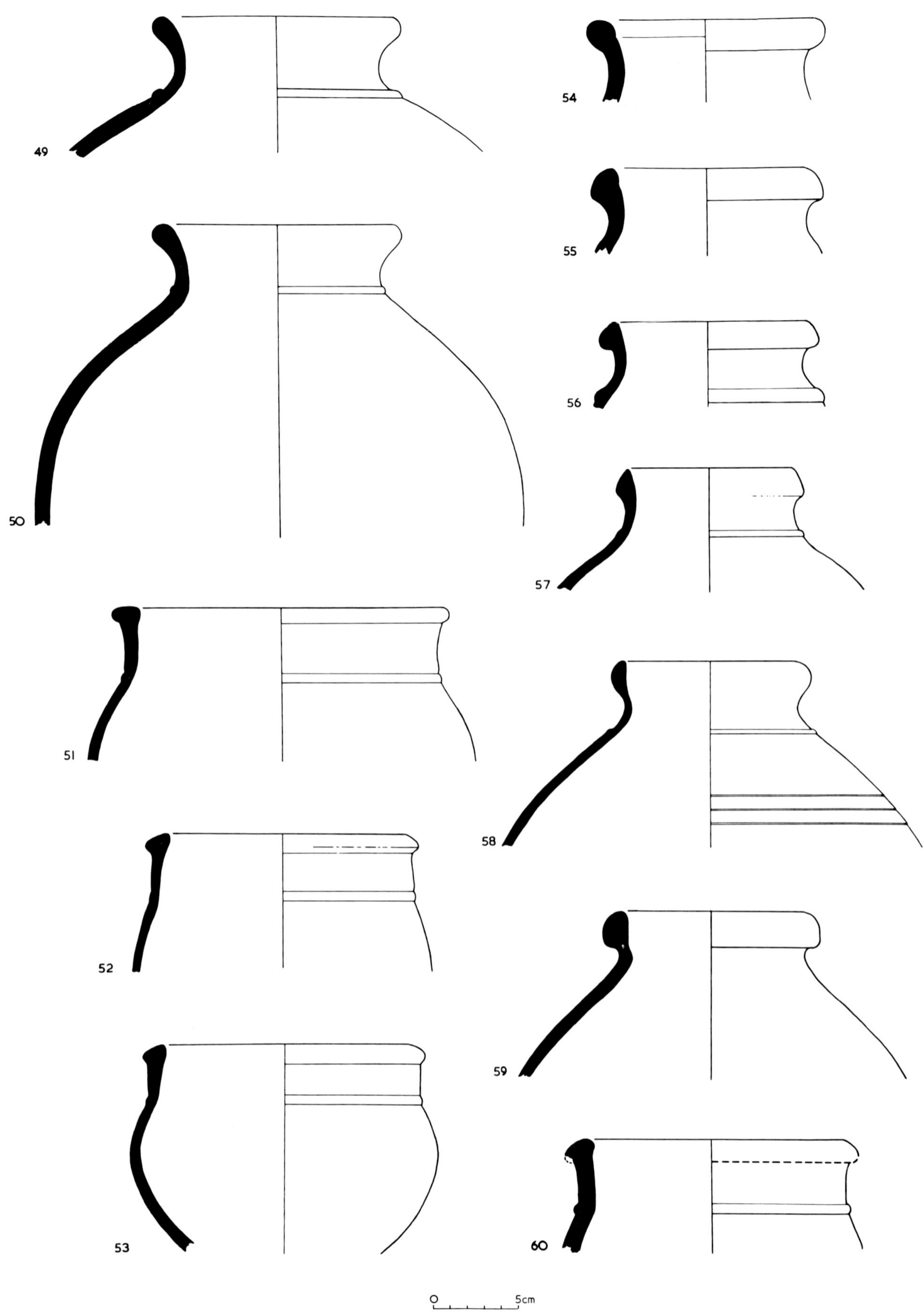

Fig. 11. Pottery from Qasrij Cliff. Scale 1:3

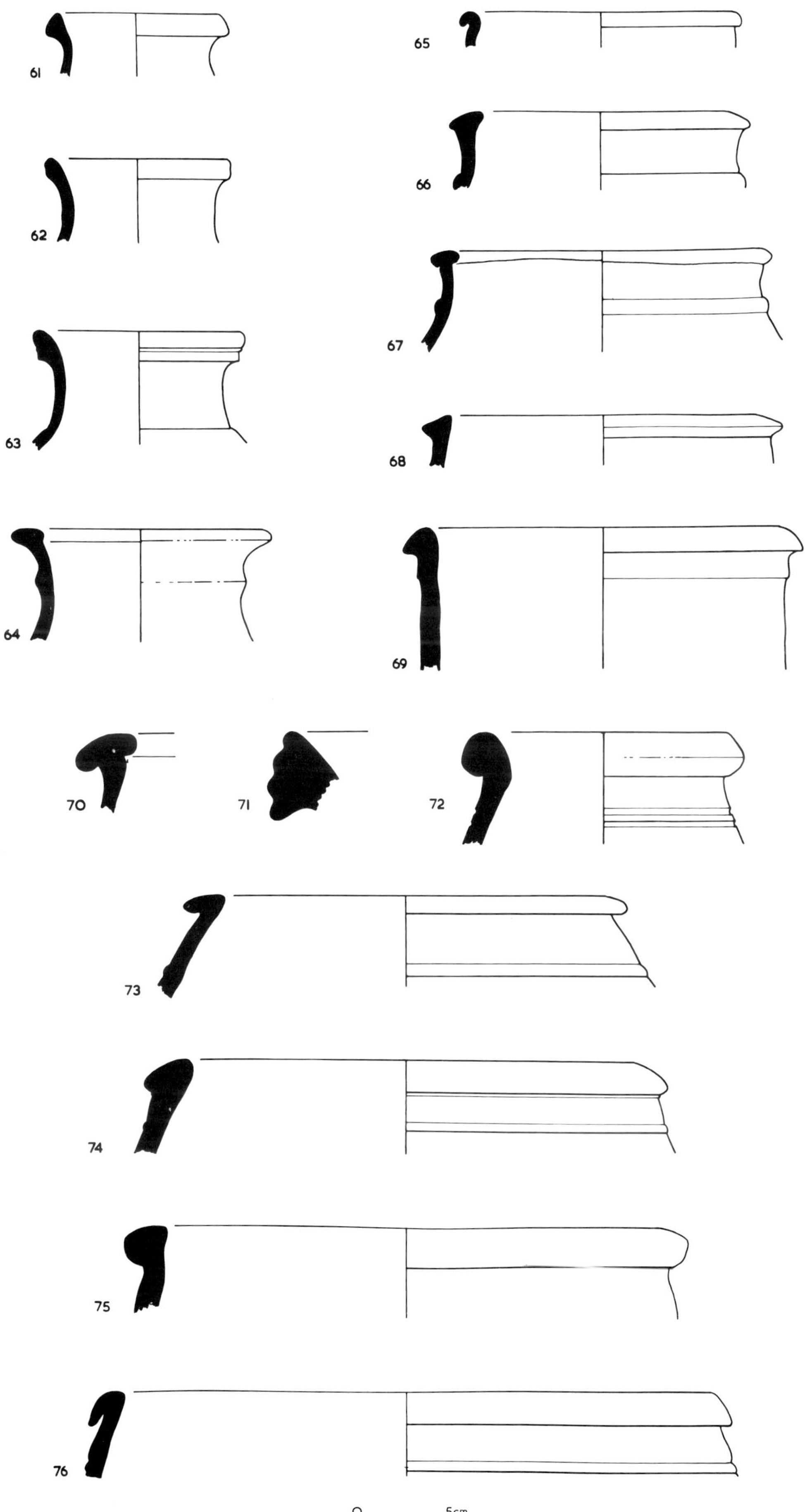

Fig. 12. Pottery from Qasrij Cliff. Scale 1:3

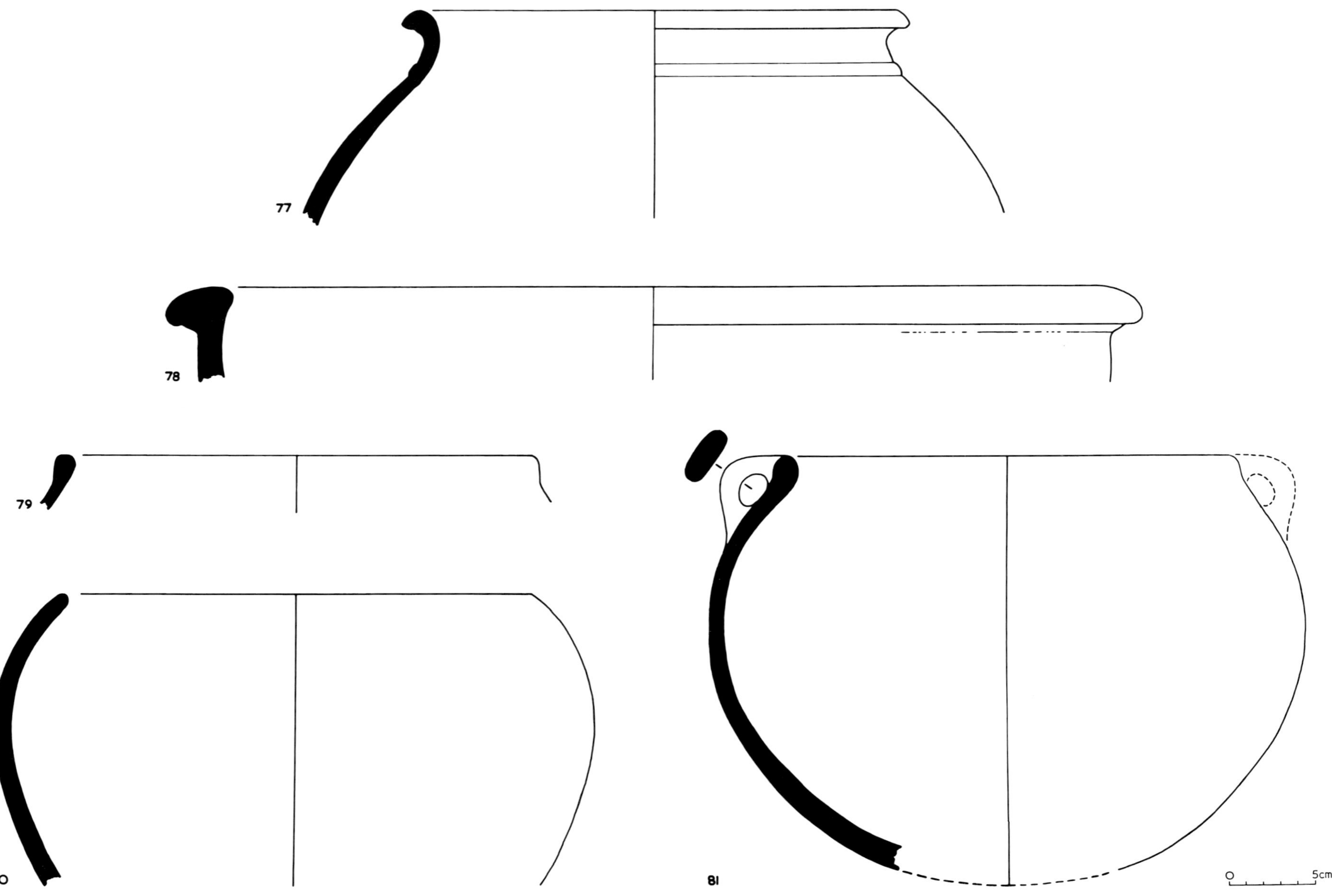

Fig. 13. Pottery from Qasrij Cliff. Scale 1:3

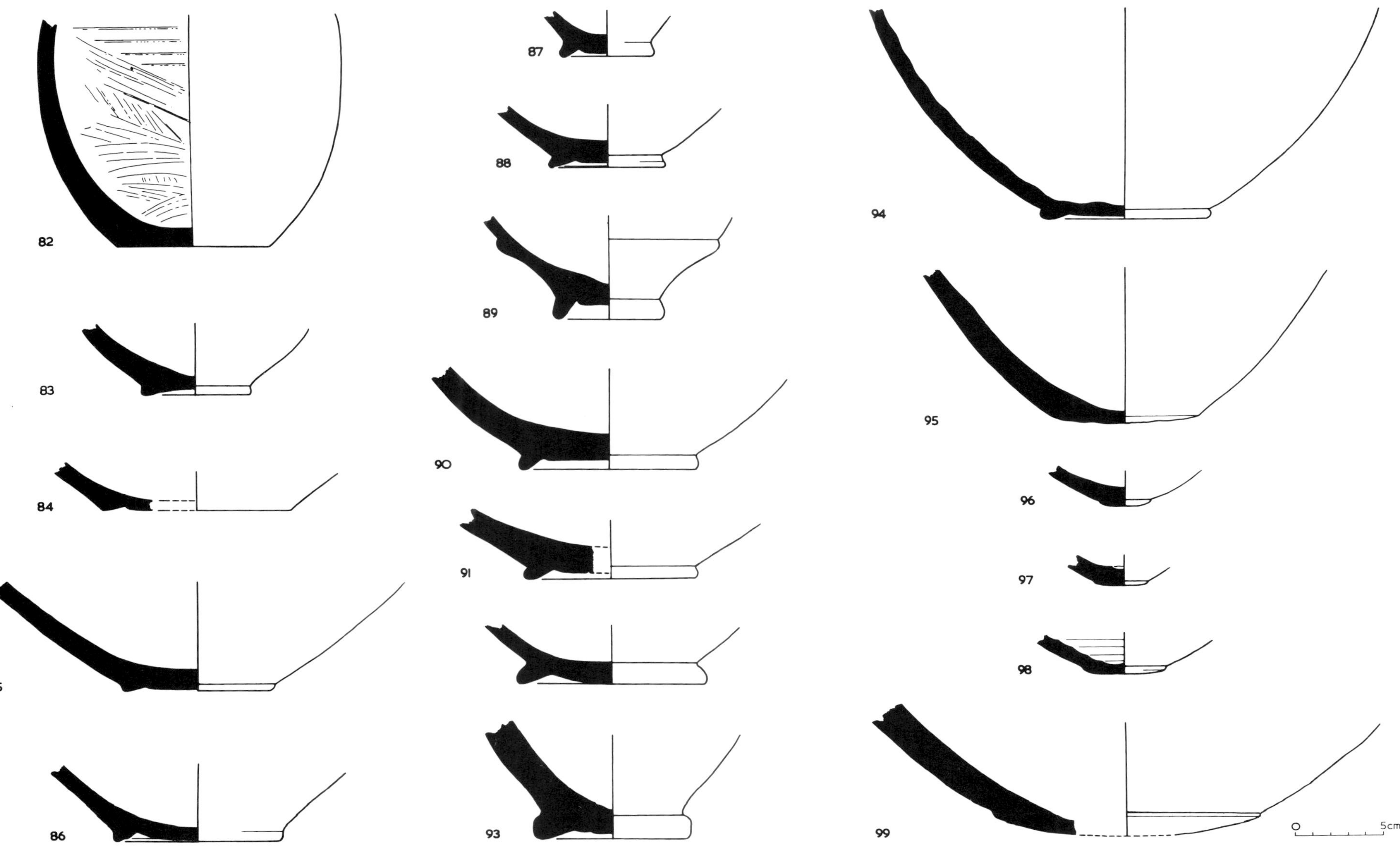

Fig. 14. Pottery from Qasrij Cliff. Scale 1:3

Fig. 15. West part of main excavated area, Khirbet Qasrij

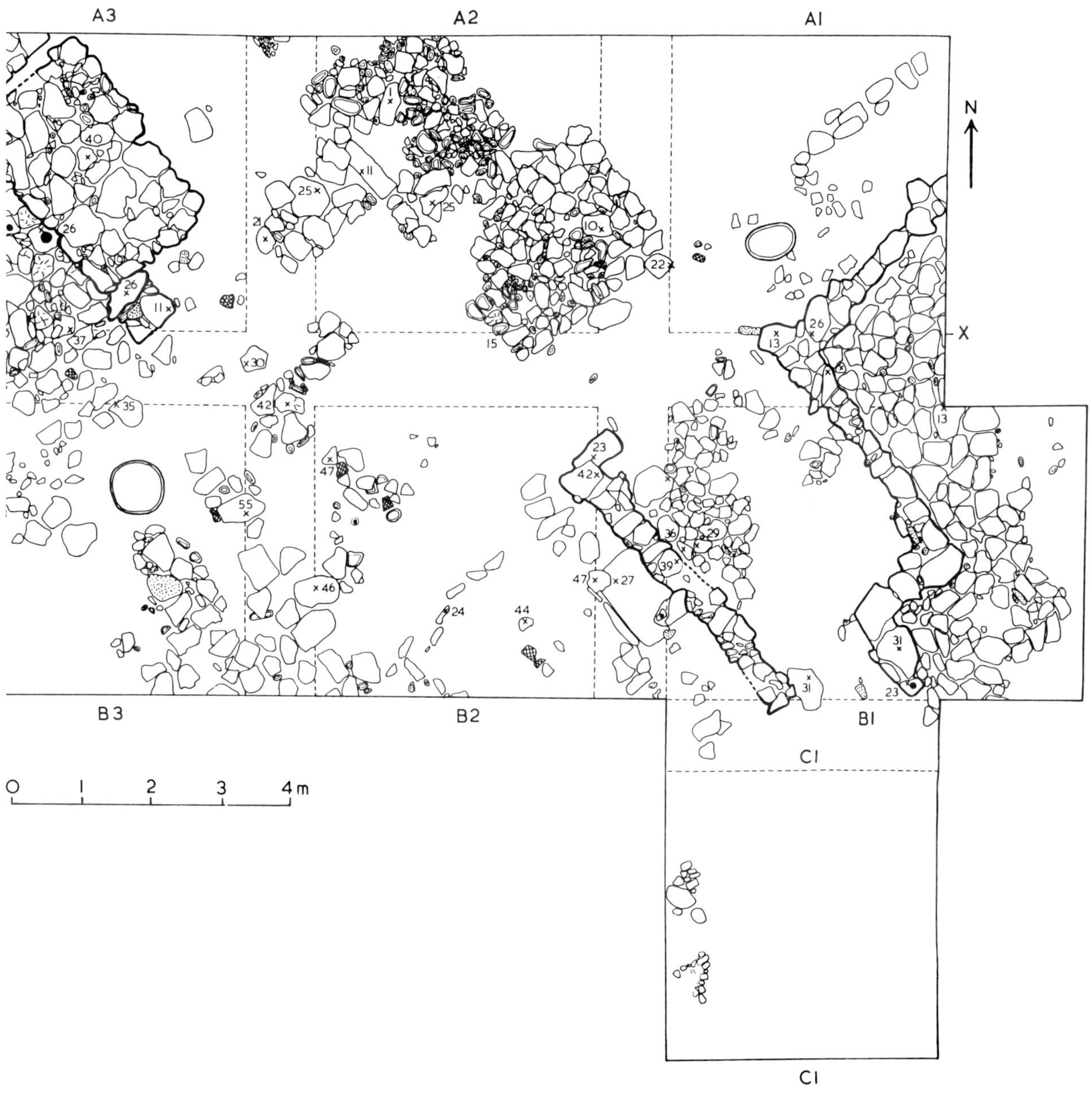

Fig. 16. East part of main excavated area, Khirbet Qasrij

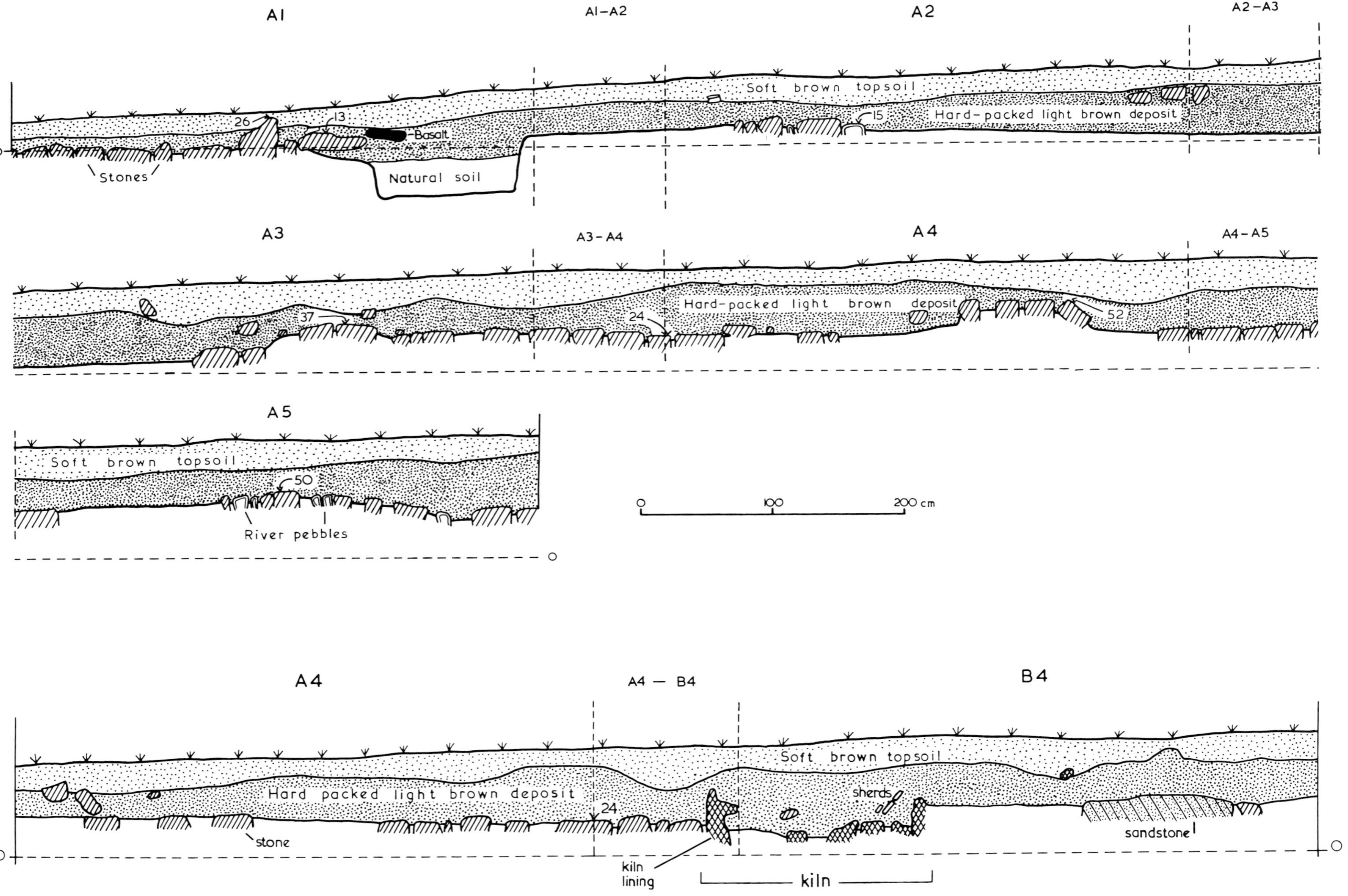

Fig. 17. Sections X-Y (top) and V-W (bottom) through main part of excavated area at Khirbet Qasrij

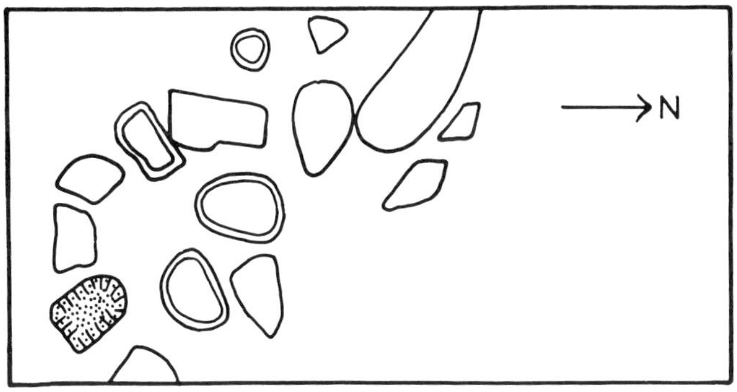

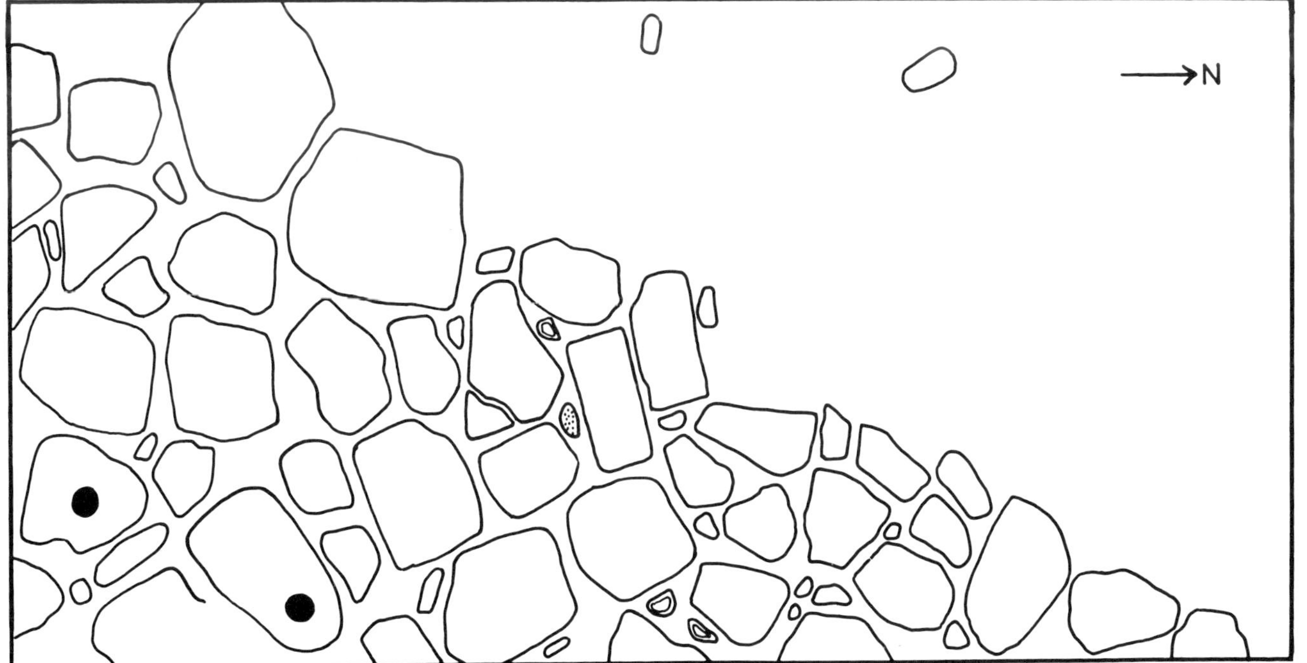

Fig. 18a. Trench KQ1, Khirbet Qasrij

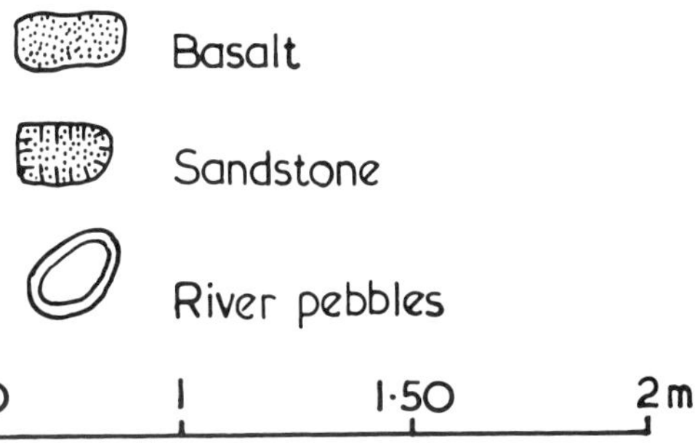

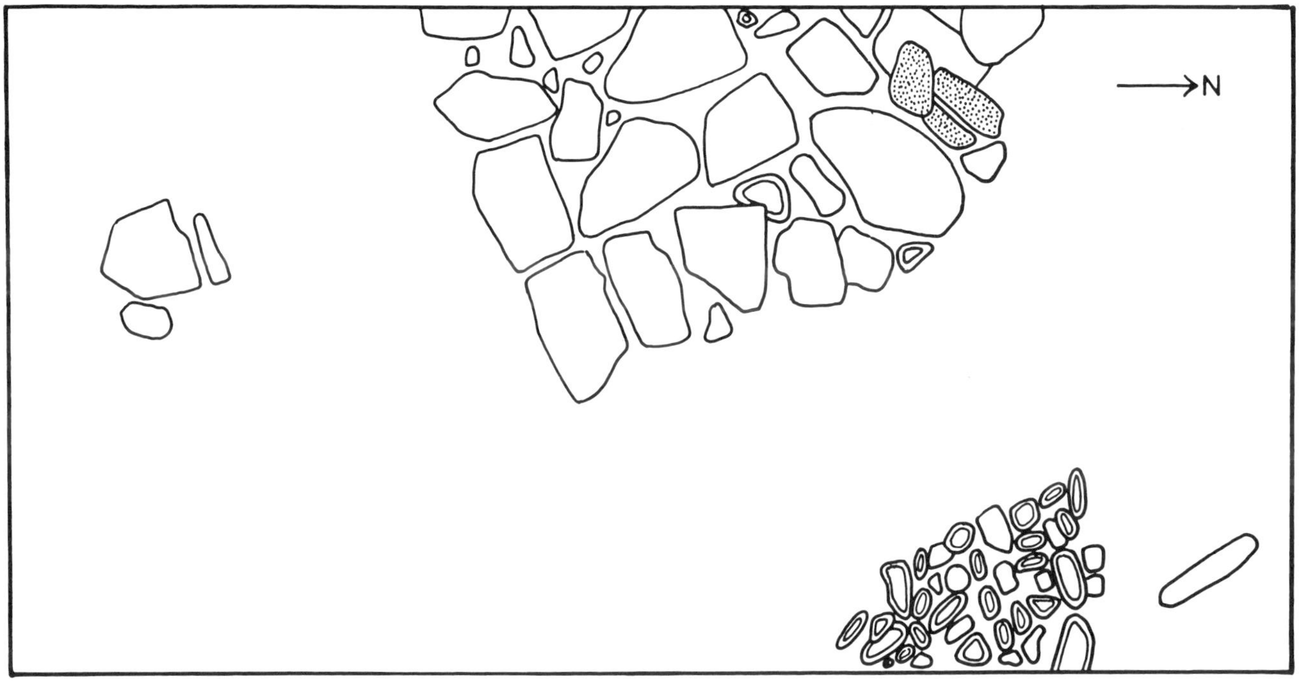

Fig. 18c. Trench WR, Khirbet Qasrij

Fig. 18b. Trench PF, Khirbet Qasrij

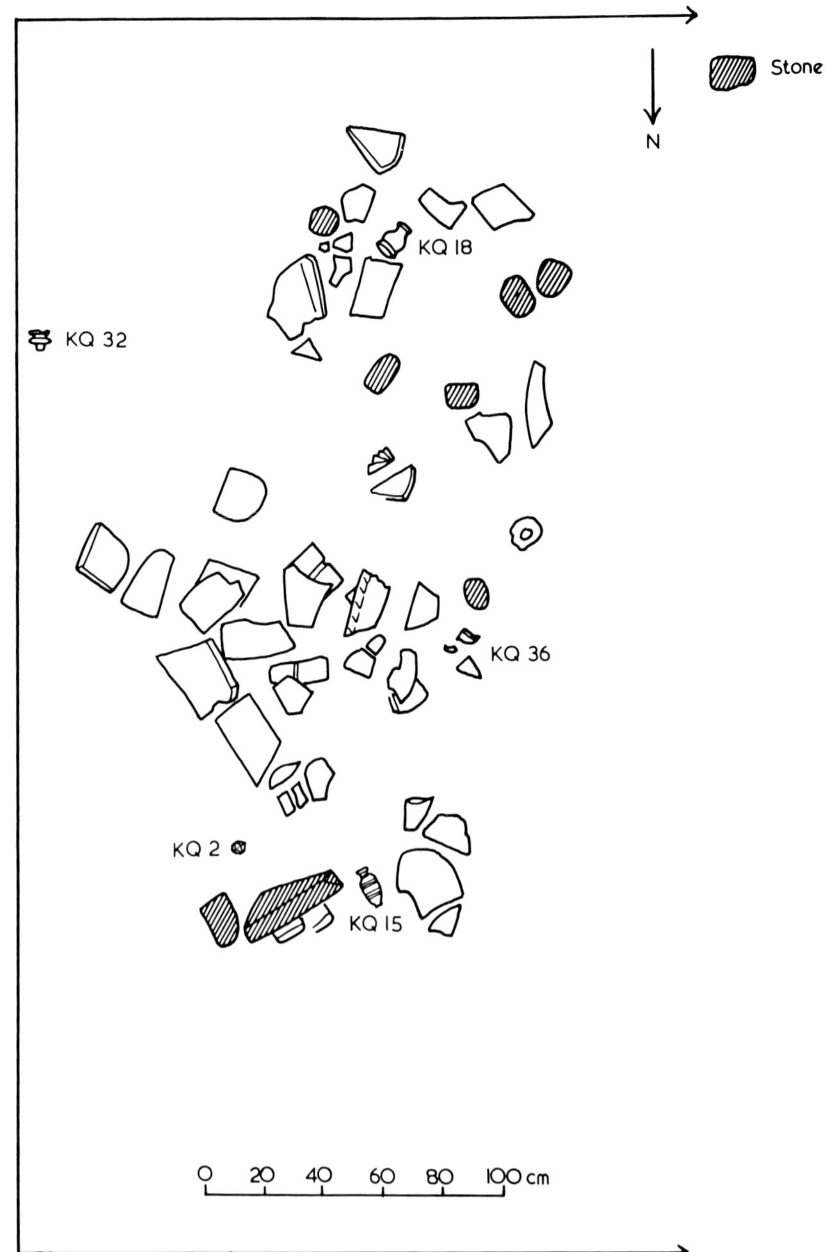

Fig. 19a. Sherd scatter in east part of trench A2, Khirbet Qasrij

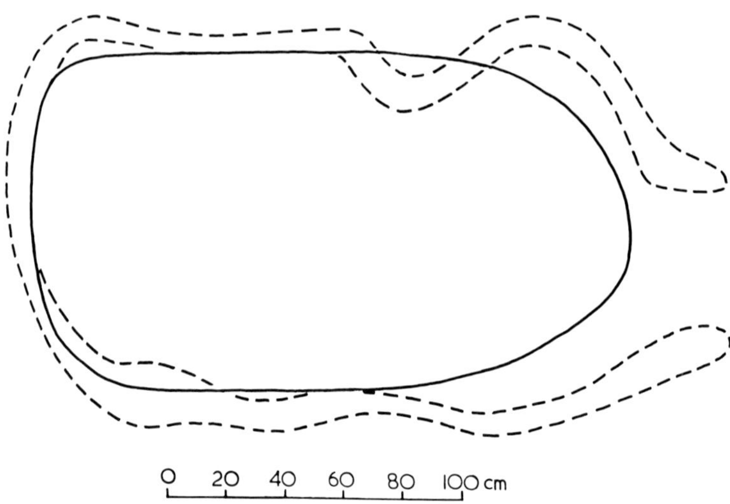

Fig. 19b. Outline of kiln at top (dotted line) and bottom (continuous line) of
fire-pit, Khirbet Qasrij

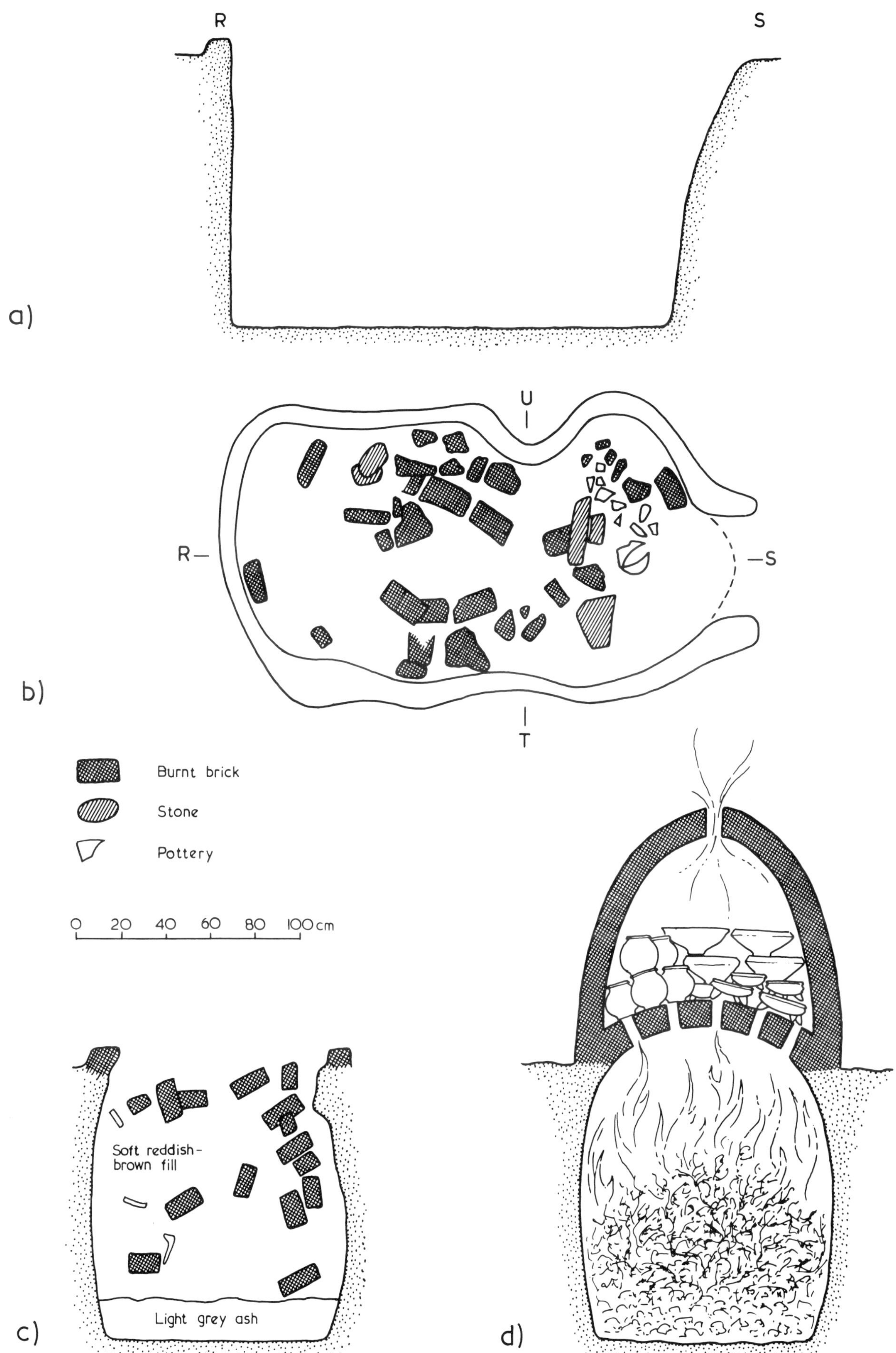

Figs 20a-d. Plan of kiln at Khirbet Qasrij, showing filling of rubble and pottery (b), sections through kiln (a, c), and hypothetical reconstruction (d)

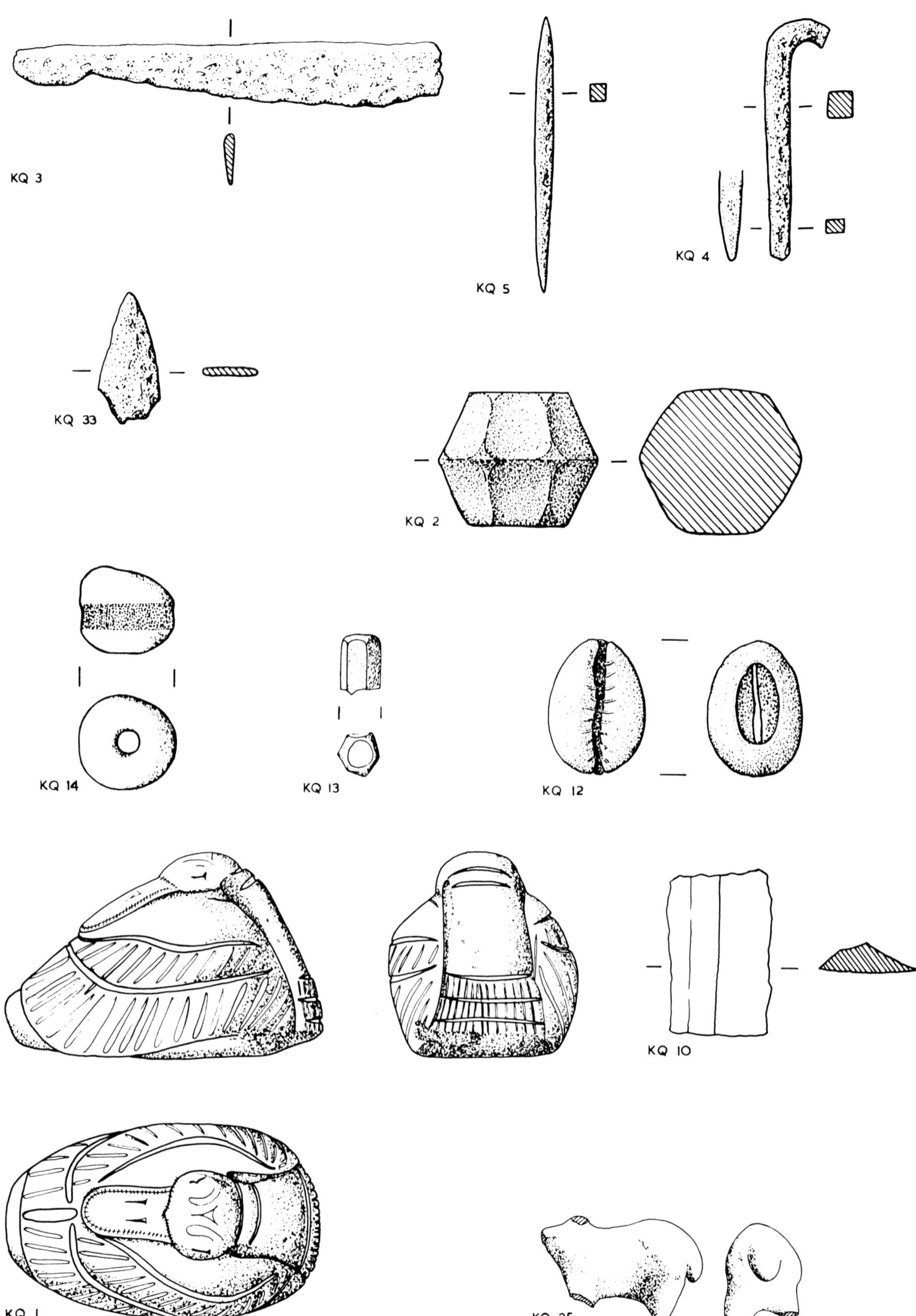

Fig. 21. Small finds from Khirbet Qasrij. Scale 3:4, except KQ12-14, which are 3:2

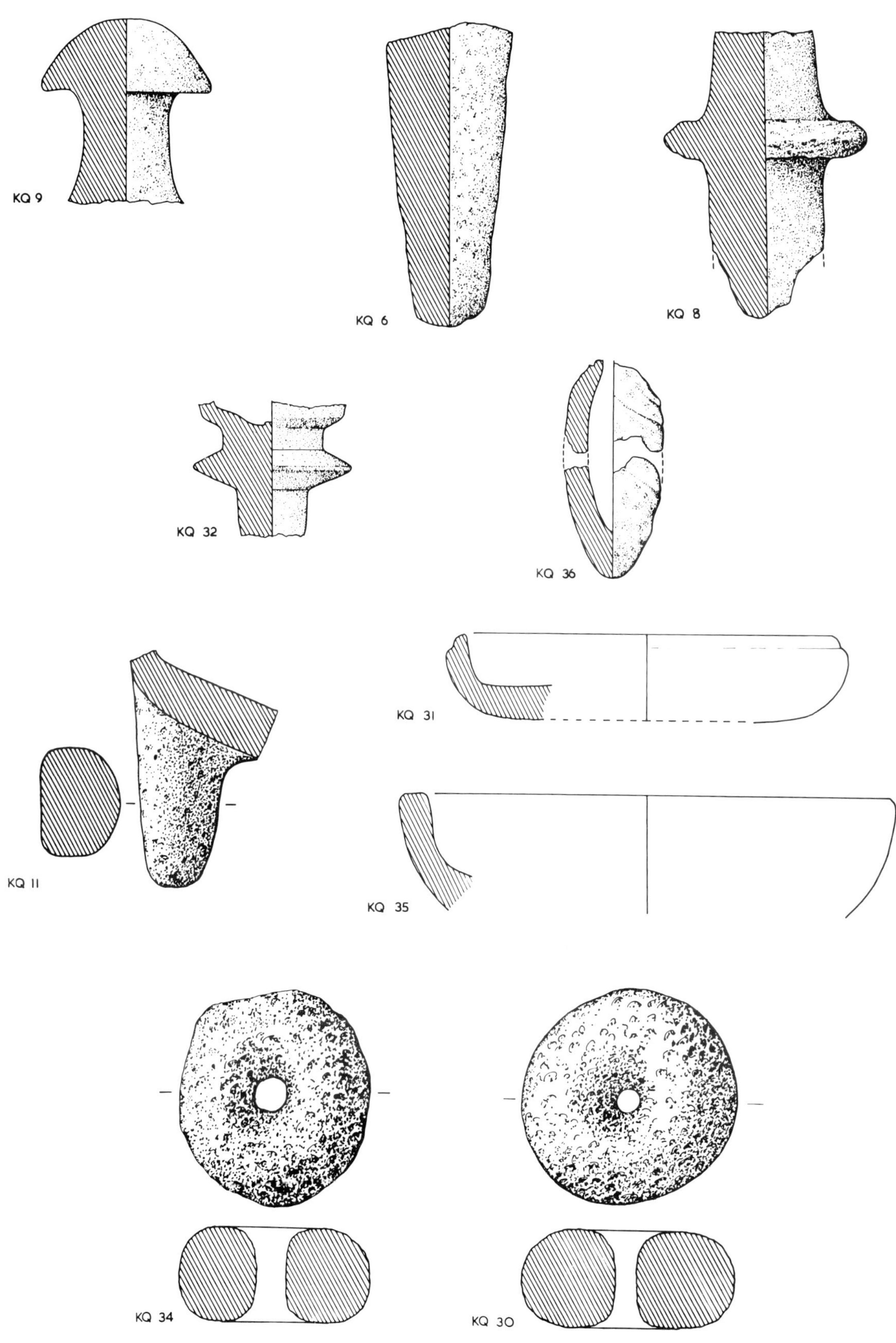

Fig. 22. Small finds from Khirbet Qasrij. Scale 1:3

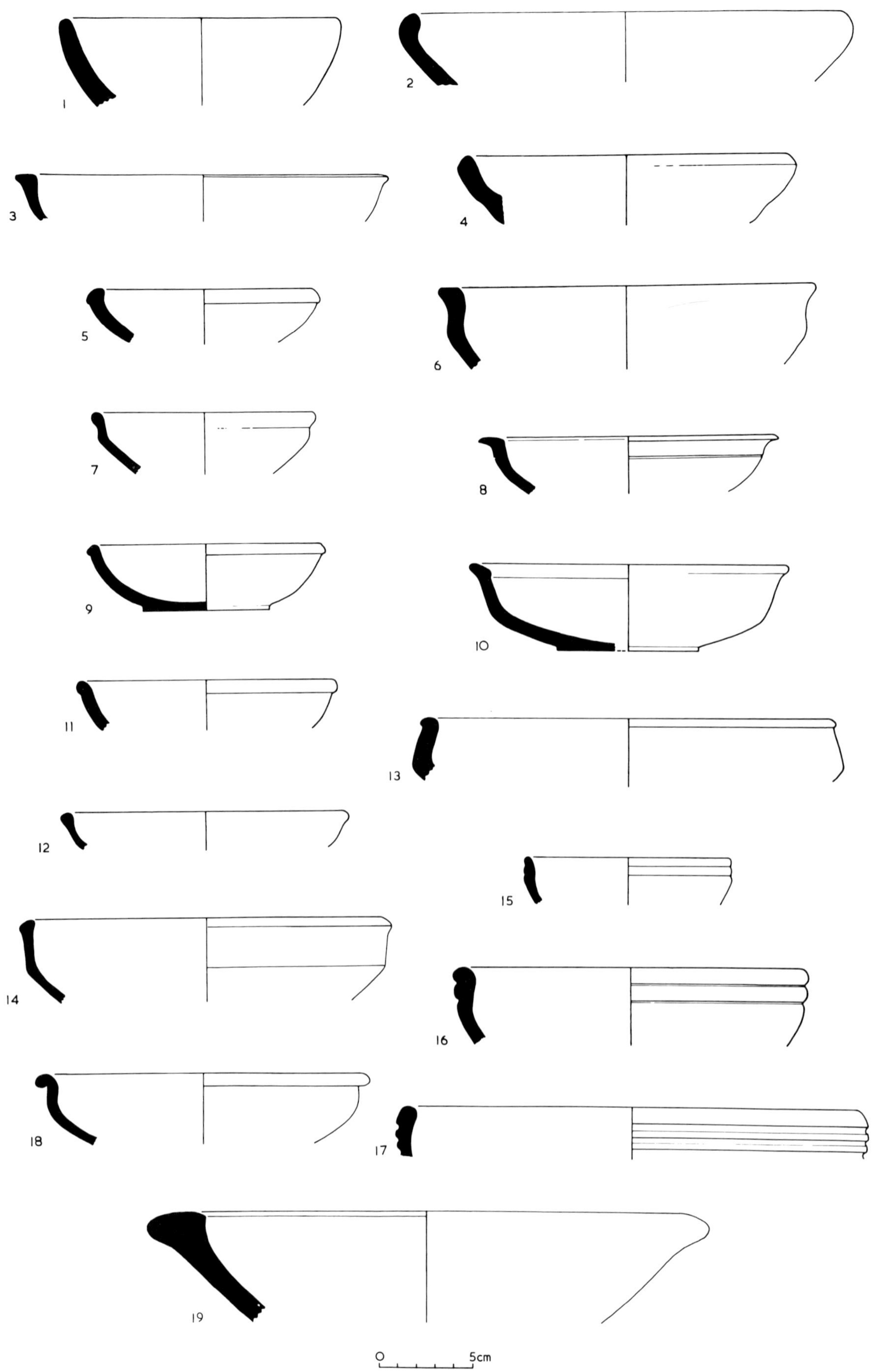

Fig. 23. Pottery from Khirbet Qasrij. Scale 1:3

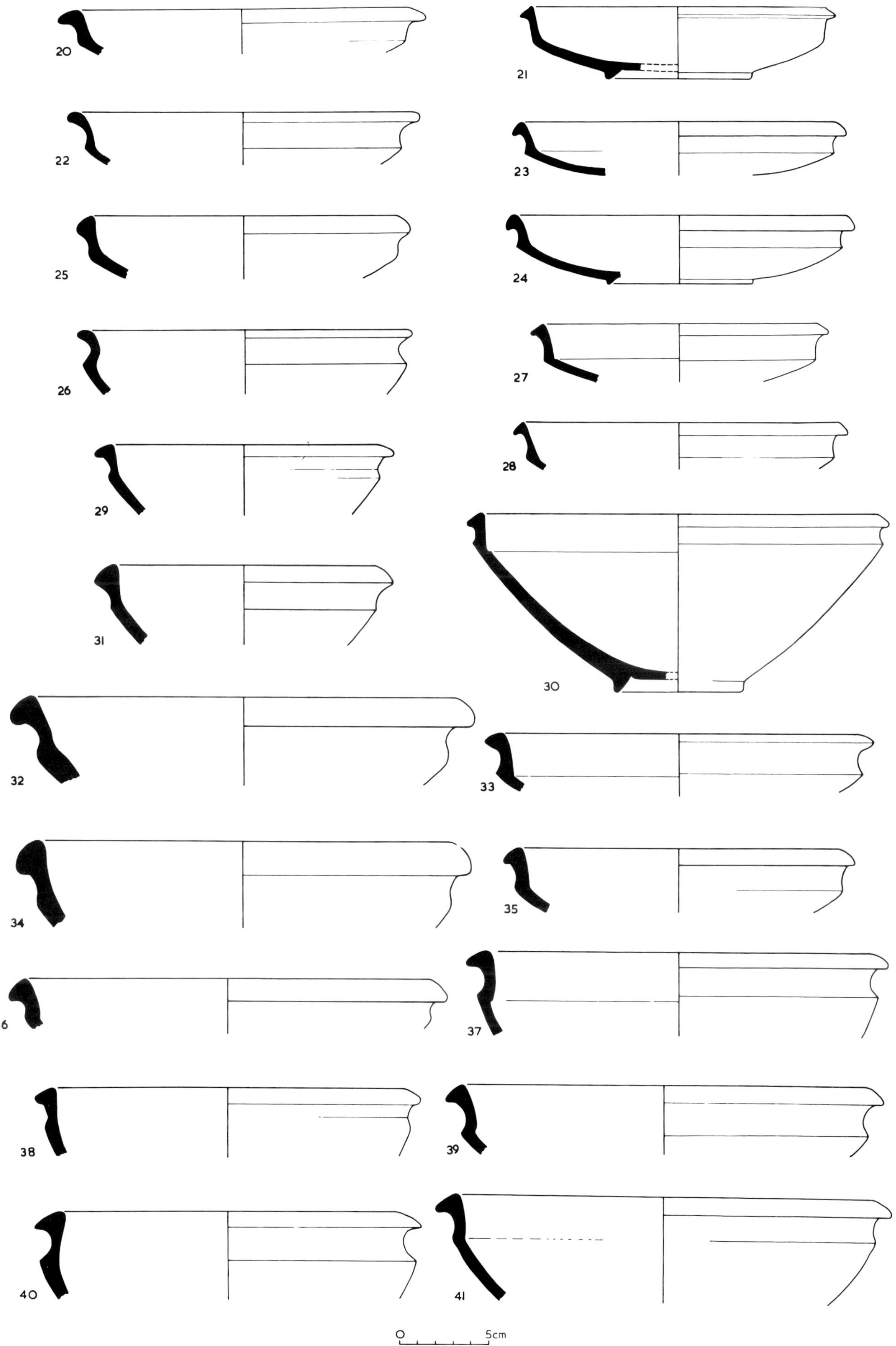

Fig. 24. Pottery from Khirbet Qasrij. Scale 1:3

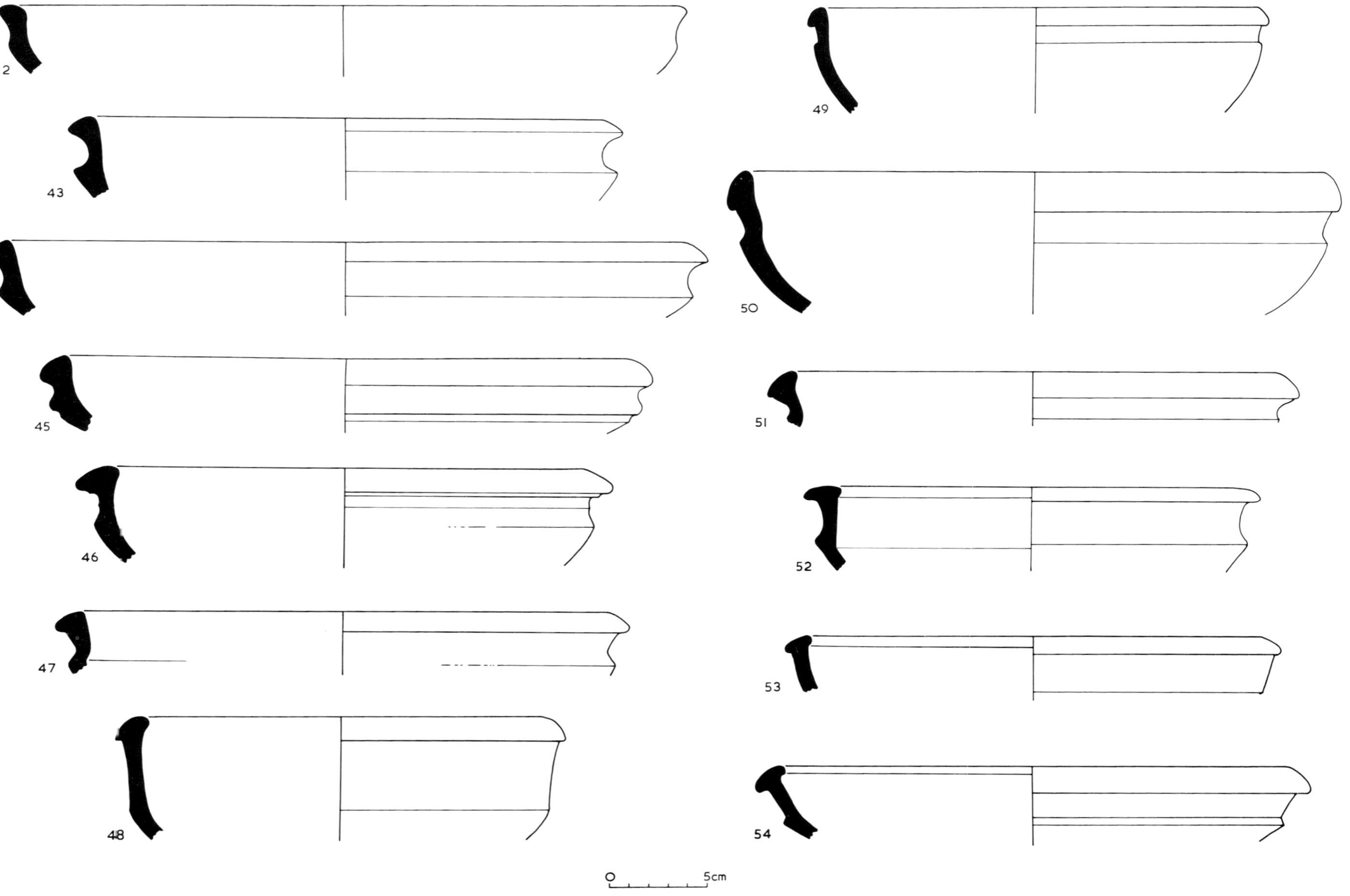

Fig. 25. Pottery from Khirbet Qasrij. Scale 1:3

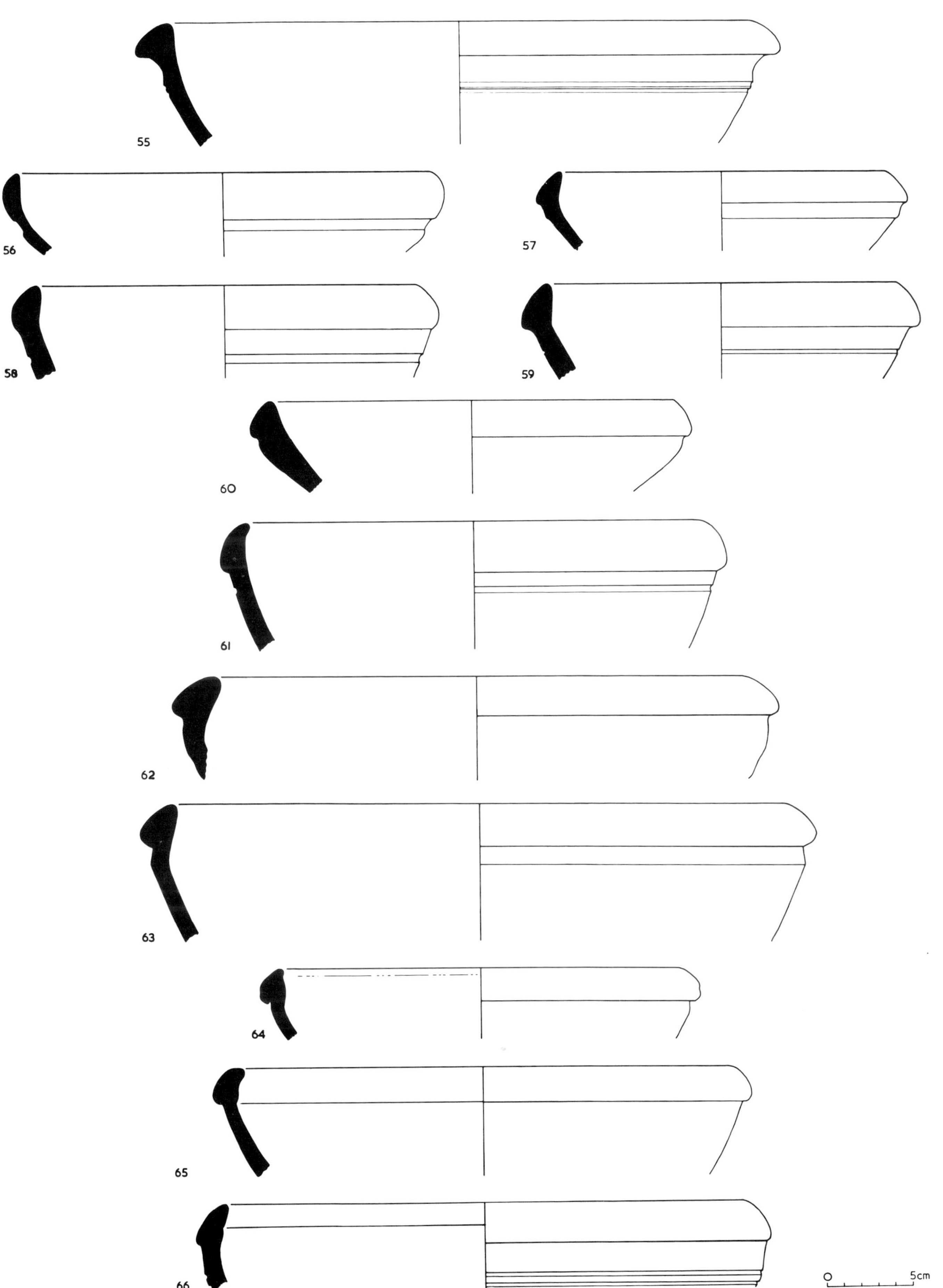

Fig. 26. Pottery from Khirbet Qasrij. Scale 1:3

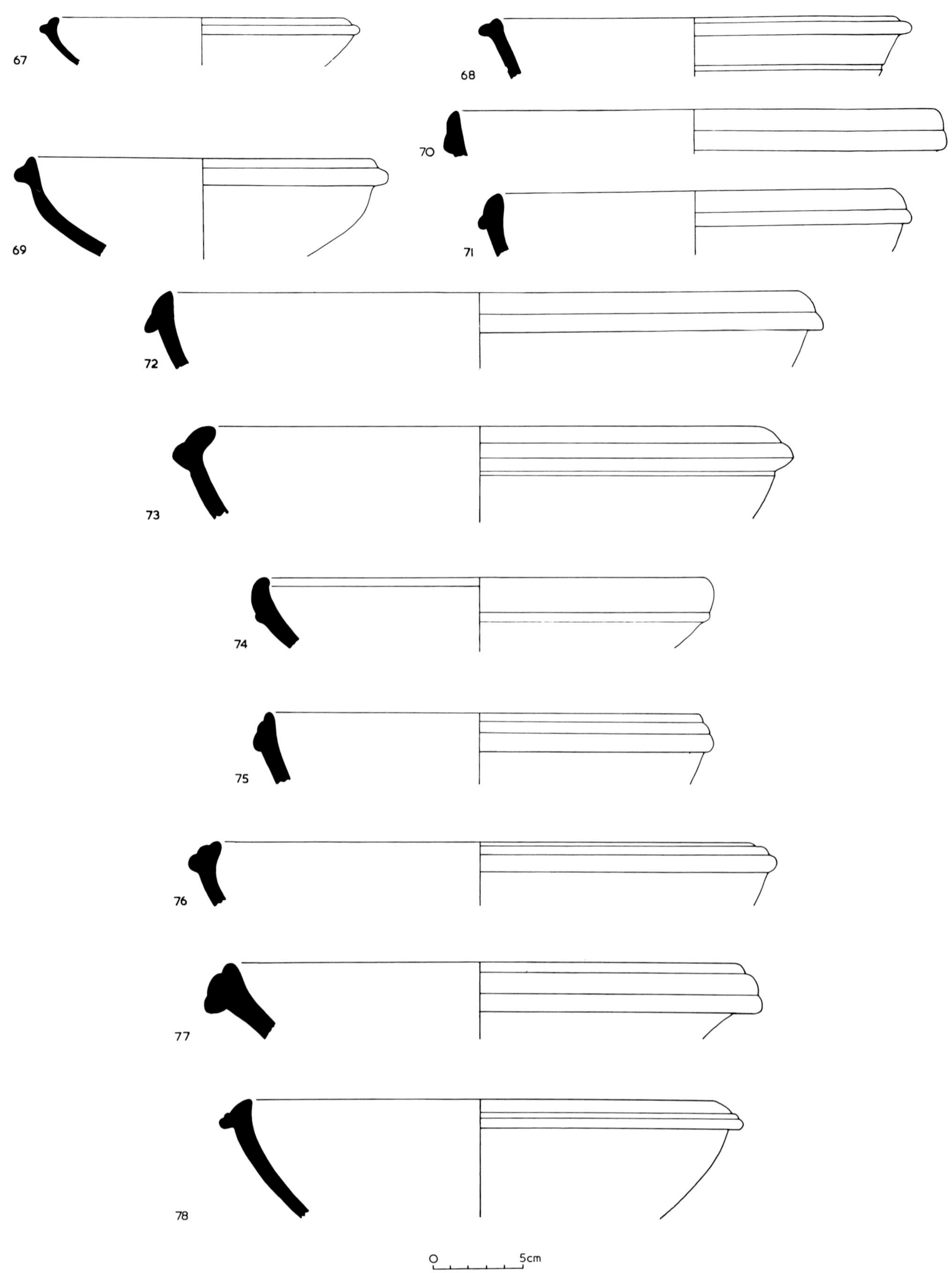

Fig. 27. Pottery from Khirbet Qasrij. Scale 1:3

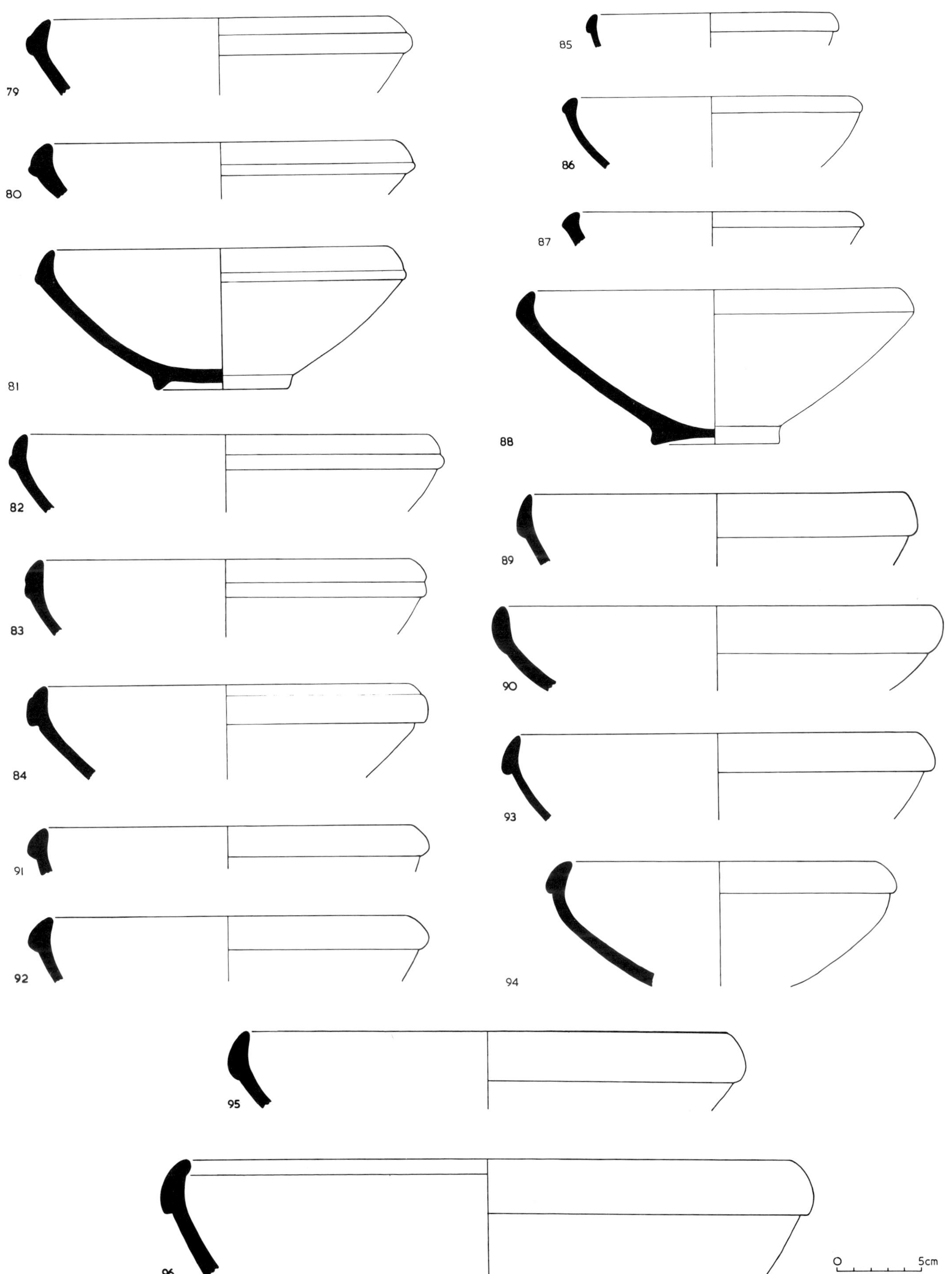

Fig. 28. Pottery from Khirbet Qasrij. Scale 1:3

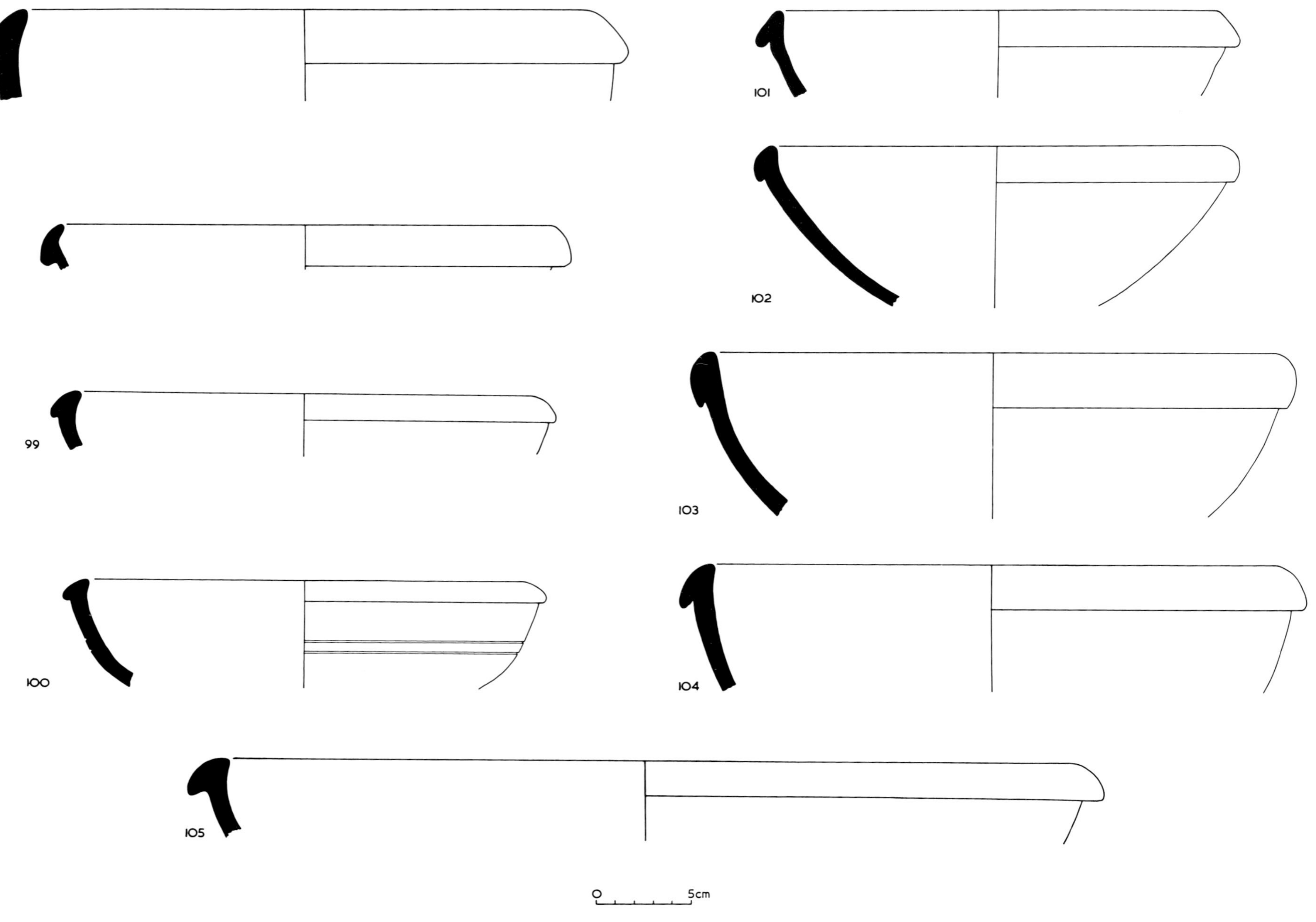

Fig. 29. Pottery from Khirbet Qasrij. Scale 1:3

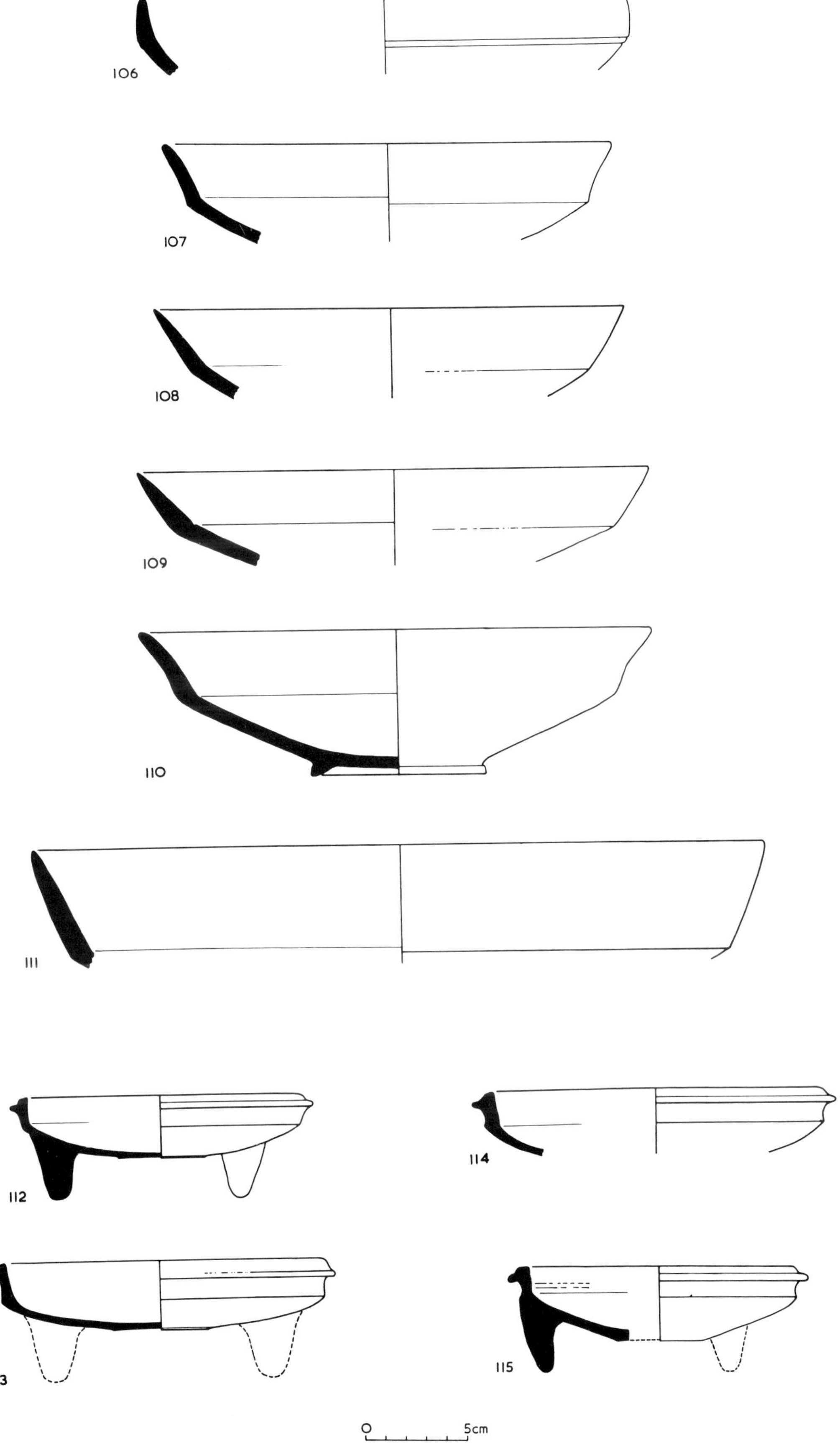

Fig. 30. Pottery from Khirbet Qasrij. Scale 1:3

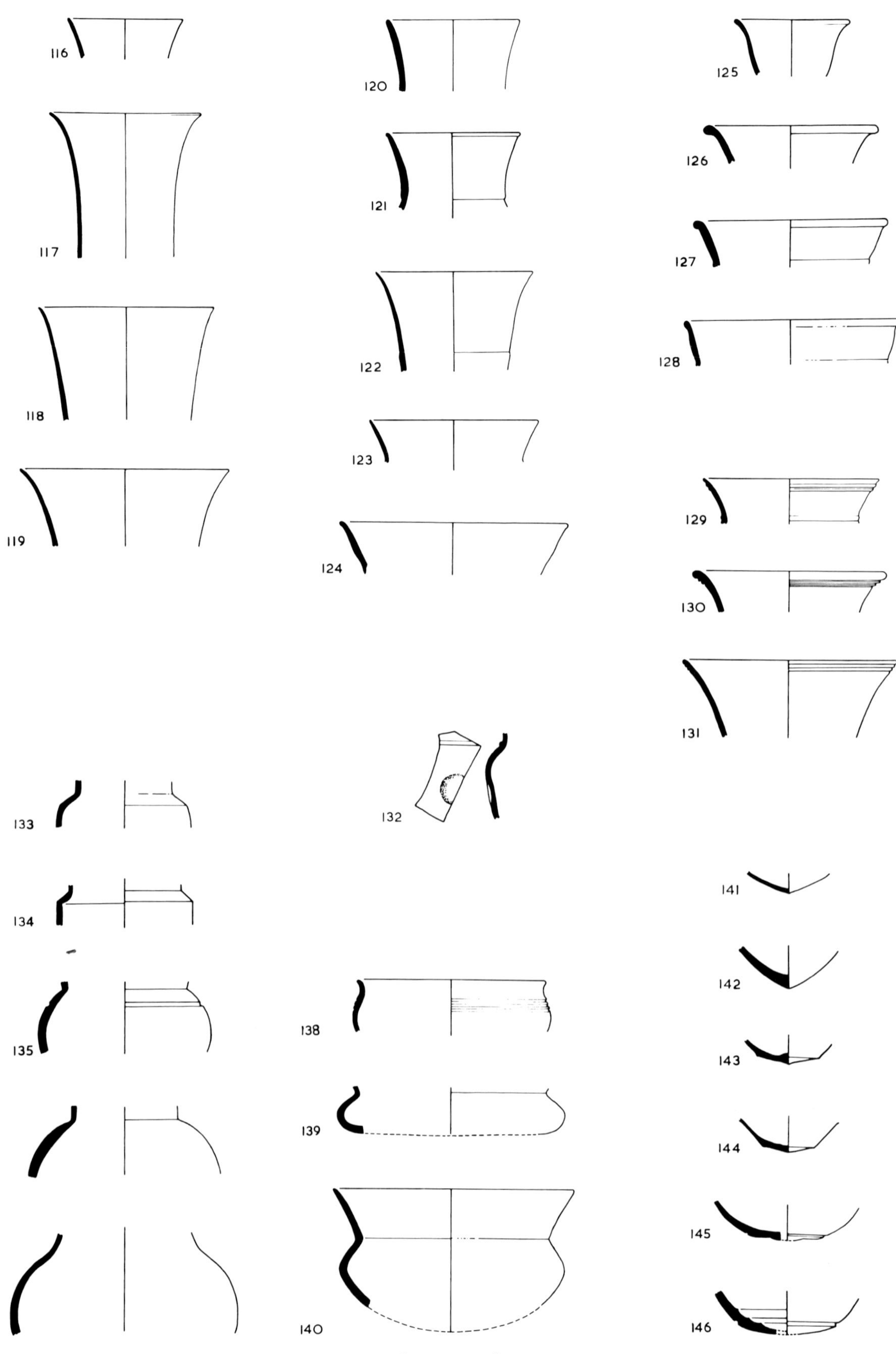

Fig. 31. Pottery from Khirbet Qasrij. Scale 1:3

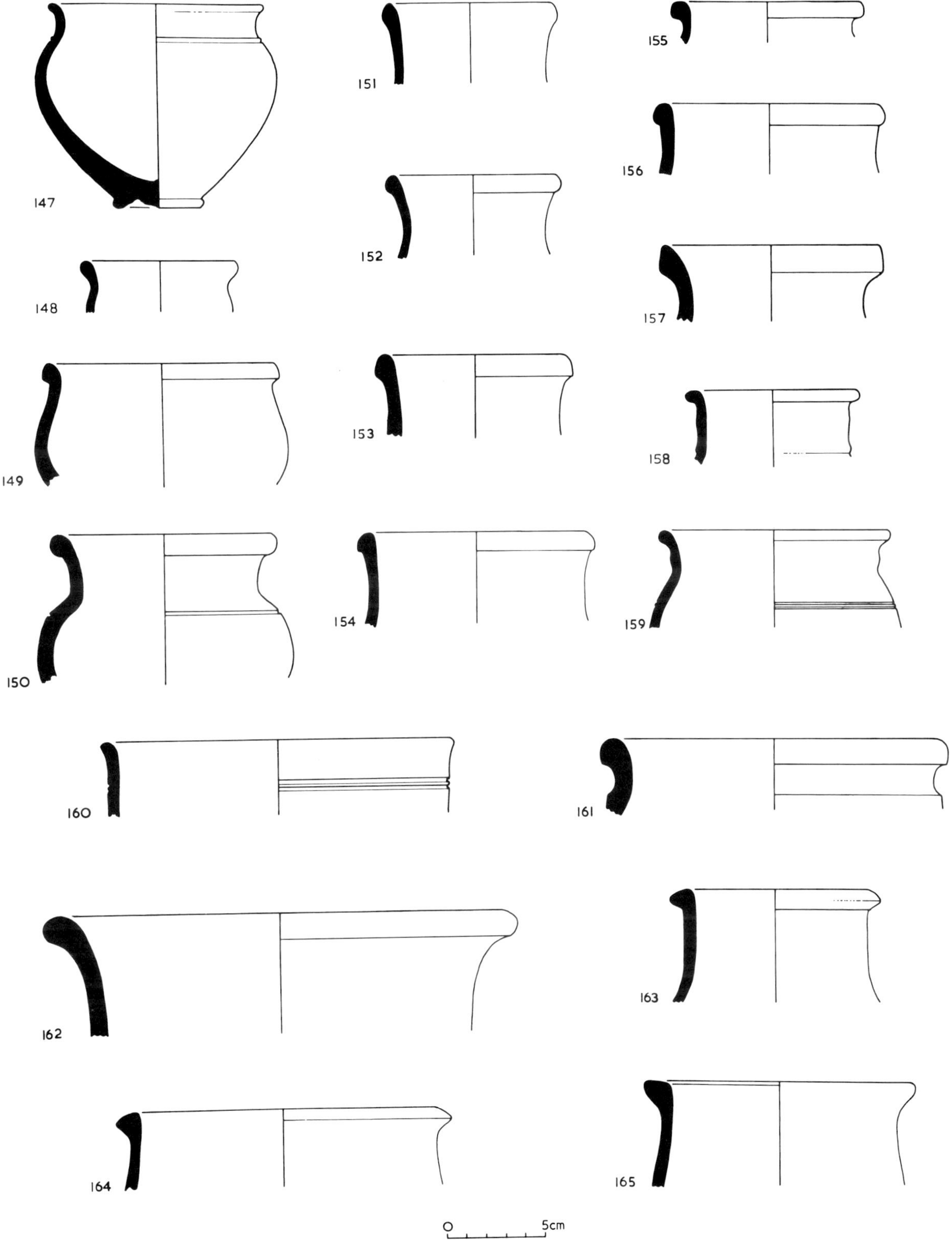

Fig. 32. Pottery from Khirbet Qasrij. Scale 1:3

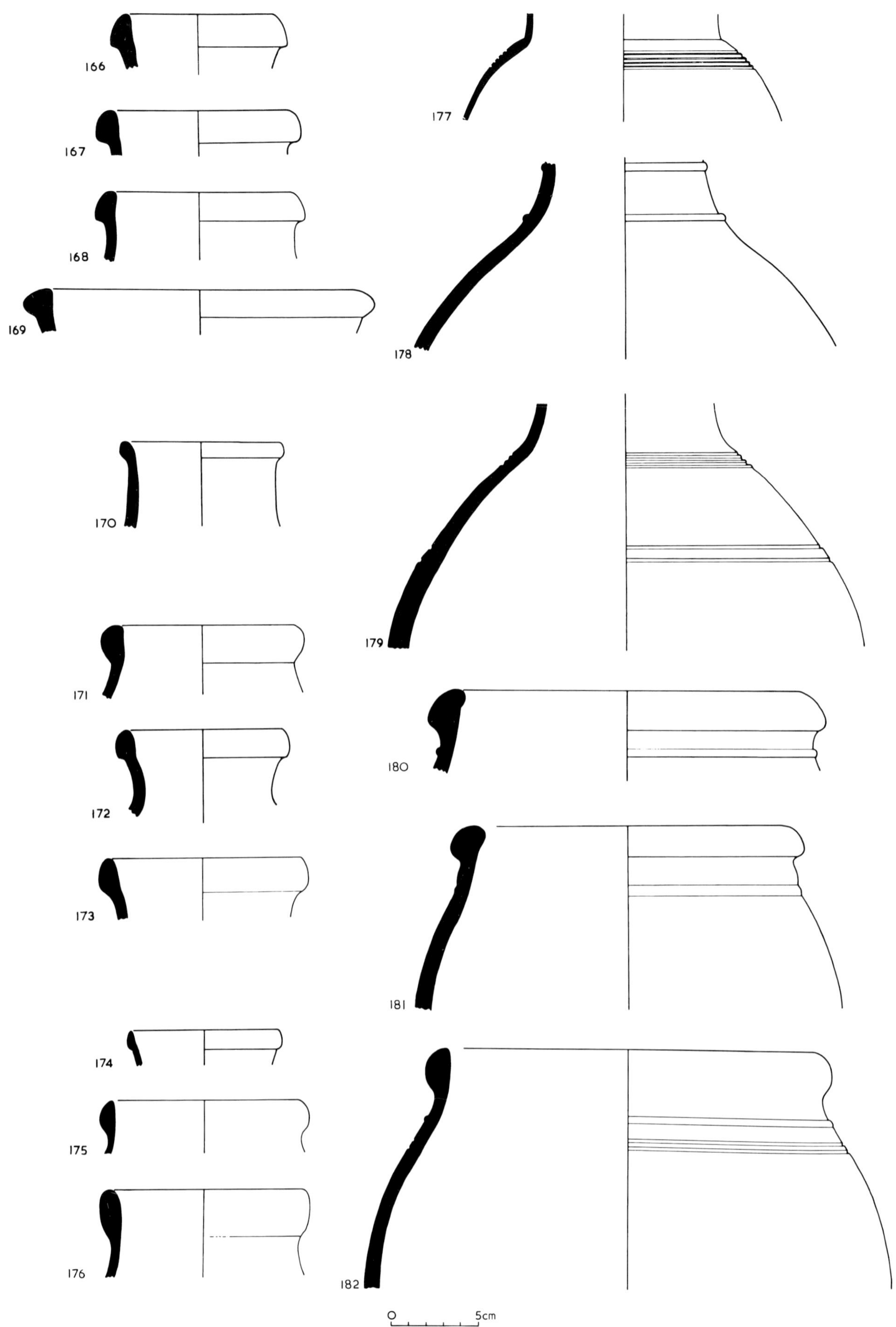

Fig. 33. Pottery from Khirbet Qasrij. Scale 1:3

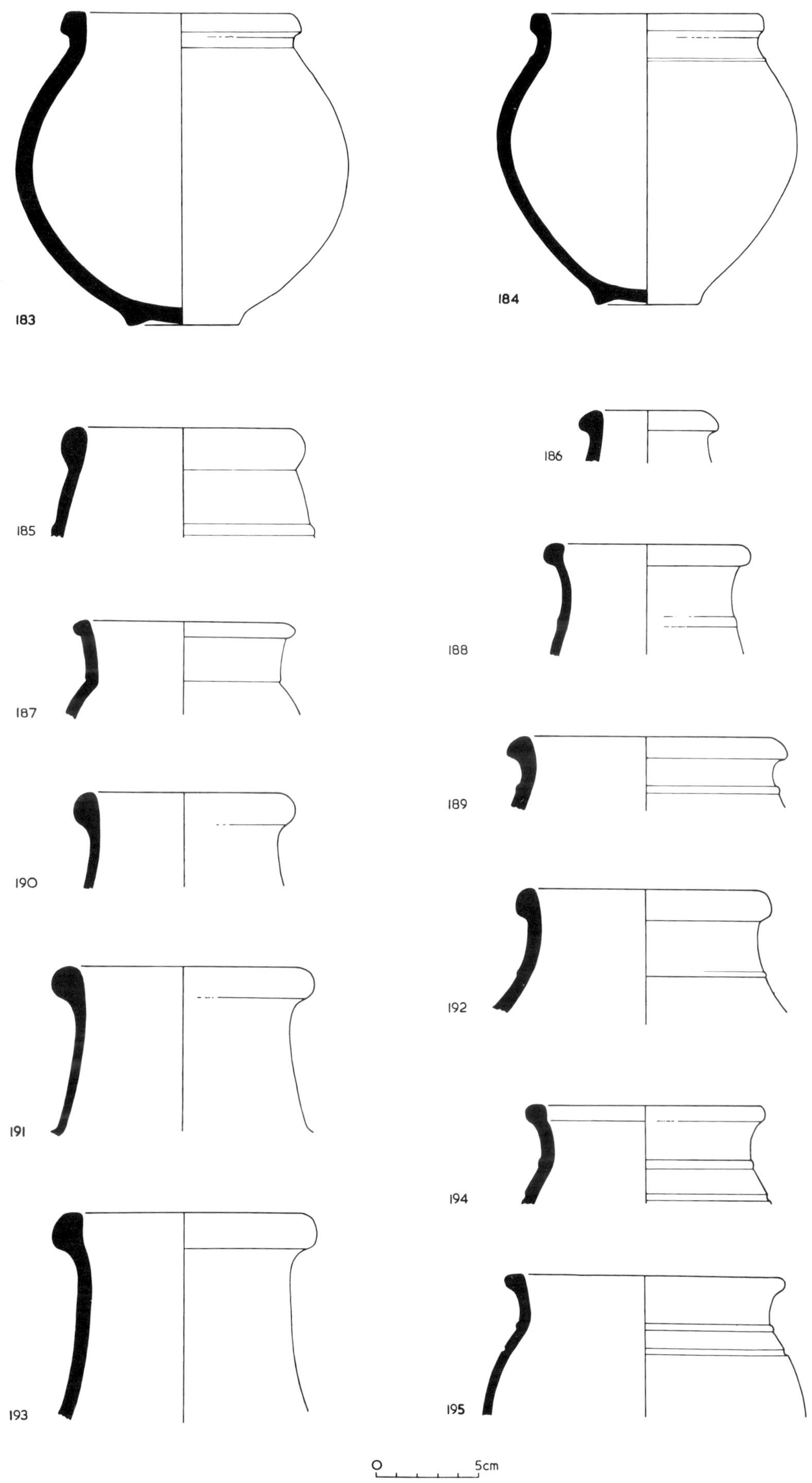

Fig. 34. Pottery from Khirbet Qasrij. Scale 1:3

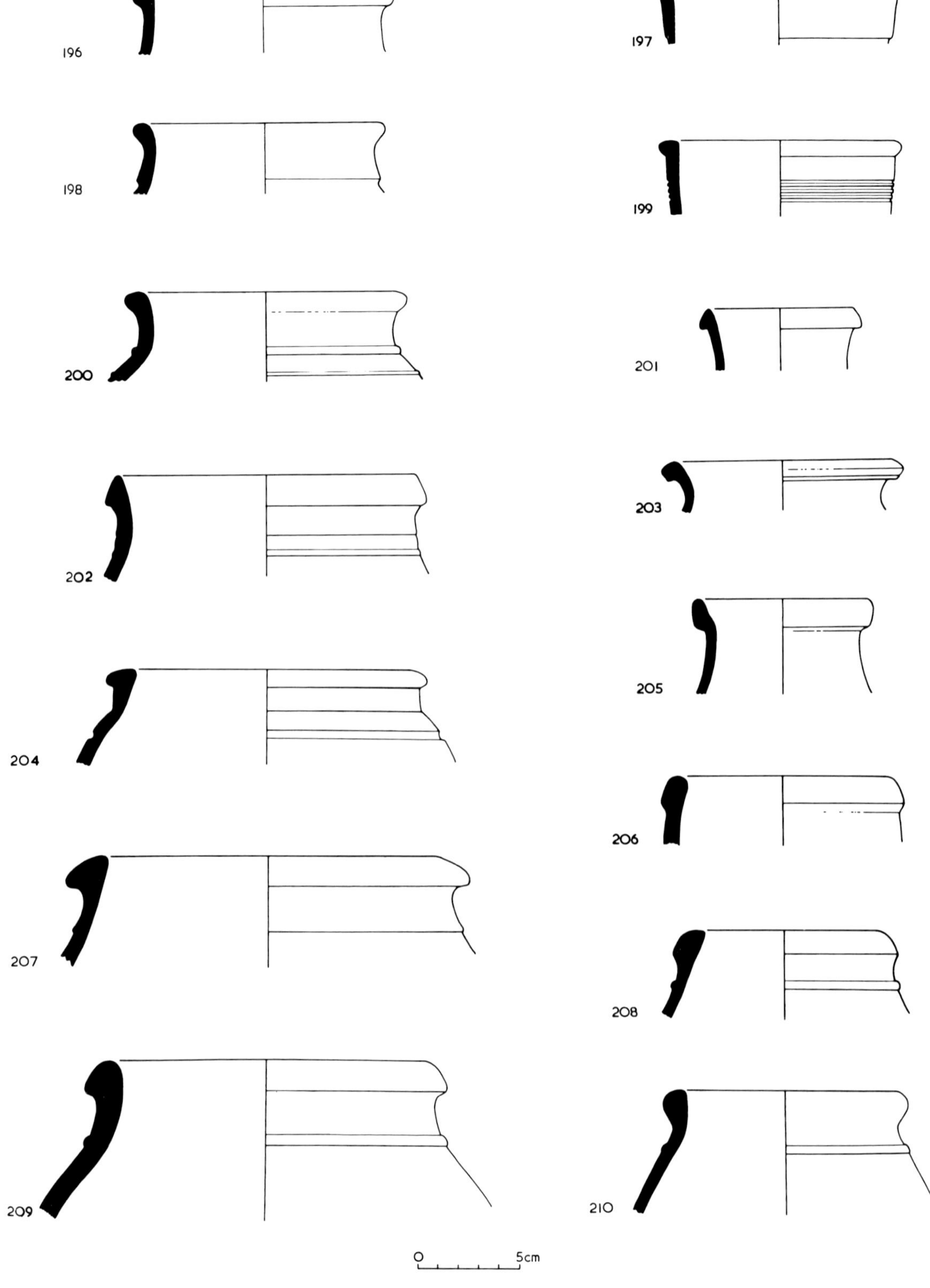

Fig. 35. Pottery from Khirbet Qasrij. Scale 1:3

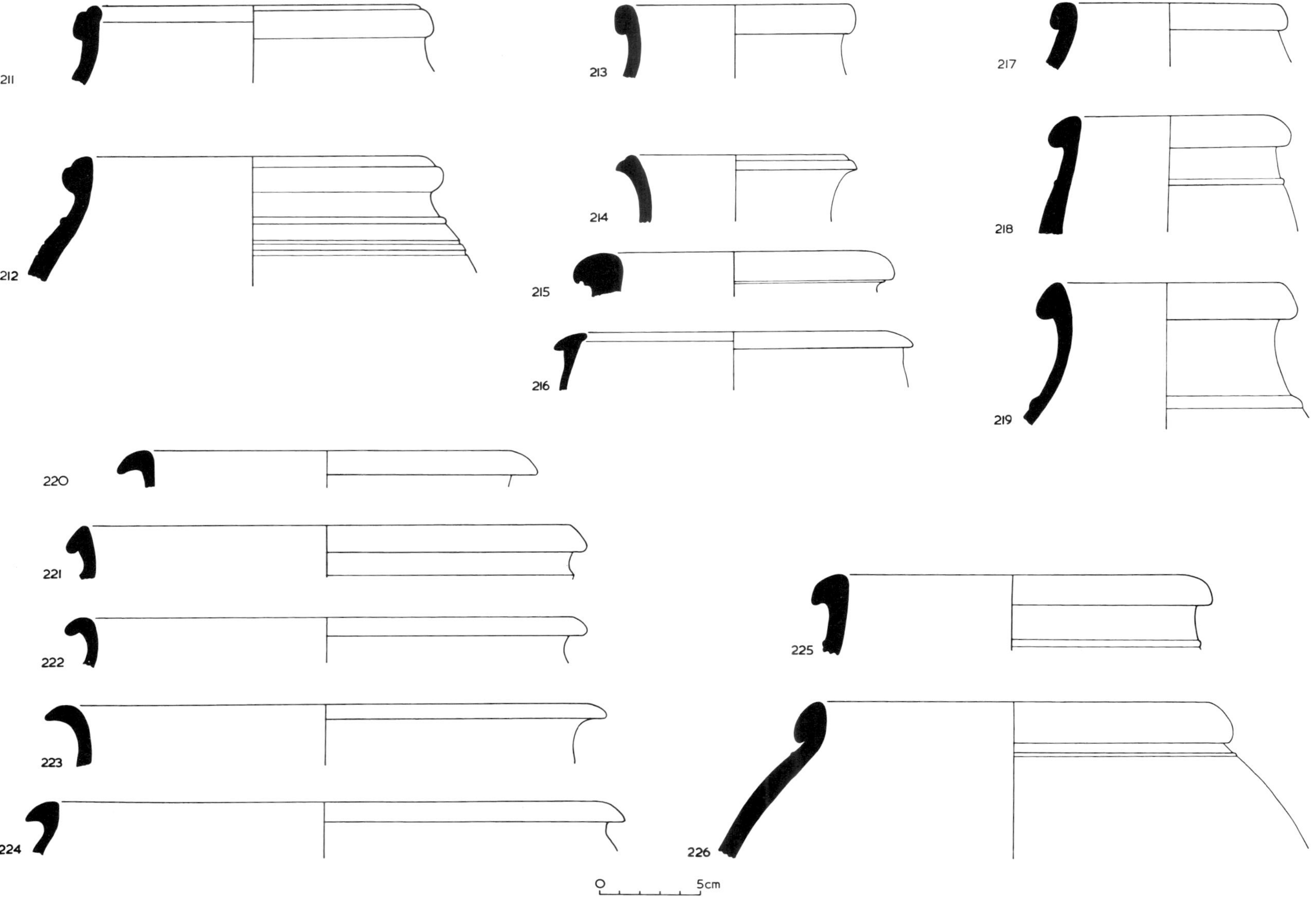

Fig. 36. Pottery from Khirbet Qasrij. Scale 1:3

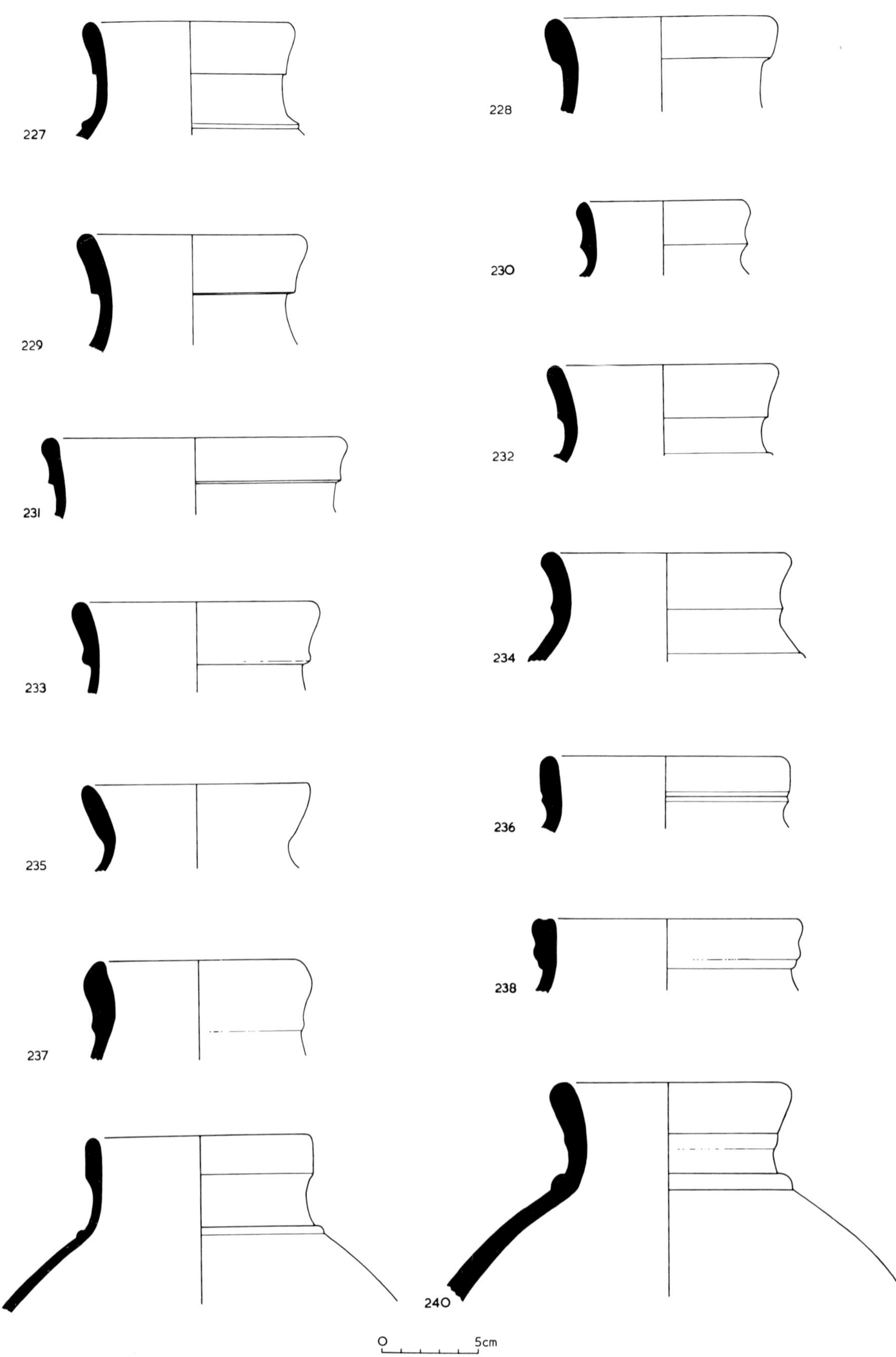

Fig. 37. Pottery from Khirbet Qasrij. Scale 1:3

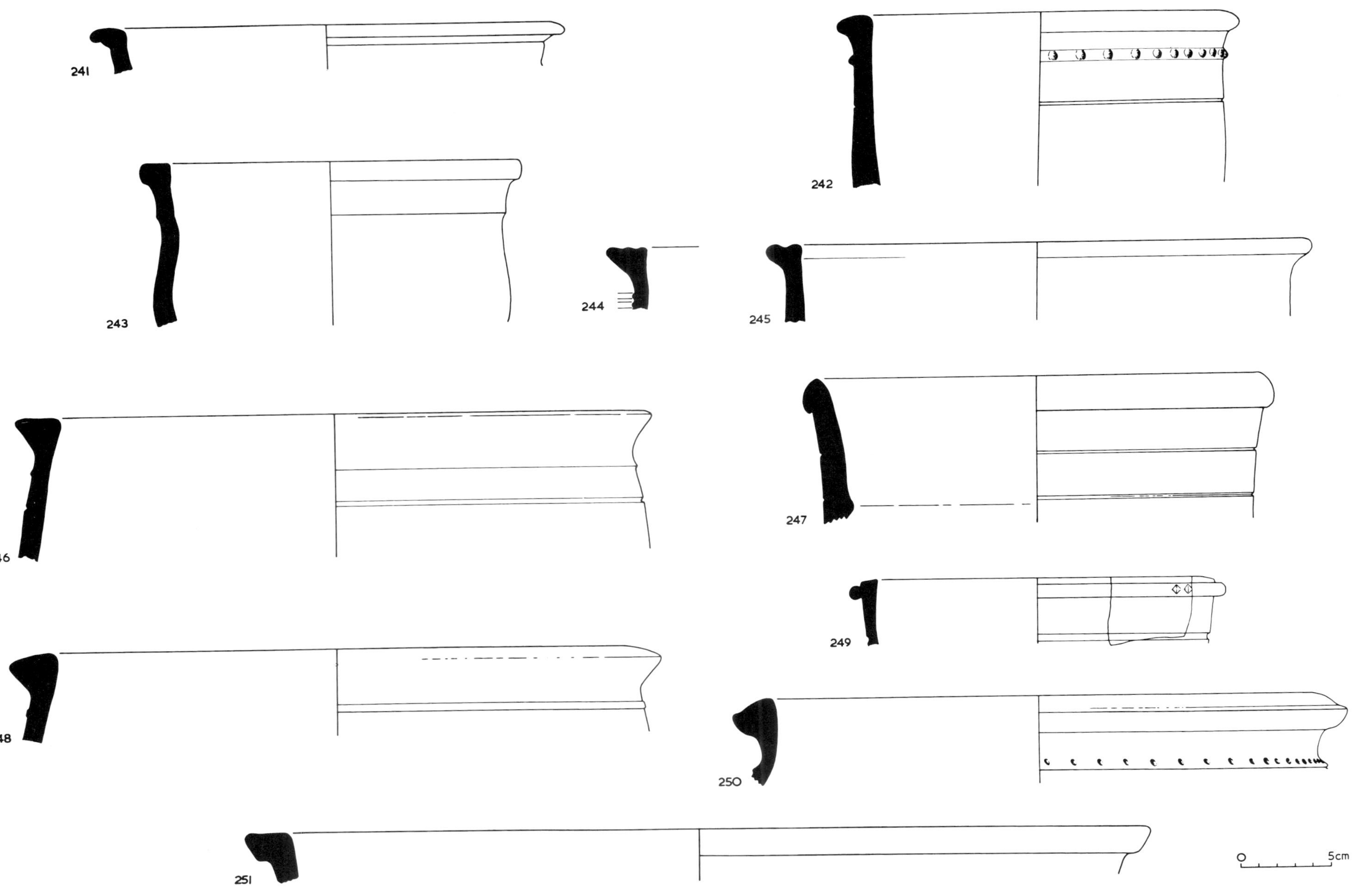

Fig. 38. Pottery from Khirbet Qasrij. Scale 1:3

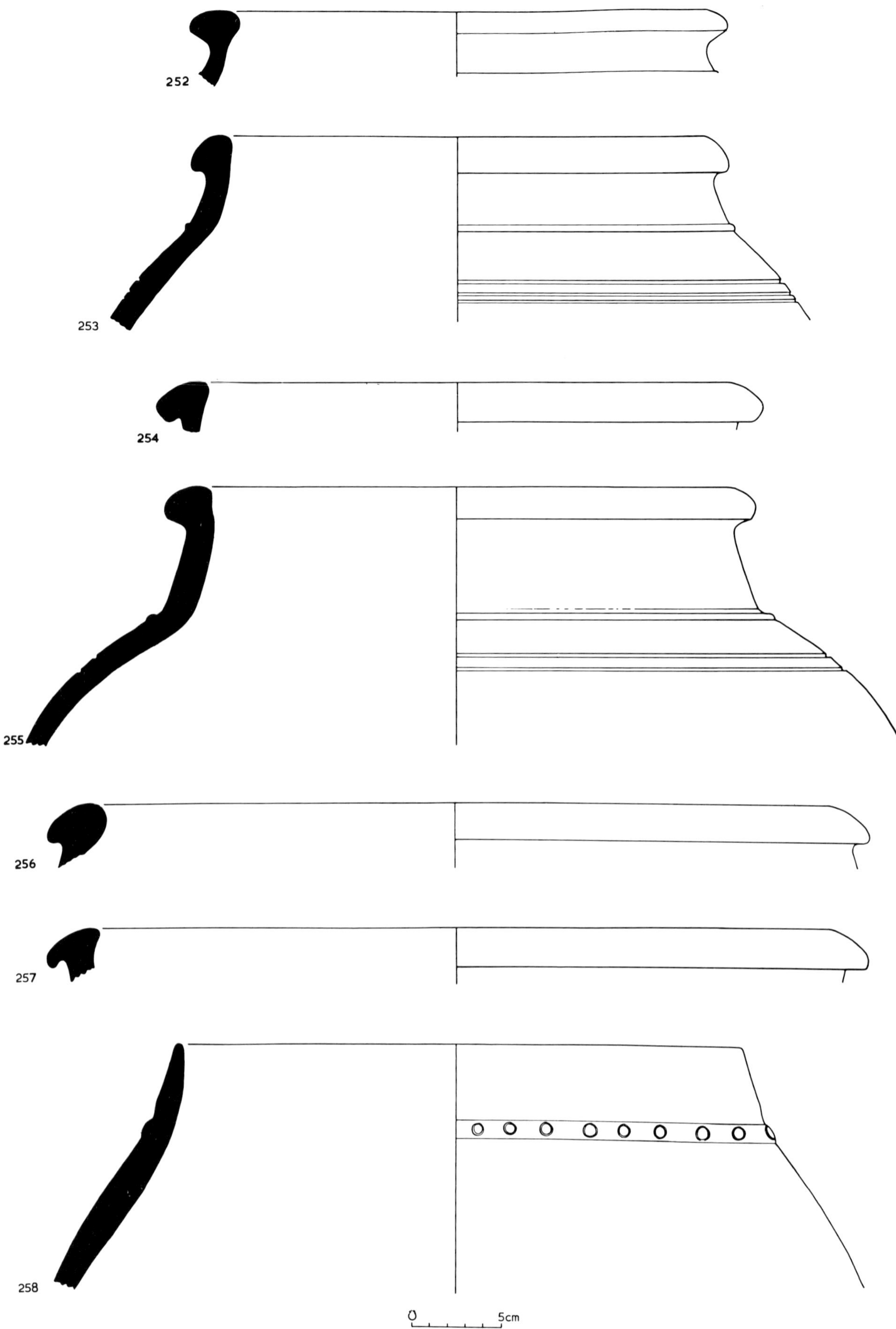

Fig. 39. Pottery from Khirbet Qasrij. Scale 1:3

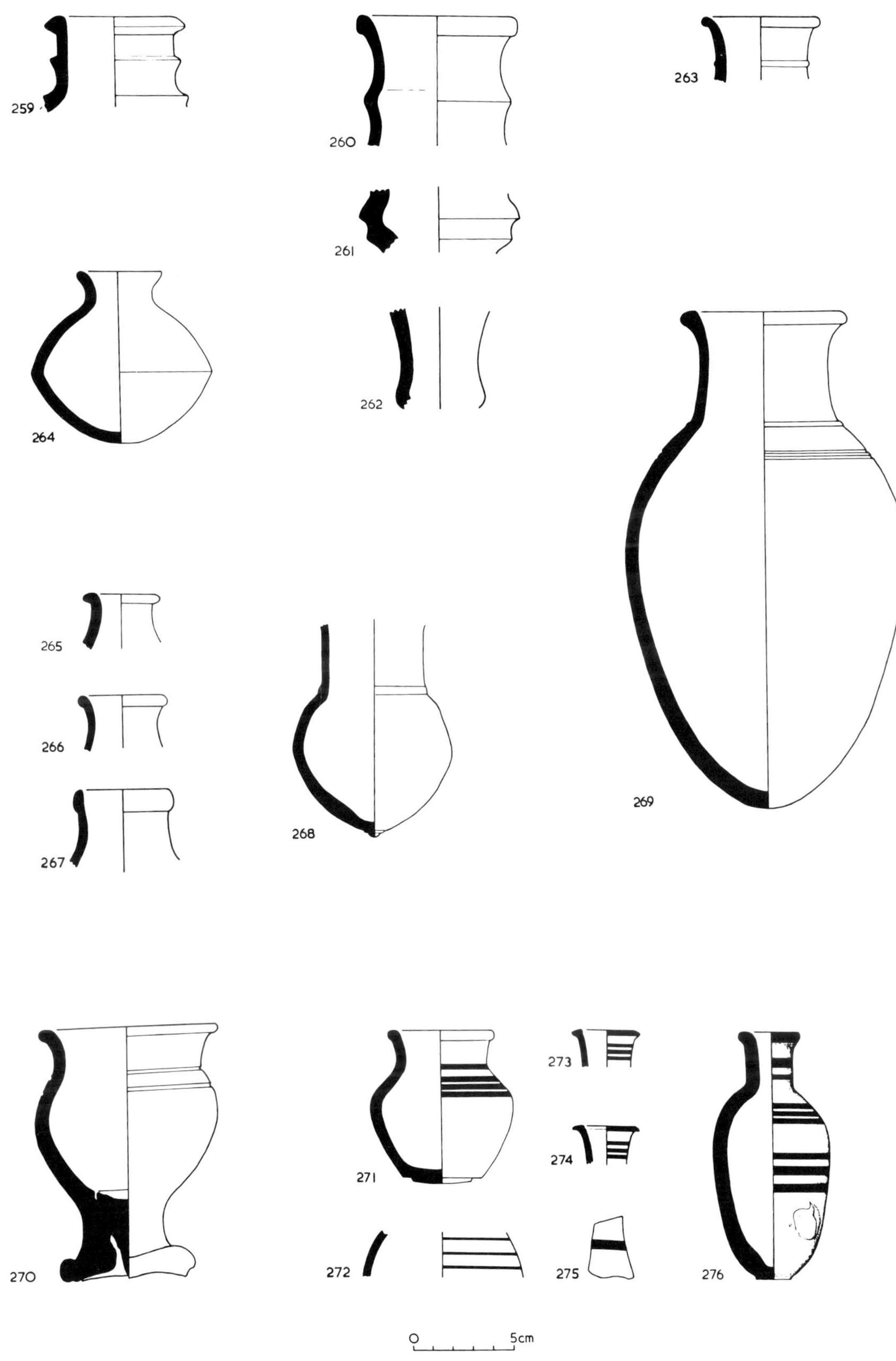

Fig. 40. Pottery from Khirbet Qasrij. Scale 1:3

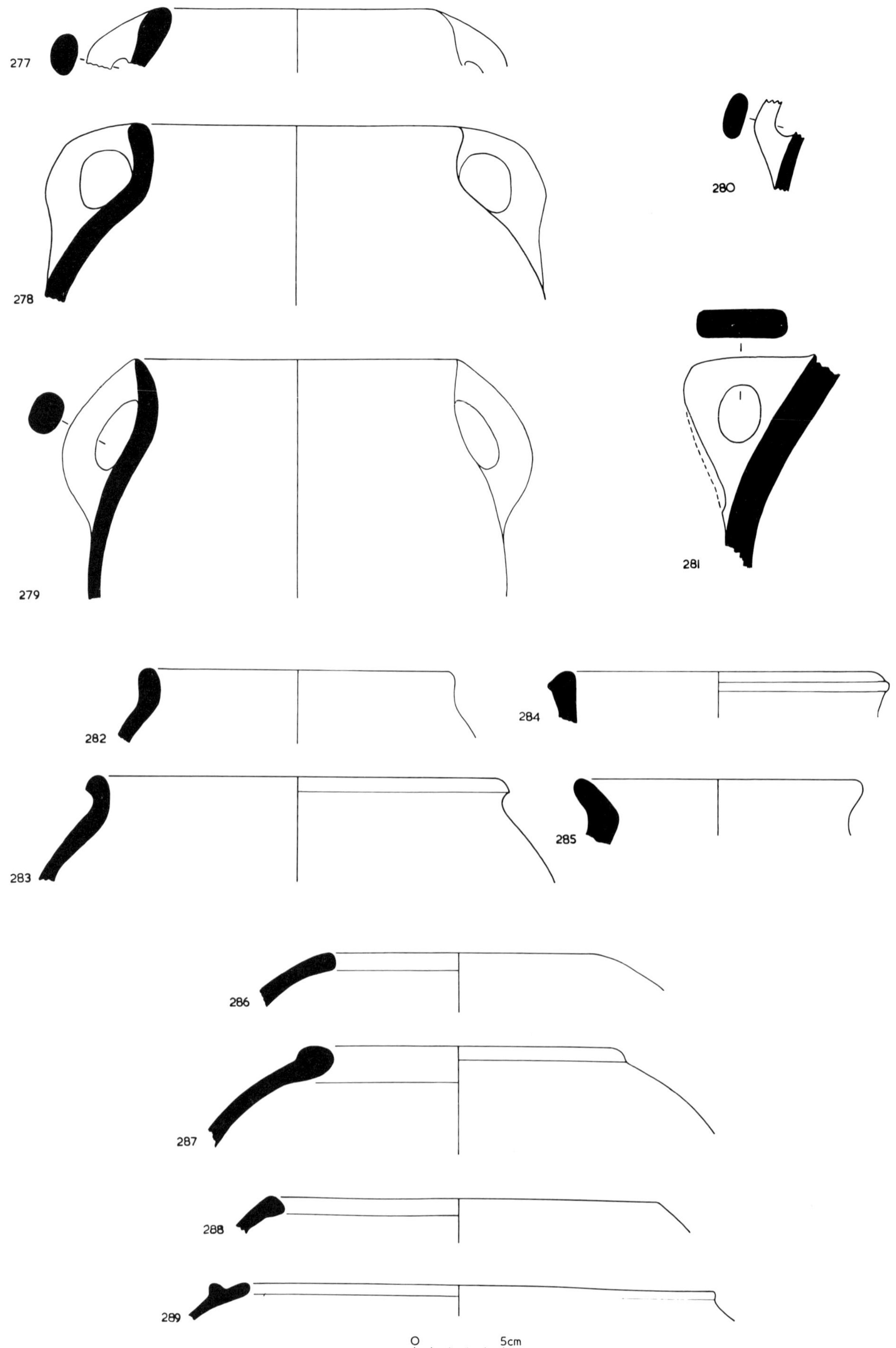

Fig. 41. Pottery from Khirbet Qasrij. Scale 1:3

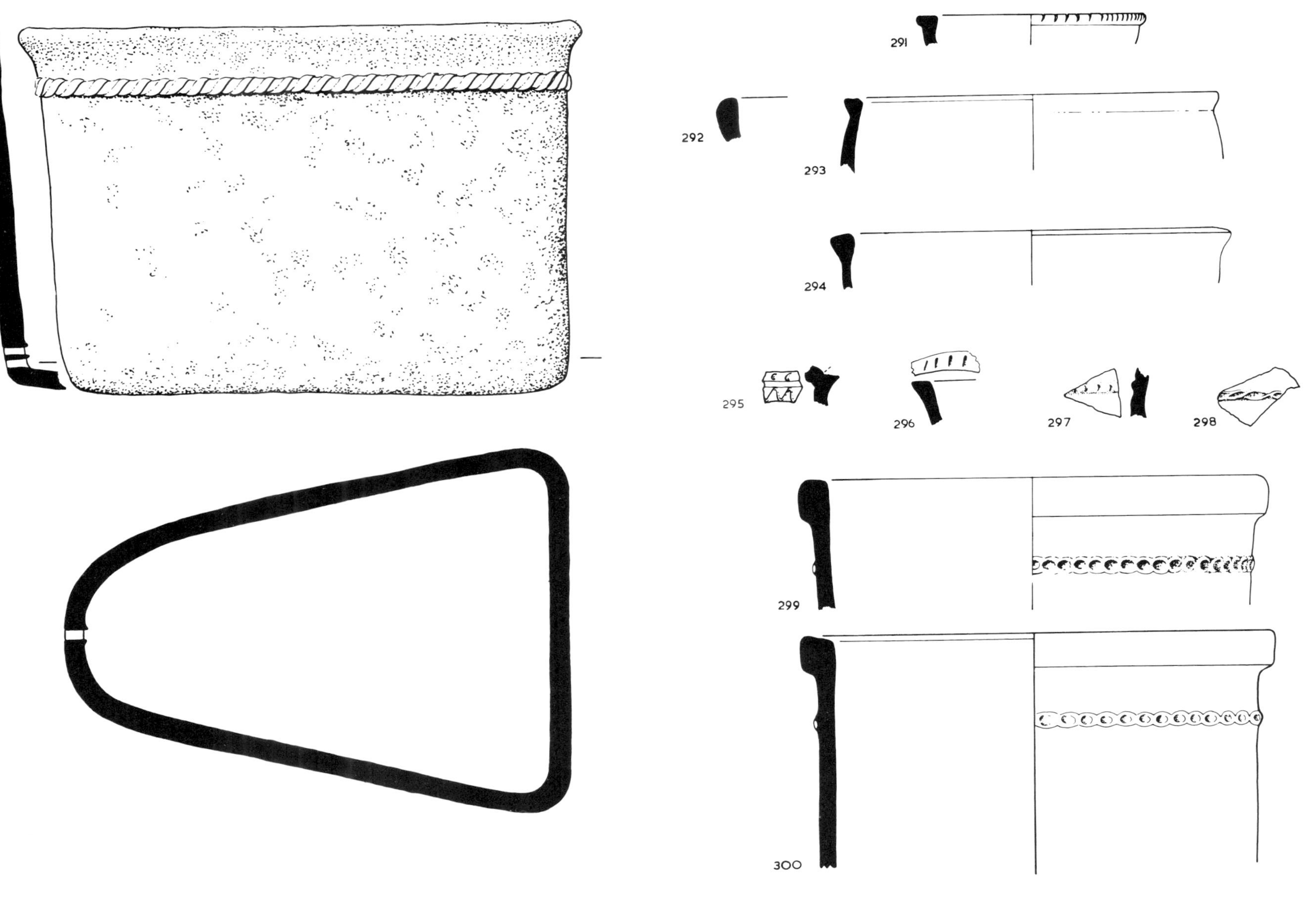

Fig. 42. Pottery from Khirbet Qasrij. Scale 1:8

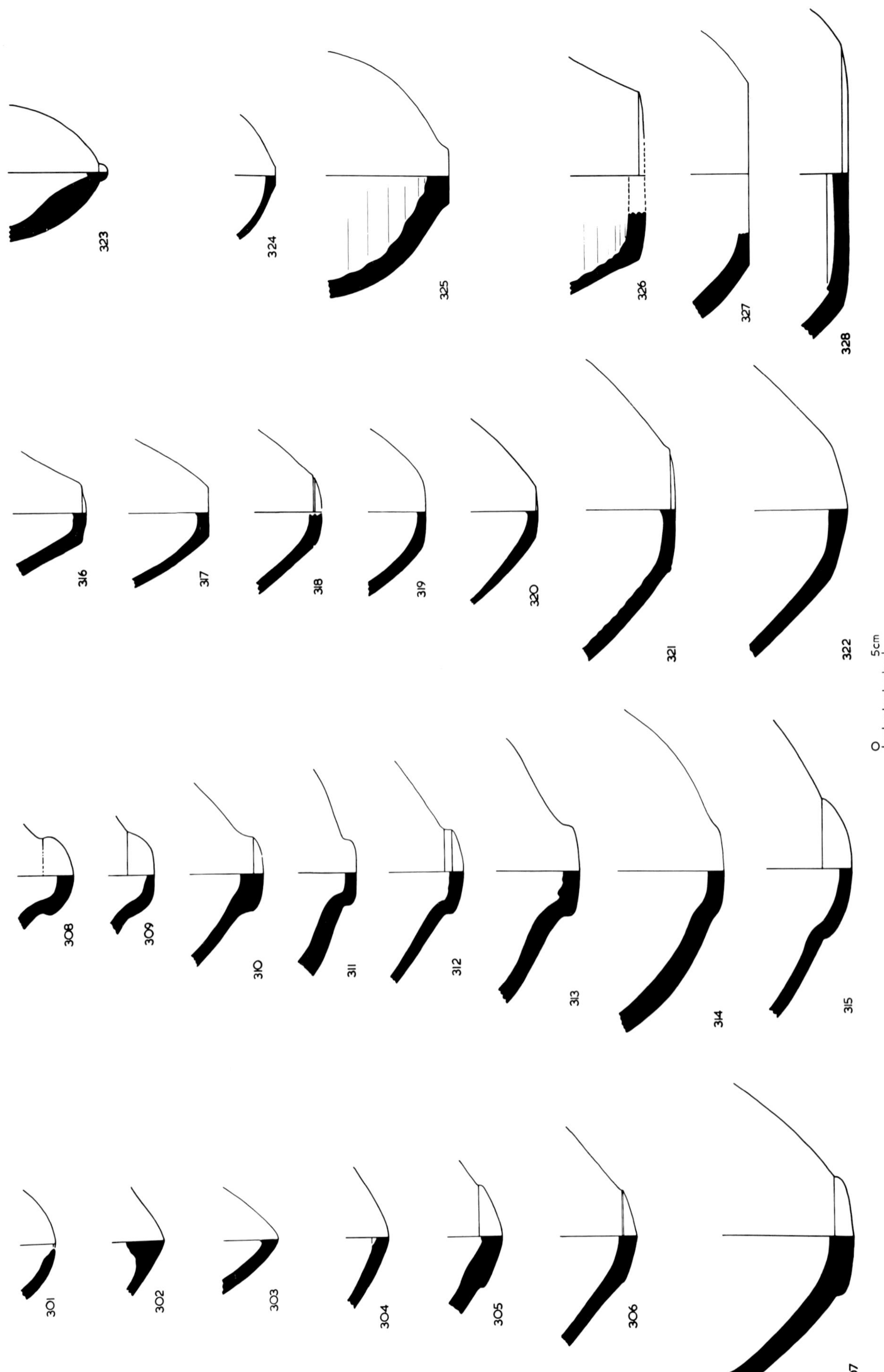

Fig. 43. Pottery from Khirbet Qasrij. Scale 1:3

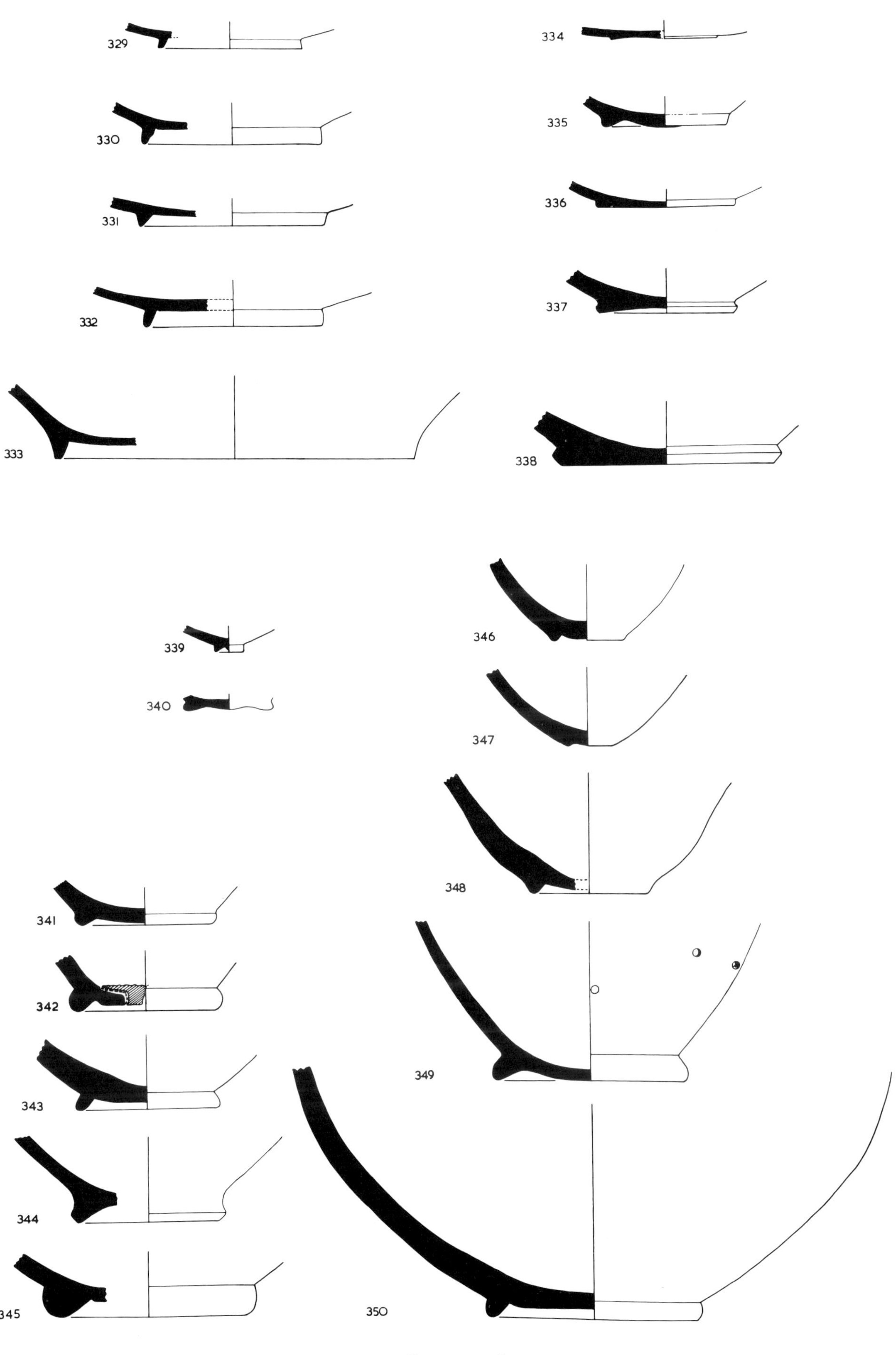

Fig. 44. Pottery from Khirbet Qasrij. Scale 1:3

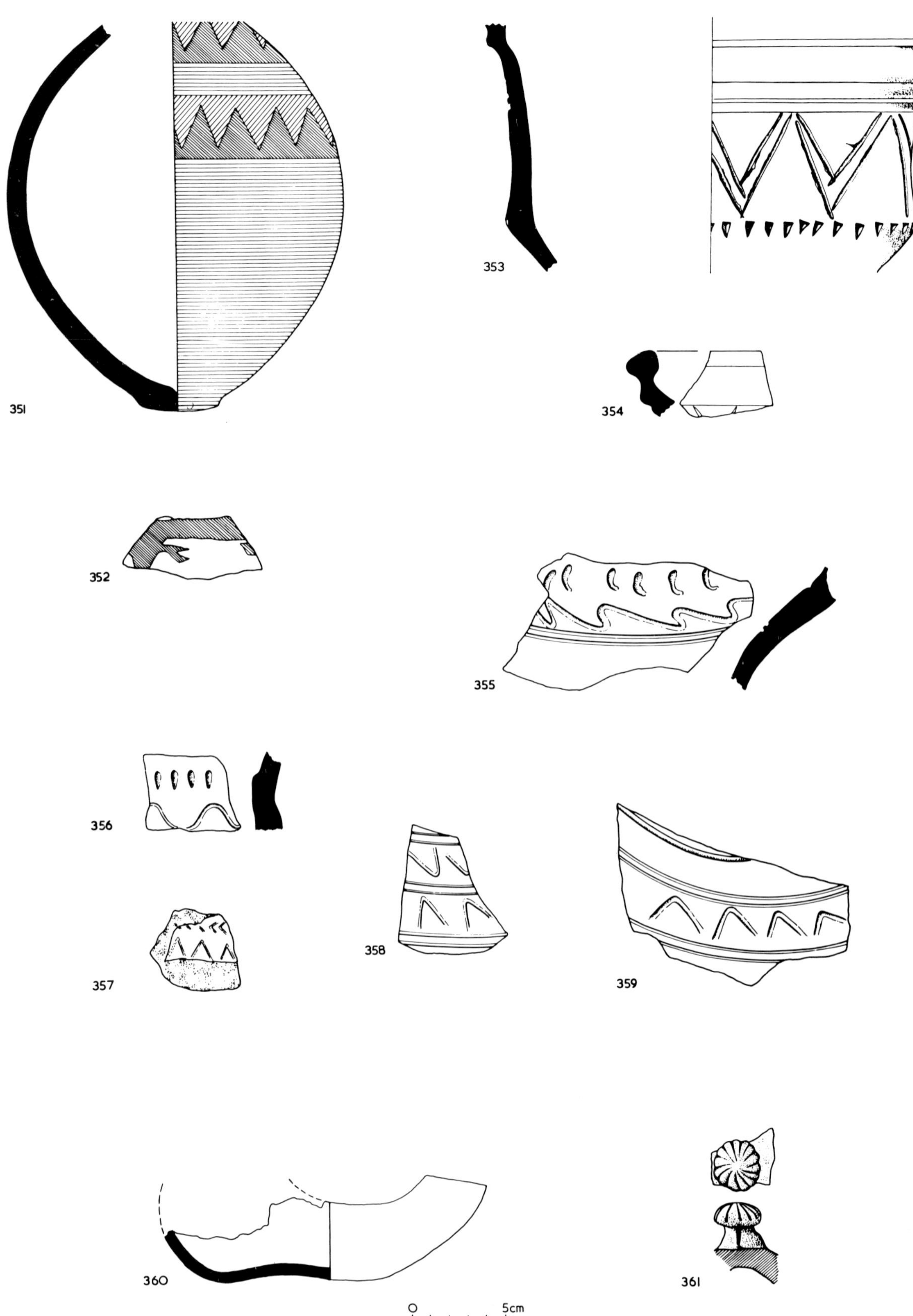

Fig. 45. Pottery from Khirbet Qasrij. Scale 1:3

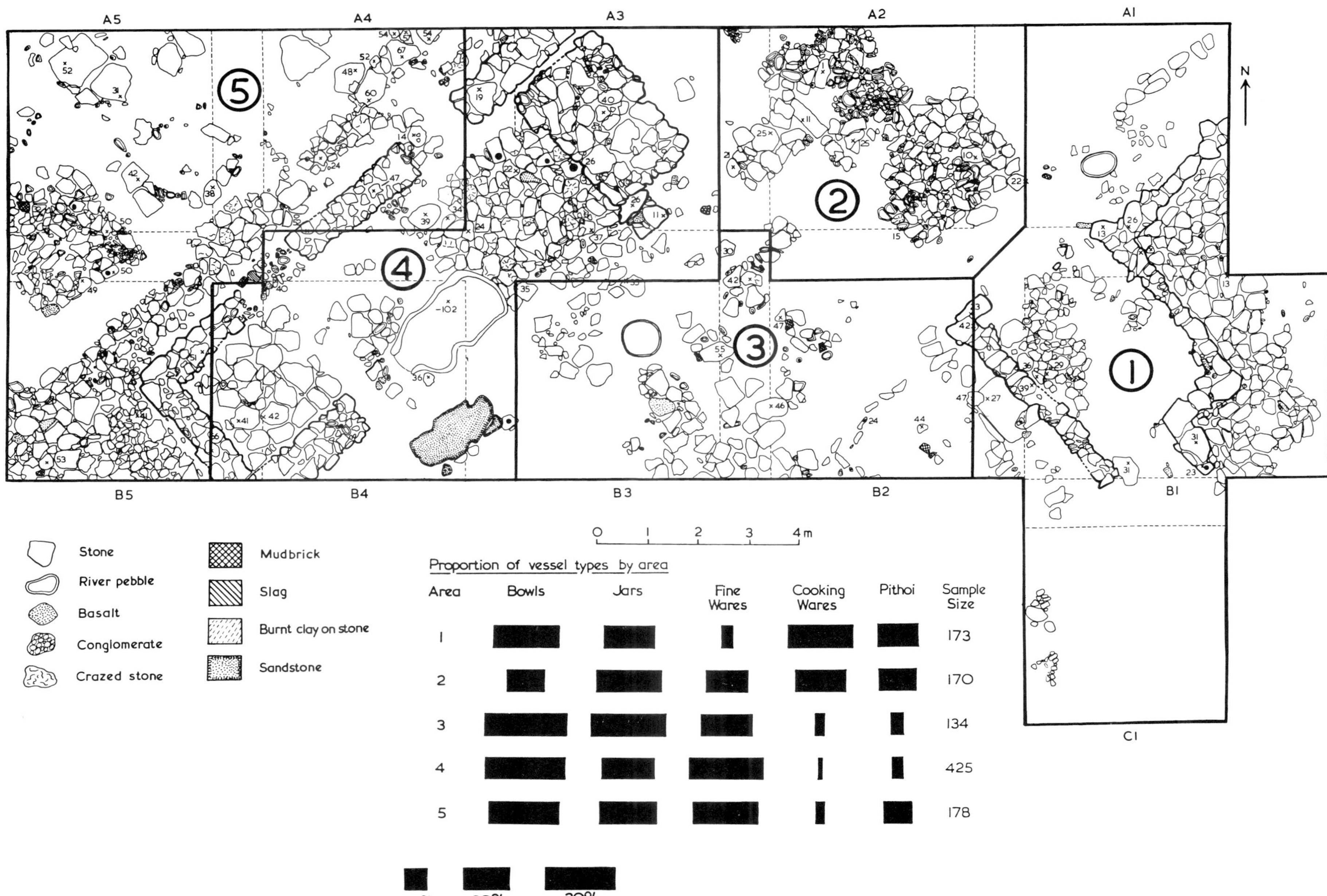

Fig. 46. Distribution of vessel types in main excavated area at Khirbet Qasrij

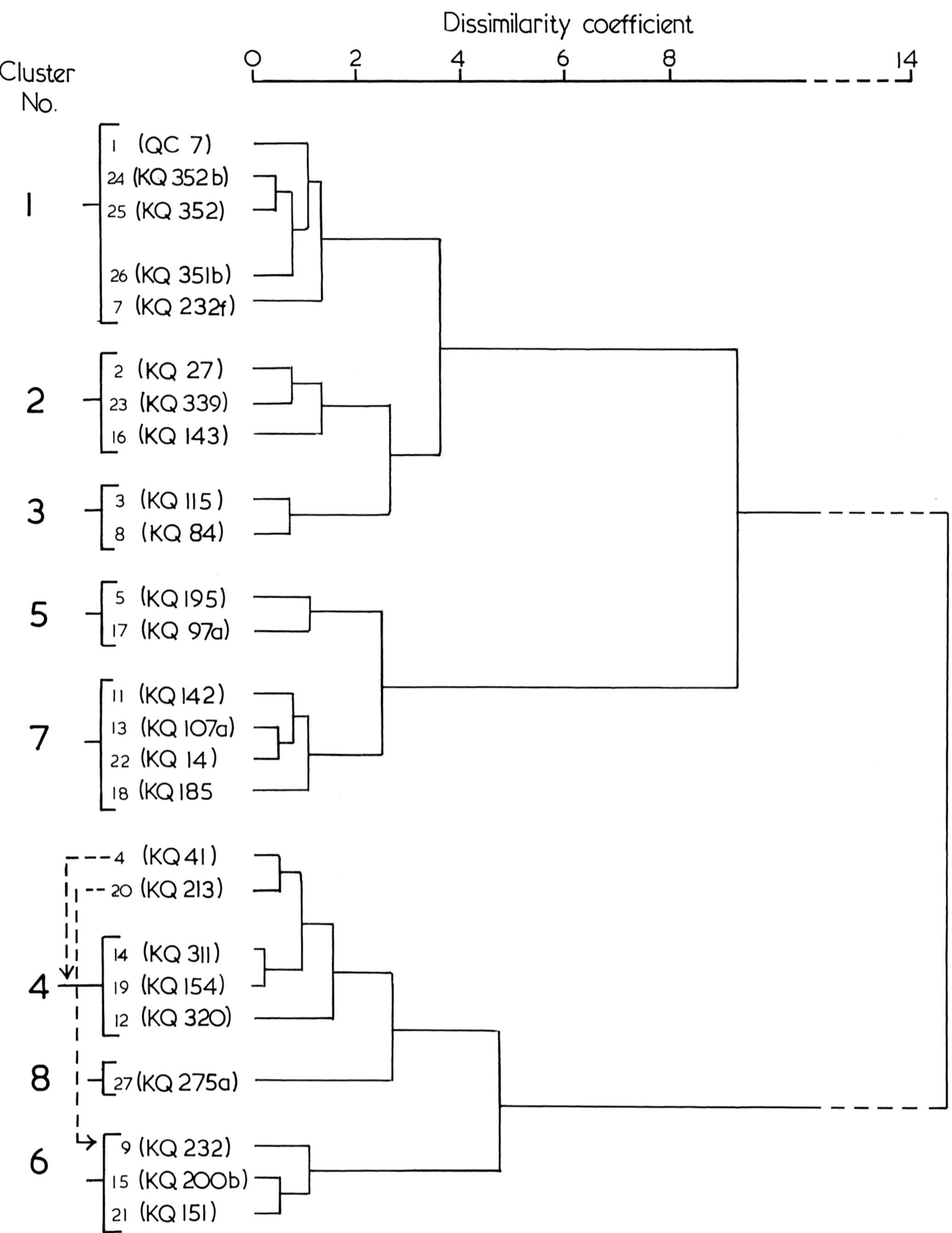

Fig. 47. Dendrogram from cluster analysis showing relationships between clusters (numbers in brackets refer to pottery catalogue entries)

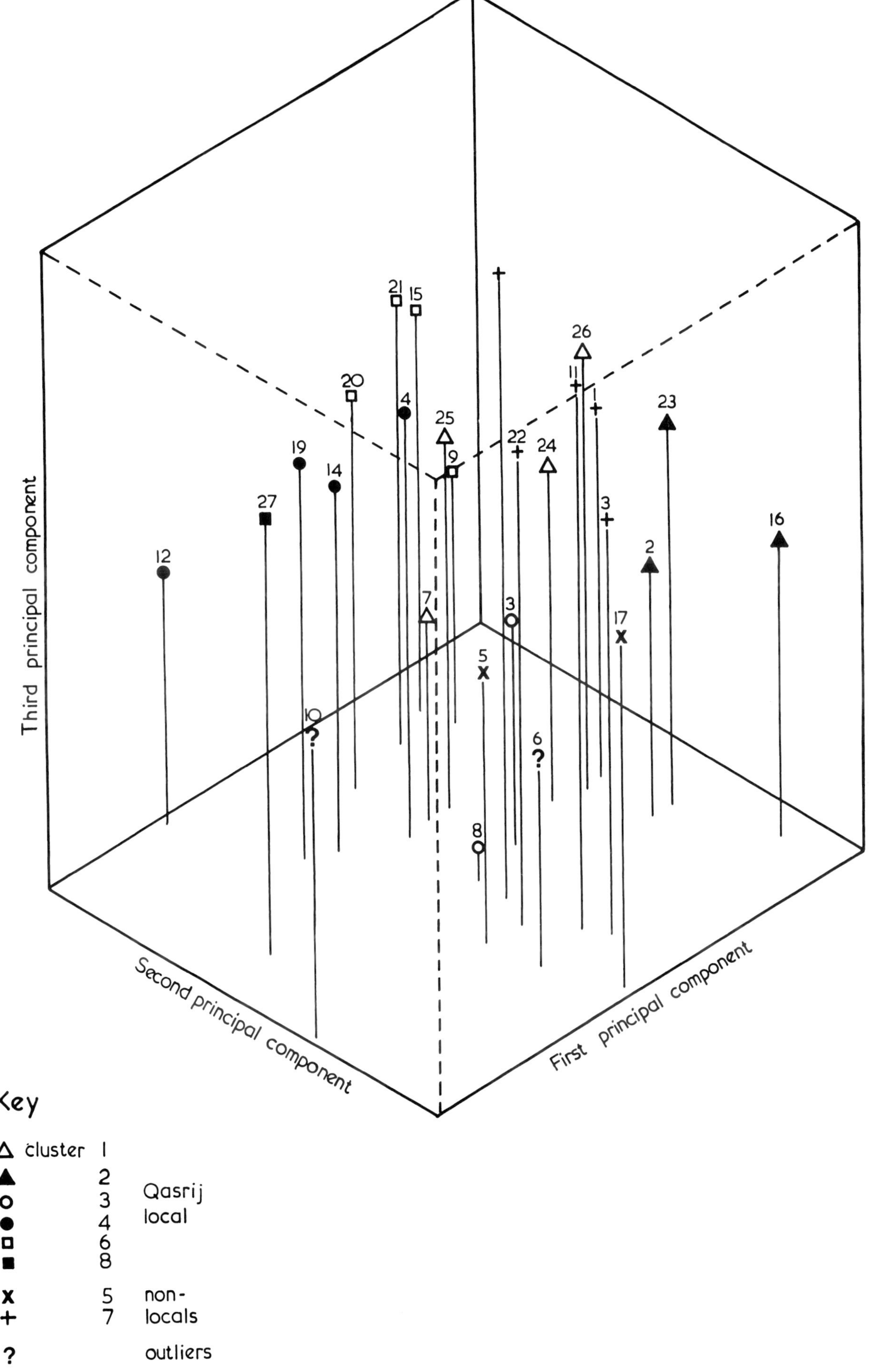

Fig. 48. Isometric drawing showing the principal components analysis, with clusters indicated by different symbols

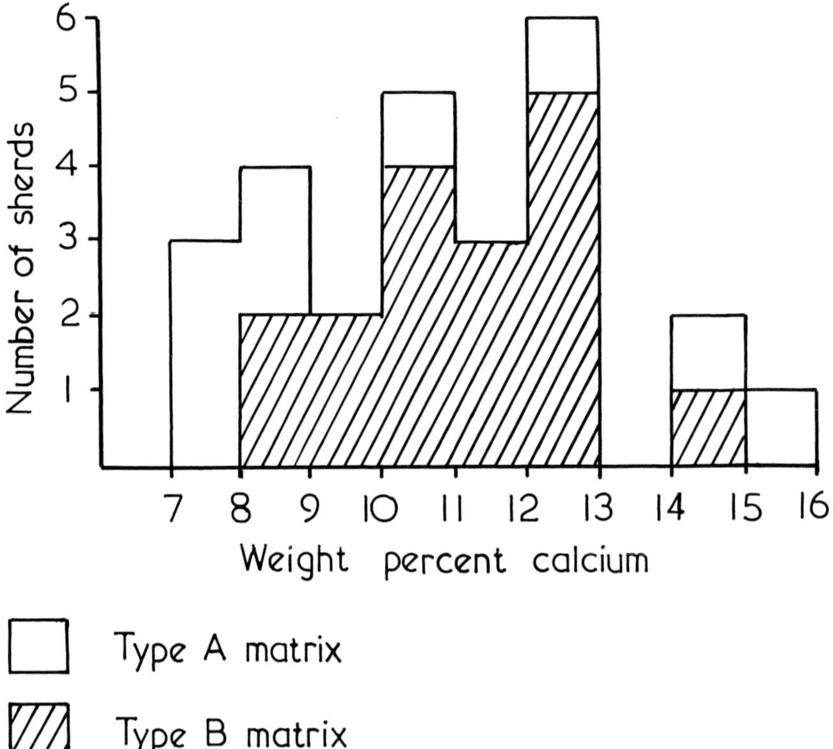

Fig. 49a. Calcium content of ceramic bodies, showing microstructure type

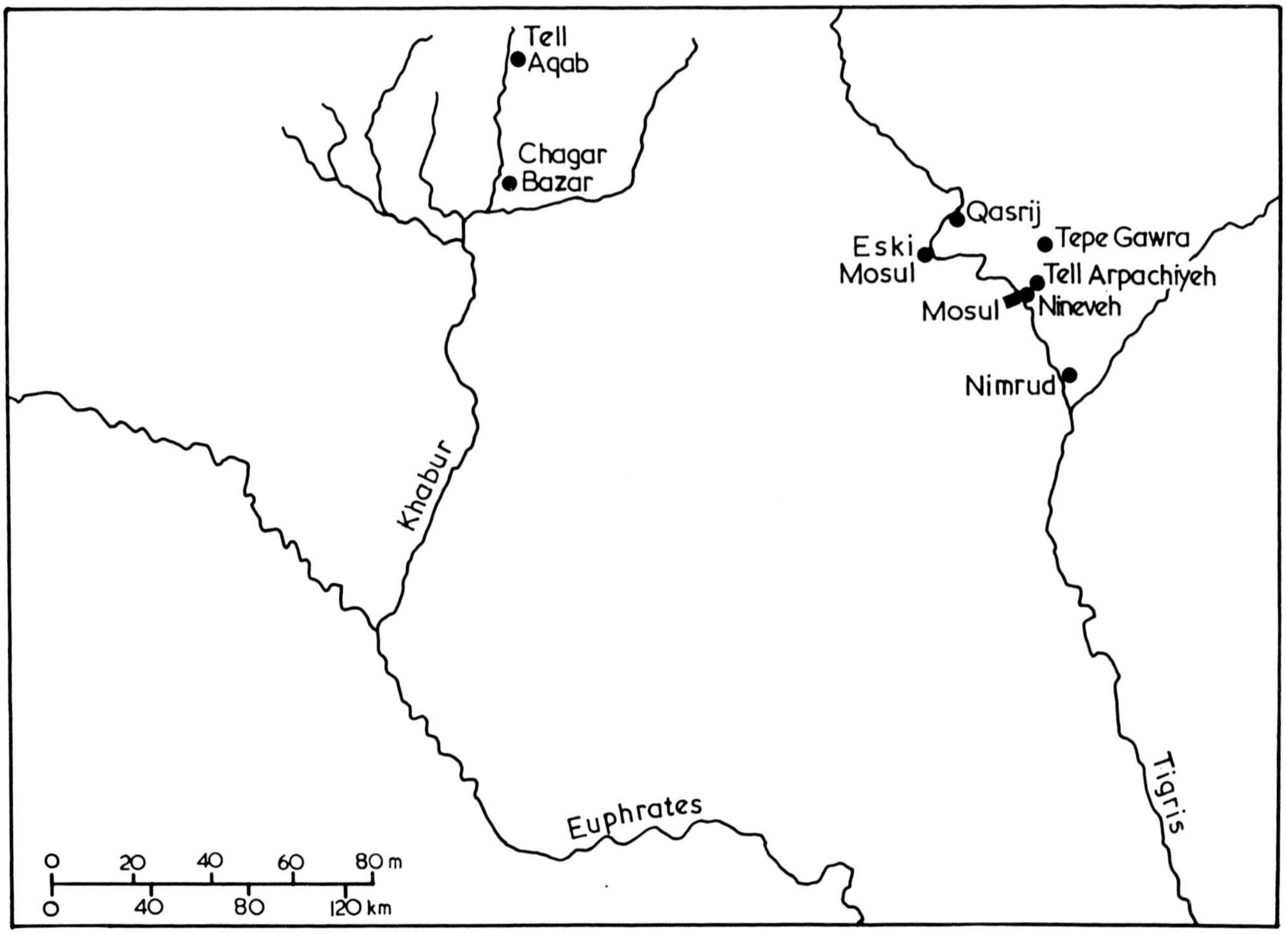

Fig. 49b. Map showing sites where neutron activation analysis of pottery has been carried out

PLATE I

a. The site at Qasrij Cliff looking west, showing the pit and the sondage QC1 on the headland

b. View of the pit at Qasrij Cliff after excavation

a. The start of excavations at Khirbet Qasrij, looking east. Wadi Qasrij and the deserted modern village of Qasrij are in the background

b. The main excavated area at Khirbet Qasrij looking west, with Jebel Butmah in the far distance

PLATE III

a. General view of the main excavated area at Khirbet Qasrij, looking west

b. General view of the main excavated area at Khirbet Qasrij, looking east

Photograph of the main excavated area at Khirbet Qasrij, taken from a kite

a. Industrial complex in the centre of the main excavated area, Khirbet Qasrij

b. Work-surface at the western end of the main excavated area, Khirbet Qasrij

a. Block of sandstone to the south of the kiln, Khirbet Qasrij

b. Drilled stones in the pavement to the north-east of the kiln, Khirbet Qasrij

a. Pottery vessels KQ16-17 *in situ*, Khirbet Qasrij

b. Painted pottery bottle KQ15 *in situ* on the floor of trench A2, Khirbet Qasrij

a. Collapsed bricks and pottery wasters in the fill of the kiln, Khirbet Qasrij

b. Mixed debris including a large number of pottery wasters in the fill of the kiln, Khirbet Qasrij

a. The kiln at Khirbet Qasrij in course of excavation

b. The kiln at Khirbet Qasrij after excavation

a. Pottery wasters from the kiln, Khirbet Qasrij

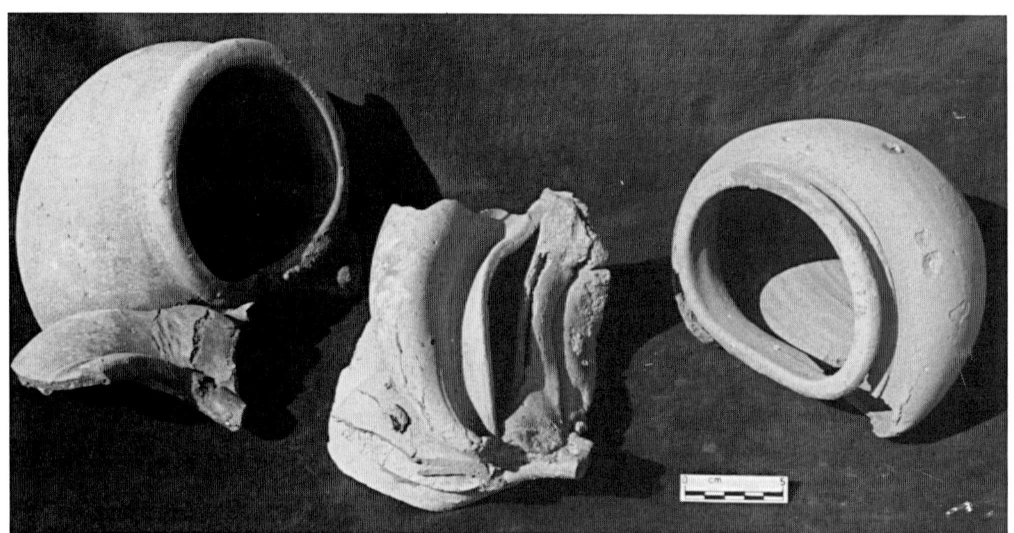

b. Collapsed jars from the kiln, Khirbet Qasrij

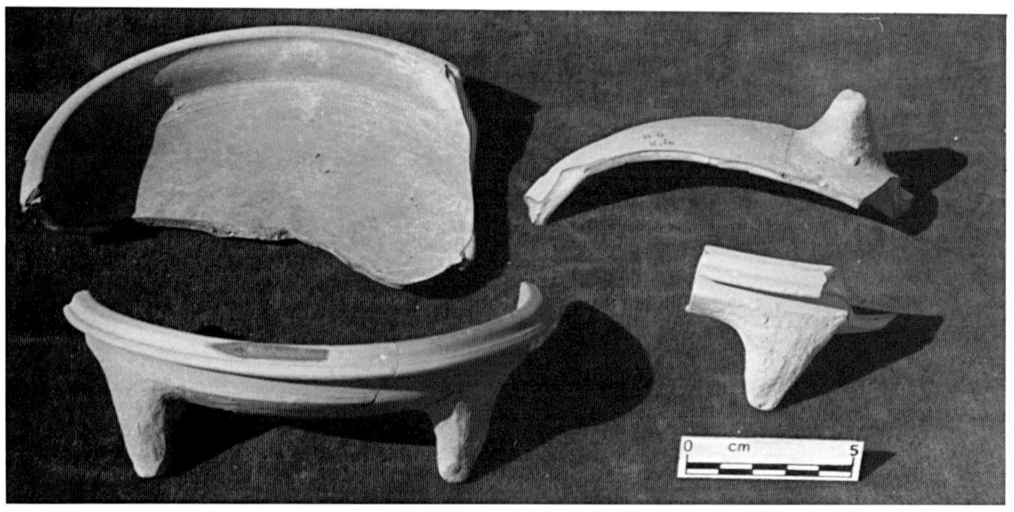

c. Grey-ware tripods from Khirbet Qasrij

b. Polychrome glazed jar KQ24 from Khirbet Qasrij

a. Painted pottery bottle KQ15 from Khirbet Qasrij

Stone duck-weight KQ1 from Khirbet Qasrij

SEM photomicrograph of a section through a fragment of Egyptian blue from
Khirbet Qasrij, showing Egyptian blue crystals (white) intermixed with
unreacted quartz (grey)

اللقى الصغيرة من خربة قصريج

KQ 1 (اللوح XII ، الشكـل 21) ـ بطـة وزن من الحجـر ، الطـول 8,25 سم الارتفاع 5,28 سم الـوزن 268,9 غرام . الخندق B3 . 50 سم تحت سطح الموقع .

KQ 2 (الشكل 21) ـ وزن من الحديد ، الارتفاع 3,4 سم القطر 4,25 سم الوزن 217,5 غرام . الخندق A2

KQ 3 (الشكل 21) ـ سكين من الحديد . الطول 11 سم ، العرض 1,64 سم . الخندق B2 . 29 سم تحت سطح الموقع .

KQ 4 (الشكل 21) ـ وتد من الحديد . الطول 6,1 سم . الساق 0,65 سم . الخندق A5 . 55 سم تحت السطح .

KQ 6 (الشكل 22) ـ ساق مسمار جداري من الفخار ، الطول 15,3 سم القطر 6,73 سم . الخندق PF .

KQ 8 (الشكل 22) ـ كسرة مسمار جداري من الفخار ، الطول 14,8 سم القطر 8,9 سم . الخندق A4 .

KQ 9 (الشكل 22) ـ رأس مسمار جداري من الفخار ، القطر 9,0 سم الخندق A4 .

KQ 10 (الشكل 21) ـ كسرة نصل من حجر الصوان ـ الطول 4,25 سم العرض 2,68 . الساحة A3-A4 .

KQ 11 (الشكل 22) ـ ساق من مرجل ثلاثي من البازلت ـ الارتفاع 11 سم . الخندق B3 . 36 سم تحت السطح .

KQ 12 (الشكل 21) ـ خرزة من الصدف ، 1,73 × 1,23 سم الخندق A2 .

KQ 13 (الشكل 21) ـ خرزة من الصدف، الطول 0,75 سم . العرض 0,55 سم ، الخندق B5 ، 24 سم تحت السطح .

KQ 14 (الشكـل 21) ـ خرزة مدورة من الـزجاج . صفراء اللون مع خط اصفر غامق حول وسطها . الارتفاع 1,05 سم القطر 1,26 سم ، الخندق B4 ، 48 سم تحت السطح .

KQ 25 (الشكل 21) ـ كسرة من دمية حيوان من الفخار . الطول 4,25 سم الارتفاع 2,5 سم . الخندق A1 .

KQ 30 (الشكـل 22) ـ قطـع حجـر (بـازلت) مدورة مع حفرة في وسطها . القطر 11,5 ، لعلها دولاب الموازنة المنصوب على المحور الذي يدعم دولاب الفخار . الساحة B2-B3 .

KQ 31 (الشكل 22) ـ كسرتين لحافة اناء من حجر البازلت . القطر 21,5 سم ، الساحة B1-B2 .

KQ 32 (الشكل 22) ـ قسم من حامل للفخار، الارتفاع 6,75 سم . الخندق A2 . 23 سم تحت السطح .

KQ 33 (الشكل 21) ـ رأس سهم من الحديد . الطول 3,29 سم. الساحة A2-A3-B2-B3 . 45 سم تحت السطح .

KQ 34 (الشكل 22) ـ قطعة مدورة من حجر البازلت، في وسطها حفرة مماثلة لـ KQ 30 . القطر 11,1 سم . الساحة B2-B3 .

KQ 35 (الشكل 22) ـ كسرة حافة من اناء من حجر البازلت ، القطر 26,0 سم . الخندط C1 .

KQ 36 (الشكل 22) ـ قطعة مجوفة بيضوية الشكل من الطين عند وسطها حفر صغيرة. الخندق A2 .

الخـلاصـة: خربـة قصـريـج موقـع مسـاحـتـه اكثـر من 5 كيلومتـرات شملت الحفريات مساحة صغيرة مركزها المنطقة الصنـاعيـة . وتـدل كل الاكتشـافـات عن اهمية الموقع ، منها ثلاثة مسامير ومن الفخار من النوع المستعمل في القصور أو المبـاني الـرسميـة . من الارجح ان الطبقـة المكتشفـة في خربـة قصريج تعود الى النصف الاول من القرن السادس قبل الميلاد . ان معلوماتنا عن هذه الفترة عند سقوط الامبراطورية الاشورية والفترة التي تلتها مباشرة من تاريخ شمال العراق قليلة جداً ، ناتجة عن عدم التعرف عن اي موقع او طبقة اثناء التنقيبات . لذلك مجموعة فخار قصريج ذات اهمية كبيرة . يحوي هذا الكتـاب على ثلاث ملاحق . الاول ، (بقلم ر. ك آبـريتشـارد R.k. Uprichard يصف فيها الطرق المستعملة في تنظيف وترميم الفخار واثار اخرى . الملحق الثاني (بقلم م. س. تايت M.S. Tite) يتعلق بتحليل كسرة من «النيل المصري» Egyptian Blue من خربـة قصـريـج . امـا الملحق الثالث فيلخص نتائج التحاليل لنماذج الفخار بواسطة الامتصاص الذري والمقطع الرقيق (بقلم فريستون وهيوز I.C. Freestone & M.J. Hughes) .
نقدم الشكر الى الدوائر الرسمية العراقية لموافقتهم على استعارة النماذج لدراستها .
ونقـدم شكرنـا مرة اخرى لمؤسسـة الاثار والتراث العامة العراقية ، لمعاونتهم ومساندتهم ولولاهم لما استطعنا انجاز عملنا هذا .

اجـزاؤه ربمـا كانت مسقوفة ومن المحتمل انها تشكل وحدة سكنية هذا مع العلم ان الجدارين المتزاويين والممتدين باتجاه شمالي غربي ـ جنوبي شرقي يعودان الى غرفة قياسها ٢٫٧٠ × ٣٫٨٠ ، وعند الزاوية الغربية وجدنا مدخل وصنارة باب حجرية .

بالاضافة الى الحفريات الرئيسية قمنا بحفر اربعة خنادق (الشكل 3) . عند الخندق KQ1 ، ٢ × ١ متر (الشكل 18a) وتحت السطح و٥٠ سم وجدنـا صخور مبعثرة لعلها تعود الى تبليط أو اساس لجدار . اما الخندق KQ2 فكان خالي من اي اثر . لكن الخندق PF ، ٤ × ٢ مترويقع حوالي ٢٣٠ متراً الى الغرب من الحفريات الرئيسية احتوى على تبليطين من الحجر اكتشفـا قرب سطـح المـوقـع (الشكل 18b) . الخنـدق WR ، ٤ × ٢ مترويبعد ٣٤٠ متراً جنوب غرب الحفريات الرئيسية يحتوي على تبليط متكامل (الشكل 18c) وعلى حجرين مع حفرتين مستديرتين في وسطهما . قطر الواحدة ٨ سم .

لقد كشفت التنقيبات في خربة قصريج على كمية كبيرة من الفخار فبالاضافة الى الجرار الكاملة كان هناك ١٢٬٠٠٠ كسرة ، معظمها يحتوي على شوائب نباتية ورمل خشن (grit) ، بينما الفخار من جرف قصريج احتوى على شوائب نباتية فقط . والميـزة الاخـرى لفخـار خربة قصريج هو النسبة العالية (٢٠٪) من كسرلونها اصفرفاتح . هناك عدد كبيرمن الاواني المتنوعة الاشكال: اواني جؤجؤية (الارقام 20-54) ، اواني حافاتها مضلعة (الارقام 76-78) ، أومائلة الى الخارج (الارقام 107-110) ، واواني ذوات ثلاث قوائم رمادية اللون (الارقام 112-115) . وتقارن هذه الاشكال بالشبيهة لها بين الفخار من مدينـة نمـرود . امـا الاواني ذوات الحـواف السميكـة أو المائلـة الى داخل الانية فمن الصعب وجود شبيه لها بين فخار العصر الاشوري المتأخرولعلها تعود الى الفترة التي تليه . وهناك اواني رقيقة الصنع (الارقام 116-146) بينها الاستيكانات وكـؤوس وقـدح واحـد من طراز «القصـر» ، جميعها تعود الى اواخر العصر الاشوري ، بالاضافة الى الكسرذات الحواف المـائلـة نحـو الـداخـل واشكـال اخرى (الارقام 147-226) اما الاواني ذات الحواف المثنية فهي تعود الى الفترة اللاحقة من العصـر الاشـوري . امـا القـواريـروالاواني الصغيرة (الارقام 259-269) فمن بينها الاناء رقم 276 ، وهومزين بخطوط بنية اللون (الالواح VIIb-XIa) والجرة رقم 271 مزينة بخطوط حمراء ـ بنية ، وكلا الجرتين اكتشفتا سوية مع الجرة رقم 264 (اللوح VIIIa) وكلهن من العصر الاشوري المتأخر . ولنفس التاريخ يعود اناء مزجج يقارن بمثيل له اكتشف في معبد نابو في نمرود (اللوح XIb) بالاضافة الى المصباح الانبوبي الشكل (رقم 360) .

يعـود معظم فخـار خربة قصريج الى العصر الاشوري المتأخر . لكن هناك بعض اشكال الاواني تعود الى العصر الذي يليـه ، منهـا الاواني ذات الحـواف المائلة الى الداخل أو العريضة (الارقام 79-100) والاواني ذات الحواف المثنية (الارقام 227-240) . وقد كشفت التنقيبات عن طبقة واحدة في خربة قصريج نستدل منها قصر المدة لاستيطان الموقع . بالاضافة الى ذلـك لم تكشف الحفـريـات عن اثار اخرى مختلفة سوى كسرة فخارة واحدة من العصر الاسلامي (الرقم 361) ولذلك فان فخـارقصـريـج يكـون مجمـوعة متجانسة تعود الى فترة واحدة ، والارجح الفترة التي تلت العصر الاشوري استناداً الى الفوارق (بالاخص بالنسبة للمادة واللون) بين فخار جرف قصريج وخربة قصريج . ومن الممكن مقارنة بعض الاشكال مع فخـارمن القرن السـابع من نمرود ويعود بتاريخه الى قبل سقوط المدينة في ٦١٢ ق.م. واعتماداً على ذلك نقترح ان تاريخ خربة قصريـج هو النصف الاول من القـرن السـادس قبل الميلاد . ومعززاً لهذا التاريخ هوطرازابطة الوزن المؤرخ الى العصر الذي يلي نهاية العصر الاشوري .

شهر اذار ١٩٨٣ للموسم الاول ، وشباط واذار ١٩٨٤ . واشتغل في التنقيب حوالي تسعة عمال وعامل واحد من الشرقاط . ازيل التراب من مساحة قياسها ٢٦ × ١٤ متراً . ثم نقبنا خندقين ٢ × ١ متراً على بعد ٣٠ و٥٠ متراً عند الجهة الشمالية من المنطقـة الـرئيسـيـة . واضـافـة الى ذلك فقد حفرنا خندقين اخرين ٤ × ٢ مترو WRوPF عند حدود الموقع للتعرف على مساحة المستوطن (الشكل 3) استظهرت الحفريات ان المستوطن يتكون من طبقة واحدة ضحلة . والدلائل على اي ترميم أو اعادة بنـاء معـدومـة . ولـذلـك فكل الظواهرتبين قصر المدة لاستيطان الموقع . مع العلم ان معظم الاثار اكتشفت قرب السطح . ووجد التبليط والعتبات المبنية على الصخر في كل المجسات (ما عدا KQ 2 ا) على عمق يتراوح بين ٥ و٦٠ سم تحت سطـح التـل . امـا في الحفريـة الرئيسيـة كانت التربة على السطح طرية بنية اللون ، سمكها حوالي ١٦ سم ، وتحت هذه الطبقة ترسبات طينية لونها بني ، تغطي التبليط (المقطع، الشكل 17) . قُسم الفخار والعظام واللقى الصغيرة المكتشفة من الخنادق الى قسمين : الاول (1) اللقى من التربة العليا ، والثاني (2) من طبقة الترسبات الطينية .

ان اهم اكتشاف في الحفريات الرئيسية (الشكل 15-16 والالواح IIb, IIIa-b,IVc) مجمع صغيرمحوره «كورة» لعمل الفخار . يقع البناء في الـزاوية الشماليـة الشرقية من الخندق (B4) وبعضه يمتد الى الاكوام المجاورة . (الشكل 19b, 20a-b والالواح VIII-IX) . البنـاء بيضـوي الشكل ١٢,٥٠ × ١,٣٨ متراً عند السطـح ، ترتفع بقايا الجدران حوالي ١٩ سم من سطح التبان . امـا المـوقد فيقع تحت التبان بحوالي ١,٢٠ متراً والقاعدة حمراء من شدة الحرق قياسها ١,٩٣ × ١,١٢ متراً . جدران الموقد ملطخة بالطين سمكها بين ٥ و٧ سم، ومتحجرة من شدة الحرارة، ومحفورة عامودياً ما عدا الجهة الجنوبية الغـربيـة فهي مائلة قليـلاً حيث تحـوي فتحـة المـوقـد لوضع الوقود وجمع الرماد . لدعم وتقوية تبان الموقد . عند قاعدة الموقد طبقة سمكها ٣٥ سم متكونه من رماد فاتح اللون ، فوقها ترسبات ناعمة لونها احمر بني مخلوط مع كسر آجروطين محروق اصفر اللون . عند قمة الحوض ستة آجرات محروقة ، مرتكزة على جوانبها على شكل نعل الحصان ، قد تكون بقايا قبة لسقف الموقد او تبليط الفرن (oven) . ومن المحتمل وجود حفر في ارضية الموقد كي تتسرب النارمن الحفرة. لكن الارضية نفسهـا قد تهـدمت. ووجـدت كسـرات فخـار حوالي ٣٠ wasters منهـا جرار مختلفـة محـروقـة (اللوح Xa) وثـلاث جرار (اللوح Xb) . واخيراً هناك عدة اشكال من الفخار اكتشفت في الموقد ، من بينها الفخار المسجل تحت الارقام ٢٠، ٣٠، ٨٨، ١٠٧ ـ ١١١ و٢٣٢ .

كانت الارضيـة الى الجهـة الشمالية الشرقية والجهة الجنوبية الغربية من الموقد مبلطة بالحجارة . وبالقرب من الجهة الشمـاليـة الشرقيـة عتبة مبنية من الحجر مستطيلة الشكل ٣ × ٢ متر ، تعلوعن الارضية بحوالي ١٥ سم ، اما الغرض منها فغيرواضح ، وقد تكون لوضع الانية عليها عند تجفيفها قبل حرقها . وهناك حفرمدورة على حجارة التبليط عند الجهة الجنوبية الغربية مقابل العتبة قياساتها ٨، ٩، ١٤ سم على التوالي . من المستبعد انها كانت صنارات باب لعدم وجود مدخل بالقرب منها ، من المحتمل اعتماداً على ان المجمع متخصص بصناعة الفخار ان تكون الحفرقواعد لمحور عجلات الفخـار . الى الغرب من المنصـة والرصيف والموقد جدار اسسه واضحة والباقي ارتفاعه حوالي ٢٥ سم عند نهاية الجانب الجنوبي الغربي يلتف بزاوية ٩٠° ويمتد الى بعد ٢,٣٠ متر ثم يلتف مرة اخرى ليلتقي بالموقد ليشكل مستطيل يحيط المجمع .

الى الجهـة الجنوبيـة من الموقد وعلى بعد ٦٥ سم كتلة من الحجر الرملي مقاسها ١,٨٥ × ٠,٩٠ متر، سمكها ١٠ سم والارجح انها كانت تستعمل كلوح مسطح لعجن الطين . الى الشرق من الموقد وعلى بعد ٢,٢٥ متر قاعدة من الفخاركبيرة كانت على الارجح تعود الى زير لخزن الماء ، بالقرب منه وجدنا بطة وزن (اللوح XII) في الطبقة التي تعود الى المنصة الحجرية .

الى الغرب من الجدار المحيـط بالمـوقد ارضية مرصوفة بالحجر وعند نهاية الجهة الغربية من ساحة الحفريات ارضية اخرى مرصوفة بالحجارة ، مربعة الشكل ٢,٥٠ × ٢,٣٠ متر، لعلها كانت مكان للعمل. وفي احدى الحجارة حفرة عميقة مدورة تشبه الحجارة مقابل المنصة . الى الشمال الشرقي من الارضية والجنوب الشرقي من زاوية الخندق A5 ، وجدنا بعض الحجارة مرصوفة بشكل دائري لعلها كانت بالوعة حيث هناك انخفاض عند الوسط .

الى الشرق من الموقد في القسم الشمالي من خندق A2 ، تبليط اخرمن الحجر لعله كان مكان للعمل . مستطيل الشكل ٤,٩٠ × ٢,٧٠ متراً . احتوى التبليط شرق الخندق على كمية من كسر الفخار (الشكل 19a) وكسركبيرة عند لصقها شكلت تابوت صغير .

عند الجهـة الشرقية من الحفـريات الرئيسية وخاصة في الخندقين A1 وB1 يلاحظ اختلاف التخطيط حيث ان بعض

تنقيبات جرف قصريج وخربة قصريج

يحوي هذا التقرير على التنقيبات التي قامت بها بعثة المتحف البريطاني برئاسة الدكتور جون كيرتس في جرف قصريج وخربة قصريج . يقع الموقعان ضمن منطقة مشروع انقاذ حوض صدام . ولمؤسسة الاثار والتراث العراقية المزيد من الشكر لمنحنا فرصة التنقيب وتزويدنا بالعمال والمعدات والسكن . ونخص هنا بالشكر الدكتور مؤيد سعيد رئيس المؤسسة والدكتور بهنام ابو الصوف المدير العام للدائرة الشمالية وممثلي المؤسسة السيد محمد زكي والسيد عبد السلام . ونرد شكرنا الى البعثة الاثارية البريطانية في العراق وبالاخص مديرها الدكتور مايكل روف ، حيث شاركناهم السكن وزودونا بالمعدات والعديد من المساعدات الاخرى .

جرف قصريج هو موقع صغير يعود الى العصر الاشوري الحديث يقع على الجانب الشرقي من نهر دجلة حوالي ١٥٠٠ كيلومتر شرق قرية بابنيت (الشكل ٢) .

استمرت التنقيبات خمسة ايام بين ١٠ و ٢٢ آذار ١٩٨٣ ، قام بالتنقيبات ثلاثة عمال احدهم من الشرقاط . وقد اظهرت التنقيبات عن حوض كبير ذو جوانب مستقيمة قطره ٣٫٧٠ متراً (اللوح Ia-b) وعمق ما تبقى منه ٢٫٢٥ متر . والارجح انه كان اعمق اصلاً . اما ارضية الحوض فهي مسطحة وعليها حفرتان الاولى (Pit A) قطرها ٩٥ سم وعمقها ٢٠ سم والحفرة الثانية (Pit B) قطرها ١١١ سم وعمقها ٣٥ سم (الشكل ٤) . ووجدنا الجانب الشمالي الشرقي من الحوض قد تأكل نتيجة اخدود عميق من وادي قصريج . بعد نقل الاثار والتراب من الحوض ، صنفت اللقى الى ثلاثة مجموعات (١ - ٣ ، الشكل ٥) اما المواد التي التقطت من سطح الموقع او كان من الصعب تخصيصها الى اي مجموعة صنفت «مواد متفرقة» كانت معظم مواد الدفن في الحوض مخلوطة مع رماد . وقد غطت ارضية الحوض طبقة سميكة من رماد غامق اللون وفوقها رماد فاتح اللون مخلوط مع كسر اجر ، والميزة الظاهرة هي خطوط من الرماد على طول الدفن . احتوى الدفن على اكثر من ١٠٠٠ كسرة فخار خاصة في المجموعتين (٢ - ٣) . من ضمن المواد التي اكتشفت في المجموعتين عظام حيوانات : خروف ، ماعز ، خنزير ، كلب ، وقط ، قد تعود الى حيوانات ذبحت للاكل . والمواد الاخرى المكتشفة منها كسرتين كبيرتين لأجرة من اللبن سمكها ١٠ سم وآجرة مفخورة غير مكتوبة سمكها ٦ سم وعرضها ٣٣ سم . واللقى الصغيرة تشمل خرزة زجاجية اسطوانية الشكل (الشكل KQ 26: 6a) وقسم من قبضة من الحديد (الشكل KQ 37: 6a) وقطعة من حجر الصوان (الشكل KQ 28: 6a) وعجلة من الفخار (الشكل KQ 27: 6a) .

وقد استطعنا لوجود الكمية الكبيرة من كسر الفخّار تلصيق واعادة اجزاء من الاواني اوكلها تقريباً (الشكل ٧ - ١٤) ، فهناك عدد من الاواني الجوجؤية (nos. 3-31) وامثلة متعددة من حافات الاواني (nos. 49-78) وكسر لاواني الطبخ (nos. 79-81) واستيكانات (nos. 34-37) وكؤوس (nos. 42-47) . الميزة الملحوظة في فخار قصريج هو وجود الشوائب النباتية مخلوطة مع الطين . ويعود عهد هذه الاواني بعد المقارنة مع فخار مواقع اخرى وخاصة فخار نمرود الى العصر الاشوري المتأخر ، بين القرن التاسع والسابع قبل الميلاد . ولغياب بعض الاشكال للاواني الفخارية المعاصرة لسقوط نمرود (من ٦١٤ - ٦١٢ ق. م.) من قصريج يؤدي بنا الى ان نؤرخ الموقع الى القرن الثامن قبل الميلاد .

من الواضح ان الحوض استعمل لرمي النفايات بعد الانتهاء من الغرض الاصلي له . ويمثل الفخار المكتشف وحدة متكاملة ، ومن المحتمل ان الحوض امتلأ ضمن فترة قصيرة . ونتسائل هنا عن الغرض الاصلي من وجود الحوض . فالاكثر احتمالاً كان مخزن للحبوب . حيث هناك ادلة من بلاد وادي الرافدين ومواقع اخرى في غرب آسيا في الماضي والحاضر لخزن الحبوب في مخازن محفورة تحت سطح الارض . ومعظم الاحيان تلطش جوانب المخازن بطبقة من الجص ، وعند امتلاء الحوض بالحبوب الغير مطحونة تغطى بالحلفة أو قشور الحنطة ويحكم غطائها بطبقة من الطين . ونتيجة لهذا الافتراض توقعنا وجود مستوطن قريب من المخزن . فقمنا بحفر مجسين ٢ × ٢ متر . الاول عند قمة الجرف والاخر غرب الحوض على بعد ٨٦ متراً . ولكننا لم نجد في المجسين اثار سكن . من المحتمل ان المستوطن قد تأكل اما من نهر دجلة (الذي قد غير مجراه عبر الزمن) او من الوادي شرق الموقع . وهناك ادلة ان الموقع كان مسكوناً في العصور الحجرية لوجود قطع من حجر الصوان .

خربة قصريج موقع يعود الى الفترة التي تلي العصور الاشورية ، يحده من الشرق وادي قصريج وهو الموقع ١٢ في خارطة المواقع الاثرية لسد صدام . وهو موقع كبير يمتد غرباً حتى وادي خرابة ، طوله حوالي الخمسة كيلومترات ، ولا يمتد شمالاً نحو نهر دجلة كما تعرفنا على ذلك من خلال خندقي الجس عند جرف قصريج . بدأت التنقيبات في خربة قصريج في